PINBALL GAMES

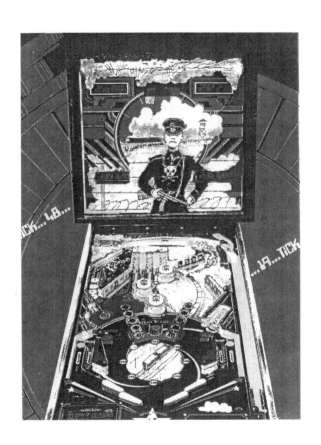

Order this book online at www.trafford.com
or email orders@trafford.com

Most Trafford titles are also available at major online book retailers.

Printed in Victoria, BC, Canada.

ISBN: 978-1-4269-2480-4 (sc)
ISBN: 978-1-4269-2481-1 (hc)

Library of Congress Control Number: 2009914200

*Our mission is to efficiently provide the world's finest, most comprehensive book publishing
service, enabling every author to experience success. To find out how to publish your book,
your way, and have it available worldwide, visit us online at www.trafford.com*

Trafford rev. 5/6/10

Cover: *Tiger Rag in the Ghetto*
Back Cover: *End of the Siege: The Russians are here.*

 www.trafford.com

North America & international
toll-free: 1 888 232 4444 (USA & Canada)
phone: 250 383 6864 ♦ fax: 812 355 4082

PINBALL GAMES

Arts of Survival in the Nazi and Communist Eras

George F. Eber
Illustrated by the author

Table of Contents

To the friends of those times—and to their memory

Author's Note

The events I describe in this book ultimately landed me, my father and step-mother, like thousands of refugees, at Pier 21 in Halifax. Early one misty morning on a retired battered troop ship, I leaned over the rail and photographed the New World as it swung into focus. We disembarked an hour later, to be greeted by Red Cross girls. We had minimum baggage, but I had a new degree in architecture, and for me a new life opened up.

In recent years, it has of course been possible to visit my former country easily, and I have done so on a number of occasions. In spring, when the tourists begin to arrive, the bridges over the Danube are illuminated with thousands of lights, and Budapest becomes once again the City of Light. I am, however, writing these pages overlooking less haunted waters—on the deck of my camp on Lake Memphremagog. Below are the kayaks, and around are geranium pots. But frequently bad news draws me inside. Television reports the cost of ultranationalism, of religious intolerance.

The events I write of here happened in my boyhood, and they have never left my mind. Years ago, I determined to write my own account of those times, and a number of starts piled up in a desk drawer. Recently, dreadful contemporary events have caused me to look again at some of those early drafts and revise them.

Reading over the pages that have accumulated, I realise that readers may often find what I have written remarkably frivolous. Many of those who shared with me the years of which I write were not as lucky as I. My excuse is that even in the worst of times, the optimism of youth still rises. When Erwin Leichter played the *Tiger Rag* in the sealed-off ghetto, his situation was not for a moment less serious—but he was vital with youth.

George F. Eber

Lake Memphremagog, Vermont.

[I] The Siege of Budapest

As soon as she understood that the siege of Budapest was about to start, Eta, my future step-mother, a supremely cool and practical person of immense girth, sailed off with her housekeeper in tow along Molnar utca. This was the first street in from the Danube embankment and for about a mile ran parallel to the river from the Elizabeth Bridge to the Francis Joseph Bridge. Near the entrance to Elizabeth Bridge was the Matyas Pinkes restaurant, close to which was the local headquarters of the Arrowcross, and leading to Francis Joseph Bridge was Custom House square. Eta's target was next to the Custom House, the Eiffel-designed, cast-iron structure which was the main market hall of Budapest. Although because of the advance of the Russian armies, the hinterland of rich farms was cut away from the market, there were still some stalls operating on the first day of the siege. Eta bought up what she could find: six scrawny chickens, all sorts of vegetables, and then, from the last of the fishermen still lingering on the riverbank with their catch, six big live Danube carp.

She brought all these dazed creatures home, filled up the bathtub, and released the carp. The chickens found their new home in the kitchen. Based on my father's advice, she also bought gallons of vegetable oil and rolls of wick. Every vessel in the house, vases, bowls, pitchers, was filled with water. A huge sack of dried beans, lard, and some Globus cans of goose liver purchased earlier from some SS soldiers were in the larder. Thus, right through the siege, in this town where women fought over the cadavers of fallen horses for a piece of

1

frozen horse meat, we had fresh fish or chicken, occasionally goose-liver pate, and from time to time a thick bean soup decorated with sautéed onions.

Thanks to Eta's prompt action, food was not to be our problem during the siege. But no sooner had we filled all possible containers with water than the flow of water from the taps stopped. The Russians had cut off the water supply, and during the first night of the siege, the electricity was cut off, too. The lights went on and off for half an hour, then died completely. By that time we had made improvised oil lamps out of sturdy drinking glasses with wicks floating in the oil. After dinner, we sat down at the table in the bay window and played poker for pretty high stakes. We could just make out the cards. Artillery fire could be heard in the distance and also the rapid hammering of machine-gun fire. It was still some distance away.

At the beginning of December 1944, the Russian armies had begun advancing on the great Hungarian plain between the Tisza and Duna rivers. A huge tank trap in the form of a giant ditch had been frantically dug on the outskirts of Budapest by the forces of the Hungarian Arrowcross government, and its propaganda machine began insisting that this ditch would stem the tide of the "eastern hordes" and reverse the fortunes of the Nazi empire. But at night, in some of the eastern suburbs, the distant murmur of artillery battles could be heard, and nobody except the most extreme Nazis believed that any magic could stave off collapse.

Besides my father and myself, Eta's apartment also housed her cousin and nephew. The cousin, Meszelenyi Laci, was a police officer from Ungvar in the Carpathian Mountains. When the advancing Russian armies caused the evacuation of Ungvar, Laci, with military orders to proceed with the retreating units to Austria, had advanced as far as Budapest, where he decided to abandon the war effort and abscond to Eta's apartment. Her nephew, Guszti, in the army engineering corps, had already reached Austria with his unit, but was sent on a detail back to Budapest, where he also decided to decamp and take refuge with Eta. Laci and Guszti were by law deserters, punishable by summary execution. I myself was equipped with false papers. According to these, I belonged to the ranks of the Hungarian Army's 502 mobile motor repair unit and was on temporary sick leave due to a minor leg wound. My documents had been obtained from an underground resistance group with the help of my cousin Pista Salusinszky, who worked at the Swedish Embassy as secretary to Raoul Wallenberg, the Swede who saved many hundreds of Jews from extermination. Between my father, Laci, the police officer Guszti, and myself, we had two pistols, two Schmeisser submachine guns, and a very dangerous situation.

Every day, as the Russians approached, the Arrowcross patrols went through all buildings looking for illegal elements, Jews, and deserting soldiers. Any young man had to be able to prove why he was not with his military unit. As soon as a patrol approached the building, Guszti and I disappeared under a pile of rubble in a light well in the kitchen, taking with us all the weaponry, while my father and Laci in his police officer's uniform were left to cope with the patrol. During air raids, everybody retreated to the basement shelter, and Guszti and I stayed in the flat. During air raids, the likelihood of visits by the Arrowcross thugs increased, because they knew that everybody would be in the shelters.

Oddly enough, in these pre-siege days, time passed quickly. We were young and cocky. At night, we listened to the illegal BBC German-language broadcasts and worried about the German offensive in the Ardennes, commanded by General Rundstaedt, the best of the remaining German generals. My father, a retired officer of the Austro-Hungarian Army, worried less; he had decided that the Germans would run out of steam. In the evenings during the blackout, Laci, Guszti, and I left the house and walked around in Pest, sometimes walking side by side with armed Arrowcross thugs. We were becoming a little careless because we believed that very soon our war would end.

One night Laci and I walked to Magyar utca, only a few blocks away, and called at Madame Frieda's emporium. We could barely find it in the pitch dark. Inside, it was well-lit and friendly, almost as it was before the war. Madame Frieda and the girls must have suspected our illegal status, but they showed no interest. There were very few guests, and when we retreated upstairs, we got the best rooms. But no sooner did we make ourselves comfortable than we heard noises and heavy banging on the solid oak front door. The door bell rang insistently, and the brass knocker crashed against the wood. Almost immediately a maid was knocking at our doors to tell us to leave: a combined Arrowcross-SS patrol was combing the area. We could hear the raiding party being received by Madame Freida in the lobby. The girls opened the windows, and we jumped down into the darkened street. It had been a close call, and for a few days after, we were more careful.

On Christmas Day 1944, we learned that the approaching Russian armies had formed two gigantic prongs and, instead

of attacking frontally, had crossed the Danube north and south of Budapest. During the night, they had succeeded in completely surrounding the city and were attacking from all sides. A German SS army of 200,000 motorised troops and a Hungarian Arrowcross army of about the same strength were caught inside this Russian ring of iron. The sounds of the artillery were booming from

Street scene in Budapest
during the Siege: January 1945

east and north and west. The siege of Budapest had begun in earnest.

On this first night of the siege, when we finally went to bed and the oil lamps were blown out, we drew the blackout curtains aside. The street was pitch black; across from us on the other side, four-storey apartment buildings loomed dark, shoulder to shoulder. I could just see indistinctly at the end of the street the little square park on its rise at the bridgehead and behind it the dark shape of the Custom House. There was no traffic. The streetcars which ran between the park and the Custom House had no electricity, and the buses and taxis were hiding somewhere. Occasionally, far away to the east and south, flares went up in the night, followed by rapid shooting. We went fitfully to sleep; all night long, we could hear the Russian bombers over the city, dropping their bombs randomly here and there. Not a real bombing raid: just the odd bomber to keep everyone awake. The sirens did not sound any more; they were silent now for good—there was no electricity to power them.

Next day, the siege intensified; the artillery duels grew fiercer. Long-range guns poured their projectiles towards the centre of the city where Eta's apartment house stood. I could hear the whistle of the shells; my father explained that the ones you heard were harmless—they flew overhead. He could also tell the calibre by the sound. Soon odd shells began exploding above us, spewing deadly shrapnel which rattled like hail on the tile roofs above. Soon everyone in the house except Guszti and myself had moved down into the air-raid shelter, taking food with them. My father commuted up and down, checking on us. The rubble in the light well had grown from the debris coming down from the roof, and we formed quite a little cave behind it for Guszti and me. The Arrowcross still patrolled the buildings, and as soon as we saw them from the window, we jumped into our hole like crabs on the beach, pulling the debris behind us on a piece of plywood to close the opening. Holding our guns, determined to use them if they should find us, we listened to the tramp of their heavy footsteps in the

5

apartment as they sometimes approached quite close. We did not move until my father came up to announce the all clear.

In the evening, as soon as it got dark, everybody came up from the shelter. Dinner was cooked, and the card game started. (Very soon I had lost thousands of pengos, and my father, a very cool poker hand, held most of my markers.) This became the routine of our days and nights. It was late in December; the artillery went on all day and night, the heavy machine guns were closer. The bombers now were flying all the time. In the lulls, some people went from street to street, bringing the news.

Basically Budapest is built on both sides of the Danube, with five major bridges connecting Buda and Pest. On the right bank in Buda, between the Elizabeth Bridge to the south and well above the Chain Bridge upriver, rises the Palace Mountain, a veritable fortress city. Here was the German command. The Russians had surrounded Buda, but were attacking on the Pest front. The plan of Pest consists of concentric half-circle boulevards with their bases on the Danube. Radial roads, like spokes of a wheel, cross the boulevards. At first, the Russians came down the spokes; these were heavily defended, as were the boulevards. But the Russians were used to siege warfare, and their troops spread out when their direct progress was impeded. They went block by block around the obstacles, breaking through basement walls, climbing roofs to get from one building to the next, thus infiltrating behind the defending lines. By the end of December, after fierce fighting, they reached the main circular boulevard, a heavily defended six-lane thoroughfare.

Every building in the city had been hit by many artillery shells, and the streets by now were full of the rubble of bricks and stones, sometimes a floor high. Through these rubble hills, pedestrians had made snow-covered footpaths, criss-crossing at the most convenient locations.

The bridges across the river were visibly mined—all except St. Margaret's Bridge which had been accidentally blown up in mid-day traffic by the Germans two months before. I saw it happen from a vantage point on Saint Gellert's Mountain, the streetcars and buses slowly gliding into the lead-coloured Danube from the slopes of the collapsed arches; then shortly the small ferry boats, propeller-driven, swarming like ducks in a pond when food is thrown in, plucking as many people as possible from the torrent.

Now on the streets, mixed with the rubble, carcasses of all kinds of vehicles began to collect, their burned-out hulks contrasting with the snow. The Arrowcross thugs speeded up their work raiding and collecting people at night, then marching them to the lower embankment and shooting them into the fast-flowing river. As the Russians tightened the noose on the centre of the city, the forces defending Pest retreated within and had less and less room to move around.

Purest chance now determined all life. One day, while I looked down at the street from behind the window curtains, I heard the droning of a heavy Ilyushin bomber flying low. Looking up, I saw it cross the sky diagonally above us. It flew so low that I could see the pilot for a split-second before it disappeared over the roof of the opposite building. In this brief moment, as my father and I watched, a cluster of bombs of the small 100-kg size tied together with chains was released and, clearly visible for an instant, disappeared into the roof of the four-floor-high building diagonally across from us. As we watched, frozen, nothing happened for an eternity; then there was a dull boom. In slow motion, the outside walls of the building with its beautiful old stonework, windows, and balconies ballooned out and collapsed in a gigantic dust storm. When the dust settled, the collapsed building lay in a heap on top of its basement. The bombs had been set to explode in the cellar after penetrating all floors. There was now a 100-foot gap in place of the old patrician residence. People ran from all around, but there seemed to be nothing that could be done. The Arrowcross arrived also from their local headquarters up the street near the Restaurant Matyas Pinkes, but when they saw there was no way to loot in the rubble, they drifted away.

7

It must have been the same night, at the end of December, that the noose was drawn so tight in Pest that a German SS motorised infantry battalion rumbled into our street, there to make its last stand with its back towards the Danube. All night we could hear the vehicles moving in through the rubble. Looking down in the morning light, I could see two large personnel carriers with tank treads pulled up on the sidewalk, tight against the walls of the buildings opposite. A few horses were tethered to these personnel carriers, a gasoline tank truck stood next to them, and a mobile field kitchen behind. In the middle of the street, soldiers in grey uniforms were in the process of setting up a light infantry-type gun, its business end facing the Customs House. All the vehicles were heavily battle-scarred. They must have started their retreat months ago in the Don basin, and they showed every mile of the road. The soldiers were fit enough, but pale and thin. They set up their command post in a command vehicle bristling with radio antennae in the courtyard of one of the buildings.

At the end of Molnar utca on the little Custom House square, many more SS soldiers were busy ripping up the cobblestones and building a barricade. Others were lifting up the streetcar rails to make tank traps, digging them in, wall high, beyond the barricades in a zigzag pattern. By the time it grew dark, the barricade was breast-high, and apart from a few guards in the archways of the buildings, the Germans were not visible.

We sat down after dinner for our usual card game. Light machine-gun fire flared up periodically, and the artillery shells were whistling overhead, but the next couple of days went by relatively uneventfully except for the occasional burst of shells. By now all our windows were blown in, and we had heavy horse blankets hung over the openings.

Then on December 30, as I peeked out the window, I saw the first of the Russian tanks. They were patrolling beyond the barricade in front of the Customs House. One of them tumbled down to the other side of the tank trap, and its turret began slowly traversing, lowering its sights. I did not wait for the shooting to start, but withdrew from the window hastily. Several bursts were fired from the tank, and the Germans returned the fire furiously. Then all was quiet. When I looked again, the tanks were gone.

That night, our poker games had additional surprises. Sitting at the window, my father drew two cards, I raised his ante, and my father met my bet. We were about to spread our hands when suddenly there was a tremendous flash and explosion; the window blanket billowed, and a flash of light came into the living room. We spread our cards, my father collected the money, and then we got up to look outside. There was total bedlam; one of the personnel carriers was on its side, its treads dangling. The horses were neighing wildly; one of them lay dying in the rubble. Soldiers rushed to carry a few wounded into the courtyard opposite. A stray Russian artillery shell had come in parallel to the street and at a shallow angle had hit the parapet below our window, spewing its deadly shrapnel across the street. Our side had escaped undamaged, and with nothing better to do, as soon as the noise outside died down, we went to bed.

Next morning, when we looked outside, we saw a crowd of women in the street, carving up the dead horse lying on its back, its legs stretched out in its final agony. Prominent among them, with a large pot and a flashing carving knife, was the red-haired daughter of the little hunchbacked tailor who lived in his store on the ground floor next door.

Our New Year's party was quiet. After a very good dinner of spicy Serbian carp followed by a dobos torta, we sat down to the obligatory poker game. We toasted the New Year with glasses of Biscuit cognac. We were not sure that we would see the end of the year, but we thought that this would be the last year of the war. The Germans across the road were also toasting, but not too cheerfully. The Russians must also have been celebrating, because apart from sporadic fire in the distance, all was quiet.

The first day of 1945 brought powerful renewed fighting, artillery and heavy machine-gun fire from the direction of the big boulevards. The Germans in their redoubt on the Royal Palace Mountain started furious shelling across the Danube towards the Russian line. The shells whistled overhead in every direction.

The siege showed no sign of ending. Our spirits sank when some civilians crossed over from Buda with reports of very determined defenders in the fortress and a rumour that a heavy German battle group was approaching from Transdanubia with the aim of breaking through the surrounding Russian forces and relieving the siege.

The news seemed to have given new enthusiasm to the Arrowcross, who went from house to house in the lulls between gunfire. One day, our cousin, Pista Salusinszky came by in a battered Mercedes with huge Swedish pennants on the fenders. At that time, the Swedish millionaire, Raoul Wallenberg, for whom he worked, was doing more than any other one person to save the Jews and other endangered persons from the Arrowcross by providing Swedish passports and refuge at the embassy and in embassy-owned apartment buildings. He and his assistants roamed the city, literally digging people out of the clutches of the murderous Arrowcross thugs. Pista was with him most of the time and as well helped his own underground friends.

Pista told us about the vengeful carnage of the Arrowcross, about executed people hanging from lampposts with cardboard signs on their chest enumerating their sins. The body of Count Gabor Haller, a well-known liberal pastor of the Calvinist diocese, hung for days from a lamppost on Apponyi Square in front of the Archducal Palace. Pista said that the sign on his chest read, "I helped hide Jewish criminals."

Before long, Pista's Swedish Embassy driver came up, urging him to get moving because it was late and the shooting overhead had begun to intensify. I watched from upstairs as the Mercedes started up, and enveloped in a great plume of blue smoke from its wood-fired mechanism—a wartime specialty—puttered away towards the centre of the city. The next few days and nights passed without incident. The

Russian advance seemed to have become stuck around the big boulevard, and we could not imagine a quick ending to the battle.

A few days later, as I was watching the scene out of our window, an SS Sturmführer sergeant came down the street, clutching his Schmeisser submachine gun. Stepping gingerly over the rubble, he was looking carefully at the house numbers. At our doorway, he stopped and came in. Guzsti and I dove into our cave as he arrived at our apartment. We could hear him banging on the door. My father opened the door and started talking to the man in German, then started laughing and calling us. By the time we dug ourselves out of the rubble, they were sitting at the card table, the Schmeisser leaning against the wall, a bottle of Schnapps on the table. It turned out that this German was not a German at all, but Dezsö Takacs from Szeged, whose father was a childhood friend of my father; they had been students together at the Piarist Gymnasium. Dezsö, a deserter from a labour battalion, had bought himself a complete German outfit complete with SS identification papers and was hiding in this disguise. He had to spend his days marching about the city, hiding in the rubble, so that his landlady and neighbours would not become suspicious of an unemployed German boarder. At dusk, he would return from battle to his lodgings.

We had a few glasses of Schnapps and listened to his story. We wished him good luck; he buttoned his tunic, straightened his cap to regulation angle, and hanging the Schmeisser gun across his chest, marched out into the gathering dusk.

But we heard more news of Dezsö Takacs a couple of days later when Pista visited again. On his daily wanderings, Dezsö as usual was walking around in the ruins of bombed-out buildings and had climbed up a footpath onto a rubble hill which was surrounded by the skeletal remnants of once-elegant old-town residences. The path was narrow and barely defined in the snow, and as he was negotiating the twisting turns, he saw an S.S. Sturmführer step out of the shade of a burnt-out archway and walk in his direction. Dezsö could not retreat without creating suspicion. As they approached each other, he noticed the German regimental insignia: here was a real Sturmführer. The German looked suspicious and demanded Dezsö's identification. "Jawohl," said Dezsö coolly, and with his left hand began to unbutton his upper tunic pocket, the regulation location for documents. "This surely is my end," thought Dezsö, but an afterthought flashed in his mind, "or his." The sound of the Schmeisser blended nicely into the cacophony of artillery fire and the hammering of the heavy machine guns. The German had a surprised look as he sunk to the ground amid the rubble, and Dezsö quickly pulled the body into the darkness of an archway of a ruined building. Then he left in the direction he had come from. It was time to give up his SS identity, and with the aid of the underground, he found a suitable hiding place.

Through his position, Pista heard all the underground news, and it was always interesting to have him spend a short time with us. This time he also told us that the Russians had broken through at the main boulevard and that in his opinion the siege was nearing its end. He thought that the Hungarian Army would surrender and that the German defenders would have no choice but to join them.

Indeed, the next day, perhaps January 10, 1945, we could hear the battle nearing. The bombing and artillery fire intensified, and firing from small arms was audible all around us. There was also a new sound: the plopping of small cannons, which was followed immediately by small explosions in the narrow streets of the inner city, not very far from us. Of course it was my father who immediately identified the sound as mortar fire. He explained that heavy artillery was not suitable for close-up battle, but that the trajectory of the mortars was such that it was possible to shoot from the street almost straight up over four- and five-storey buildings. When they reached the high point in their transit over the buildings, the tiny winged mortar bombs turned towards the earth and hit the ground almost vertically. Of course, aiming was not possible; for good luck, the Russians shot many mortars simultaneously, creating an almost hail-like effect.

The Germans in Molnar utca kept starting up their vehicles in the cold winter weather to warm them up, revving up the motors for short periods, hoping perhaps for orders to cross one of the nearby Danube bridges to the relative safety of Buda and possible escape westwards. Apparently no orders came. Instead, there was artillery fire of ever-increasing frequency from the Russian tanks, which by now were rattling back and forth at the end of the street around the Custom House, approaching right up to the tank obstacles. Our Germans were ducking and apparently could not return the fire.

The days passed. The fighting was obviously much closer; the noise, deafening. In the apartment, everything was covered by fine dust. Eta and my father, the housekeeper, and Laci now spent all the daylight hours together with the rest of the residents in the shelter and came up only when the shooting slowed down after dark. Even Guszti and I began to sneak down to the coal cellar next door to the shelter. There was no point risking being killed upstairs this close to the end. One evening we were huddling behind the coal bins, separated from the shelter only by slatted wooden partitions. Between explosions, we could clearly hear our group chatting with the neighbours on the other side of the partitions. This day the fighting had been particularly ferocious, and we had all been sitting on our respective sides for four or five hours when I suddenly heard Eta say to my father in Aesopian parable, "I wonder how our parcels are faring in the coal cellar?" My father was never too good at double talk. "What parcels?" he asked, "there's nothing there but the boys." Now this was dangerous, should he have been overheard. Nevertheless, perhaps because of the ongoing tension, we had a difficult time suppressing our laughter. The incident passed without consequences. When everybody went upstairs, we also sneaked after them. We blew out the oil lamp and fell asleep despite the noise of the bombers cruising low overhead, dropping bombs here and there. Suddenly there was a huge crash, and I was jolted awake. "That one was really close," I said, lighting a match in the dark. My father was sitting on the edge of his bed laughing. "Very close indeed," he answered, pointing at a standard lamp and table that fell down when he got up to go to the bathroom. Back to sleep we went, to wake up with the smoke of burning houses, acrid and heavy everywhere. Down to the cellar we went again. Another day of ferocious fighting, ceaseless and ever closer.

The card games had come to an end many days earlier, and so after dinner on January 17, we went to sleep early. Around midnight we woke to several, almost simultaneous gigantic explosions. (Later we learned that all the Danube bridges had been blown up). The building shook as in an earthquake. After this it was quiet, and sleep returned. But I woke up again, sometime later, to the sound of the clip-clop of many horses in the street. My father was already awake. "Where did the Germans get all these horses?" I asked. "Those are not Germans," my father replied. "The Russians are here.

Only the Russians would have horses in the front line." As always, I argued. "They can't be here; there was no fighting." "Let's look," said my father, and he drew the horse blanket aside. I looked down.

The little hunchbacked tailor had his door open, and his red-headed daughter, peering from behind, held a carbide storm lamp high overhead. This lit up the street and cast the shadow of a man four storeys high against the darkened building across the street. The shadow wore a huge fur-lined hat, and the shape of his quilted coat was broken only by his "balalaika" machine gun with its round magazine. I had never seen a Russian soldier before, but there was no doubt that was what the shadow depicted. Looking down the shadow, I could see below many others dressed like him, with the leads of their horses in their hands.

I had survived World War II.

End of the Siege: The Russians are here.

15

[II] Flashback: Growing Up on the Danube

Once Upon a Time

In 1925, Lenin was dying; Stalin was a Machiavellian plotter, waiting in the wings; and in the Landsberg Fortress, Hitler was writing *Mein Kampf*. But even if all the dark events of the future had been clearly foreseen, they would have been of no concern to a small boy growing up on the banks of the Danube. In 1925, I was two years old and had just become a "half orphan," as Hungarians say, although of this, too, I had absolutely no knowledge at the time. For many years, the terrifying personalities of the era cast only the faintest shadows over my everyday life.

My childhood went on in our large apartment in Csanady utca, directed by my loving nanny and our firm but affectionate housekeeper. My father spent as much of his time with me as he could, and my aunts and uncles, the brothers and sisters of my mother, visited frequently. Nobody wanted to tell me that my mother had died of TB in a sanatorium in Italy. Instead, they always told me that she would return soon. After a while, I asked less frequently, and although I still remembered the day she left, her absence soon seemed completely normal. Only much later did I understand my loss; by then, I remembered only that there was a time when I remembered her.

When not walking with my nanny or playing or sleeping, I spent my time looking out of our living-room window. In front of our building were vast empty lots, and beyond these, running parallel to our street, was the Danube embankment. My strongest memory from that time is the view of the Danube itself.

In April, the wind blew from the north, howling against the front of our house, rattling everything in its way that was not bolted down. On the inside of the windows, wine-coloured horsehair blankets hung on brass rings to cut down the draft during winter and spring. To see out, I had to climb up on an armchair, pulling myself up by the blanket. It was rather rough-textured, but comforting.

The Danube was a harsh grey with an angry look to it. Grey spring clouds flew over it, mixing with the black smoke of the tiny tugboats steadily towing the first barges upriver. In the middle lay Margaret's Island, where still-leafless great trees were bending and shaking. Beyond rose the hills of Buda, the Rozsadomb—the Hill of the Roses, where a Turkish Aga once grew roses—and behind, other hills rose higher. In the foreground, on the streets immediately below me, heavy workhorses were straining at their drays, the steel-rimmed wheels grinding on yellow ceramic paving tiles as the horses turned into Pannonia Street through the ornamental iron gates of Suhajda's construction yard.

Although everything looked bleak and shivery, spring was here, and soon the winds would stop their march from the north down the Danube valley. The panorama would change, but the Danube would keep its course, still controlling the picture in the window. I wondered about the river. When the leaves began to show on the trees of St. Margaret's Island, I was often taken for a walk on the embankment, and while my nanny worried only about my wandering to the water's edge and was not helpful with explanations about the river, my mind was fully occupied trying to understand it.

Sitting on the steps of the embankment, I soon found out that the tugboats coming from the left were chugging and churning slowly, while the tugs coming from the right were flying past. So the water was moving. There was "up" river and "down" river. One Sunday, my father took me for a walk under the gigantic craneways further downriver and explained that "up" river to the right was the mysterious magic city of Vienna in the far distance and "down" river, much further away, was the sea. The river was coming from a never-never land, going to a never-never land, bringing and taking things with it. What made it a river, what made it exciting, was that while seemingly always the same, it was always changing, changing.

Sometimes, as in April when swollen by the melting snows, it washed the roadway at the top of the embankment; in June, it receded to the level of the lowest stone steps, making it difficult for the fishermen, who liked to cast for their catch from this vantage point, and in winter it seemed to stop altogether. Now the river was frozen to a jagged dirty white, although my father said that under the ice the river flowed on as ever and the fish were still there, swimming as always.

One day, through my father's military binoculars, we actually saw people on the frozen river chasing and shooting at a pack of wolves that somehow followed a track right into the middle of Budapest. Safe behind the red horse blankets in our bay window, we seemed to be watching a movie. We could hear no sound—this was the era of the silent movies, so this did not seem strange—but the men pointed their rifles and the wolves fell down and little red spots appeared on the ice.

This visual contact with the Danube from behind the horsehair blankets ended rather soon. Gigantic and ugly boxlike apartments began to fill the empty building lots, and Suhajda's yard disappeared. It was time to move, and move we did to the hills of Buda, where our view of the Danube was more distant. But with this move came regular daily trips across the Danube bridges, of which there were four at the time. My world opened up, and with it my knowledge of the river.

The principal bridge for us was the Margaret Bridge, and I must have crossed it thousands of times, on foot, in streetcars, in buses, and on special occasions in my father's car. There were green parks running down to the Danube at either bridgehead, and the Buda embankment had beautiful old horse-chestnut trees as far as the eye could see. Nanny and I usually went to the park on the Buda side in front of the Stamboul Café. She liked the park—it had the right company for her—and I liked it because my favourite cousin Johnnie, a magnificent chap two years my senior, was in the habit of whiling away his afternoons here. Johnnie was unaccompanied by nagging nannies, and I admired his status.

Like my father, Johnnie's had been a career officer in the Austro-Hungarian army, in the turbulent era that followed the collapse of the empire. It was with Johnnie in the park that I conducted the first business transaction of my life. One afternoon I arrived there with my nanny, proudly carrying a miniature Flaubert rifle which my father had bought for me on one of his trips to Switzerland. It was a beautiful piece of work with an elaborately chased stock and a dully shining barrel. I could hardly wait to show it to Johnnie, who I believed would be mightily impressed. Nanny settled down on a bench, and I set off to find Johnnie.

He and friends soon came bounding out from same shrubbery, Johnnie in the lead, carrying a white flag draped from a long pole. Johnnie studied my rifle, while I inspected his flag. It appeared to have some vague pattern on it, but essentially it looked very much like an old bed sheet. "What flag is this?" I asked. Johnnie was ready with the answer: "It is a Hungarian revolutionary flag from the 1848 revolution. It belonged to my great-grandfather's regiment."

Now it was I who was truly impressed. We were all brought up on the legends of that era. And Johnnie then made what seemed like a remarkably generous suggestion, "If you would like to have the flag, perhaps I would trade it for your rifle."

That afternoon, I arrived home parading my flag just about the time my father got home from his work. "What is that?" he asked suspiciously. "Where is the Flaubert?" came his next question. When I explained how lucky I had been to trade the rifle to Johnnie for the flag, he summoned my nanny and said, "Quick, get me a taxi."

It was in this same park at the Buda bridgehead that I met my first victim of the Danube. This was at the height of the Depression, and the man must have thrown himself into the water upriver several days earlier and floated here face downward. All of us lined up on the top steps while fishermen pulled him out, and we stayed until a van from the morgue took him away. Later in my life, the river would carry hundreds of bodies away, dead not from self-inflicted wounds, but from shots in the back of the neck. At that time, however, this event cast not the slightest cloud on my sunlit days.

A side spur ran off the Margaret Bridge to Margaret's Island, and sometimes, when my father was free, he would take me to the island, riding a single-track horse-drawn tramcar down to the Polo Club, which my father, a horseman of some distinction, liked to visit. For a good Portorico cigar, the tram driver allowed me to drive his horse and ring the warning bell. This was a superb experience. In the late spring, when the weather began to get warm, we also visited the Palatinus swimming bath. At that time, this consisted of a very large, unlined sandy swimming tank with wooden changing shacks. A city ordinance permitted only old-fashioned swimming suits with shoulder straps for men. The law was strictly enforced by a team of policemen in heavy winter uniforms, shakos, and swords by their sides. As they marched up and down among the sunbathers, red-faced and profusely sweating, the sun worshippers hastily pulled up their straps, immediately slipping them off their shoulders again as soon as the coast was clear. It was after one such swimming excursion that I took my first ride on the Danube in one of the many propeller-driven steam ferries that scurried back and forth between the two embankments, stopping at St. Margaret's Island opposite the Palatinus swimming pool. This was a pleasant way to take our terrible sunburns home to the soothing ministrations of our housekeeper.

In the centre of Margaret's Island was a Victorian covered passageway that led down hundreds of yards to the Casino. This was unbelievably rickety, dirty, and full of birds among the rafters. As I grew older, it was a favourite meeting place of my set. Mounted vertically on the wooden columns were all kinds of game machines, and it was here that I played my first pinball game.

The games in this arcade were much less sophisticated versions of the Japanese pachinko games. Only much later did I see the classic American machines, but the principle is always the same. Pinball games are games of chance—chance and a suspicion of skill. You work the machine, flip the levers with all your cunning, but you never control where the ball will settle. It was good training perhaps. In time, along with many, I would play these games for life.

Driving to the Great Danube Bend

My contact up to this time with the Danube was mainly visual. In the spring of 1929, however, a new era started. My father, who was brought up himself on the Tisza river, the second largest in Hungary, decided that it was time that I got closer to the water, and on a fine Saturday we drove out of Budapest along the left bank of the river, my father, my grandfather, and myself with my Uncle Julius at the wheel of his huge Austro Daimler touring car. Our objective was a small village about 40 miles upriver along the left bank of the Danube.

Uncle Julius had arrived early in the morning at our house with his magnificent machine. It was huge, shiny, racing green in colour, with a gigantic steering wheel, old-fashioned hand-pumped horn, a tool box on the running board with the emergency brake, and two huge spare tires set on either side of the front mudguards. Its soft, butternut-coloured, real leather seats smelled as only real leather can, and there was an extra windshield at the rumble seat behind the front seats, but this hardly concerned me, because I was always permitted to sit in the front assisting Uncle Julius by judiciously pumping his horn, watching the water temperature gauge set over the radiator cap, and making myself useful. To sit up front with Uncle Julius was great fun. Unlike my father's chauffeur, he was a dashing driver, and his cars were always infinitely more glamorous than the black saloon cars my father favoured. And not only was Uncle Julius a dashing driver, he was also a most romantic figure, dressed in the most beautiful clothes, his feet elegantly shod in the best hand-tooled shoes of Budapest, his blonde wavy hair held down by his driving goggles. He was also a superb mechanic, which was very helpful in those days of motoring in Hungary. He could change tires and repair many quite complex problems (called in Hungarian "defekt") without ever getting dusty, working like a surgeon over the car with his soft kid-gloved hands.

Many of Uncle Julius' exploits were only whispered about among the adults, but enough filtered through for me to know that he was the principal or sole financial drain on my aging grandfather. Whenever my grandfather tried to put the screws on Uncle Julius, my grandmother, ever protective of her firstborn, intervened and once again induced my grandfather to come to his aid.

Only once, early in the 1920s, after a major peccadillo involving signing his father's name to a promissory note in payment for a major present to a young actress, did grandfather take firm action. As a condition for covering the note, Julius had to disappear from Hungary. He chose to go to Egypt, where at first, according to the news that filtered back, he occupied himself as a poor man's Lawrence of Arabia, exploring the desert as the driver for Almassy, a quite well-known Hungarian latter-day explorer. This venture, however, came to an end due to lack of funds. About that time, Uncle Julius, who himself was an officer with the horse artillery along with miscellaneous Austro-Hungarian cavalry officers, decided to stage the first point-to-point steeplechase in Egypt. The event proved a great success; however, rumours of serious irregularities in connection with inside betting and other less formidable charges on the part of Uncle Julius and others resulted in the scattering of this little expatriate Hungarian group.

Julius mysteriously resurfaced in Turkey, where, not surprisingly, he organised Western-type horse breeding for the new revolutionary Kemal government. True to form, however, something went wrong, and soon thereafter—I must have been about four—he reappeared in Budapest. With him in tow he had a beautiful and sultry Turkish girl (it appeared that Uncle Julius had become engaged) and also her mother who had financed Uncle Julius's return trip. The girl and her mother were formally introduced to my grandparents and soon after that hurriedly returned to Istanbul, poorer but wiser. Uncle Julius, who had been forgiven on condition of returning the ladies whence they came, had been staked to a small car dealership. This suited him well, but unfortunately Uncle Julius did not buy cars that were easy to sell; he bought racing cars, the rationale being that racing his colours would make him famous and that would be good for business.

He had come into my life in flesh and blood the previous summer. To visit my grandparents, I had arrived with my nanny at the small railway station of Oroshaza and after innumerable kisses was seated between my grandmother and my nanny in the back of my grandparents' very sober open Nash car for our drive to my grandfather's property. Our train had pulled out, and the railway gates across the road began to lift. But the gates hesitated, then descended again. Belching black smoke, the 3 o'clock freight train came majestically around the bend, blowing its whistle furiously.

It was at this moment that Uncle Julius made his dramatic entrance. He came galloping down the road and took his horse over the first crossing gate, then over the second. As he jumped off at our side, the freight train came rumbling by amid acrid smoke and great clamour.

This same Uncle Julius was now driving us across the river and out of Budapest. The road we took out of the city still had the original cobblestones from the days when the Romans were here, and in the industrial section we passed through there was formidable traffic. Heavy horse-drawn drays, taxis, streetcars, and chain-driven trucks were all interwoven in the pattern of traffic. But soon we passed the large leather tannery with its unbelievable smell and were out in the open country. The road was macadam-paved, with white milestones, and ran along the Danube's left bank. The Danube was quite different here: cleaner, bluer, younger even. It was also narrower. This was because of the large Szentendre Island which stretched all the way from Budapest for about 35 miles, splitting the Danube into two branches, the small Danube and the large Danube.

We now proceeded along the bank of the large Danube. The traffic was light here, and I could see the little whitecaps that the north wind put on the waves. The island's banks were dotted with the pumping stations of the Budapest waterworks, and between them weeping willows grew. There was little traffic on the river apart from the occasional skiff, but we passed a few floating restaurants and a real "Csarda" or country inn.

Soon we reached Vác, a major centre by our standards. After Vác, we had to turn inland because the river road was flooded and began to climb up a mountain into the forest. At the ridge, the road again turned towards the river and began to descend, leading us into what was considered the most dangerous and hazardous part of the road, a real hairpin turn with a considerable drop. It almost seemed that the lower part of the hairpin bent under the upper. Uncle Julius drove carefully here, slamming the car into low gear after a swift double-clutching manoeuvre. This caution was justified because we suddenly came upon a truck overturned, its windows broken, with several goats bleating inside it. We stopped beyond it and walked over to offer help. The occupants were gone. As I looked into the cab, I could smell petrol and felt that I had been the witness of a dramatic event. This drama in my mind was further underscored by the loud ticking of a dashboard clock, the lone witness to whatever may have happened.

We drove on in the sun until again the Danube began to show between the trees, and soon we could see the upriver point of Szentendre Island. Further upriver in a broad sweeping bend loomed mountains on both sides. On our side the mountains rose more slowly, on the other quite suddenly, into almost a vertical wall. On the top of this were the ruins of Visegrad Fortress, and at the bottom, near the bend in the river, stood Solomon's Tower, a part of ancient fortifications, and King Mathias' famous castle. Between this mountain and the riverbank was the village of Visegrad, and almost directly opposite, on our side, the village of Nagymaros. The villages faced each other across the river, and in the centre of each rose the spires of competing Roman Catholic churches, each with main squares in front, sloping down to the river bank. The only connection between the villages was the car ferry, whose stations were, and still are, located at the foot of the two main squares. On the Nagymaros side, the main boat station for the river steamers was also in this location, but in Visegrad it was further downriver at the foot of the ancient fortress.

In those days, because of their scenic aspect, the presence of the Danube, the mountains, and the protected location, the two villages facing each other at the great Danube bend were very popular summer resorts. My father had decided to survey both for suitability.

It was around eleven o'clock when we pulled up at an ice-cream parlour on the main square of Nagymaros, and while Uncle Julius was treating me to a double ice cream on the terrace, my father began negotiations with a realtor across the way. His specifications were quite exact. The house he would rent had to be far enough up the foothills so as not to be damp and must have a view of the river. Soon he was equipped with a list, and we started on our search.

First we drove along the railway dam which separated the village into two sections. It was the main man-made physical feature of the village. Built as a relief program for the numerous unemployed in the middle 1920s, it was faced with great blocks of stone. Many of the stones had the initials of

26

the builders painted on them in different colours. Somewhere among them, I was told, were the initials of Charlie, oldest son of our housekeeper, who had gone to Nagymaros on a marathon race. It was on my agenda to search for them later.

The great Danube bend.

When we left the dam, we travelled along a country road, past typical peasant houses, finally reaching what seemed to be a large parade ground or athletic field. Here the road veered towards the mountain slope. At the far end of the field, facing Visegrad, we came upon a large whitewashed building which had an old German sign on its face, "Zur Neuen Welt," or "Into the New World." Underneath also, in somewhat faded ancient German lettering, was the slogan, "Wanderer, he who goest through the wide world, come find rest at the New World." A huge mural depicting a typical German wandering apprentice in the attire of long-gone centuries completed the art work. In front, in the sun, were many tables and chairs, many occupied by red-faced farmers with big moustaches drinking the local wine.

We stopped here, got out of the car, and settled at one of the tables under a colourful umbrella. The proprietor, Anton Heininger, approached our table with the respect shown to folks who had arrived in a magnificent motor car. Mr. Heininger was also red-faced and totally bald, but he had a rather rakish military moustache and a green apron. Grandfather had a stein of beer and a small portion of goulash with some white peasant bread. We had cold cuts, and Uncle Julius and my father had some of the local red wine brought up from the cellar by Mr. Heininger in a glass gourd. Soon my father, who was in the wine business, having retired from the Austro-Hungarian army, engaged Mr. Heininger in a lively conversation. This first centred on Mr. Heininger's military career, which Father found to be to his satisfaction, then switched over to the quality of the local wines in general and the innkeeper's wine in particular. This laid the foundation of a very friendly relationship which was to last for years. Meanwhile, from the terrace, I admired the view: on the Visegrad side, the ruins of the fortress citadel silhouetted against the sky seemed like a gigantic steamboat shipwrecked on top of the mountain, like Noah's ark.

The puzzling thing to me was that everybody spoke a strange language. My grandfather explained that most of the village inhabitants were Schwabs who originated in Swabia in Germany and came here as colonisers under the scheme of one of the Hapsburg rulers. They had never assimilated, but remained a tight prosperous community, speaking an atrocious dialect of which I could hardly understand a word although I was quite fluent in German. Of course, they could all speak Hungarian, too, as education was in Hungarian.

While we were sitting there, my father went through his list of prospective houses and received the advice to visit a prosperous farmer called Takacs whose house was just around the corner, No. 4 on a street which ran up a small valley up towards the mountains. The street was called "Catfish Valley," for what reason I could never find out. The lower section was paved so that Uncle Julius could drive up in the car, and just where the pavement ran out, No. 4 was located. It was obviously a prosperous farmer family's house, built of bricks with a large garden and fine veranda. Across the road was a villa surrounded by many trees and lilac bushes, not in a farmer's style. The moment we stopped our magnificent machine, children appeared from all sides and silently began to examine us and our car.

We proceeded into the garden, where we were met by an extremely handsome grey-haired farmer, Mr. Takacs, and by his kind-looking wife. Mr. Takacs had a military bearing, having been a sergeant major in the Great War. Several of his fingers were shot away, but his grip was firm and his blue eyes smiling. Soon everybody was settled at a table on the veranda shaded by all kinds of creepers running up on strings, and Mr. Takacs brought up some wine from his own vintage. The business was quickly settled, hands were shaken, and we were to move into the house for the summer, while Mr. Takacs would move into his summer house in the back of the garden, nestling under his vineyard.

On the way back to the main square, we stopped at a local truck owner's place recommended by Mr. Takacs, and Father made some arrangements. He was very happy to have found a nice house with a most magnificent view in a sunny spot which would even catch the late afternoon sun, and he was also pleased to have found an honest Hungarian farmer with military background, which was very important to him.

Once we reached the main square, my father suggested that we take the ferry to Visegrad. The car was driven onto a large pontoon, and a graceful little propeller boat, appropriately named *Szep llonka* ("La belle Helene") chugged across to Visegrad with us. The pontoon was guided to a landing stage, and we drove up a very steep incline to the village. Soon again we were sitting in the shaded garden of another inn, not quite as interesting as the one in Nagymaros. The view from here was also fine, but not as romantic as from the other side, and the sun here had already disappeared, while Nagymaros was basking in its last rays. And we could see from here that above the village of Nagymaros, where the streets stopped, there was inviting terrain: hills covered in green leafy trees, above which was a plateau from where the mountains rose further, covered with evergreens.

After numerous glasses of wine and raspberry juice, for me, it was time to go. We drove back to the steep ferry ramp. Uncle Julius stopped the car at the top, and because the ferry was on the opposite side, all of them got out for a little walk. I however, took the opportunity to be in charge of the car. As my father stopped at the ferry ticket office, the car began slowly to roll towards the river. I first noticed trouble when I saw all three of them yelling and running towards me. The car gathered momentum, leaving them behind. I did not fully realise the danger of the car running into the swift current from the empty landing dock, but I saw that action was needed. So I stood up and, as I had seen Uncle Julius do many times, grabbed the ribbed end of the emergency brake and pulled as hard as I could. The car stopped just in time, with the front wheels inches from disaster. I was very proud and did not understand the fuss and concern. The ferry came, and we wended our way back to Budapest. Of this trip, though, no matter how hard I try, I can't remember anything. Obviously no more interesting things happened.

The First Summer

June came, and with it the day of moving out to Nagymaros. My nanny, our maids, and the housekeeper had been preparing things for days in advance. Large wooden crates were ordered, and into these went all the things that would not fit into the leather valises: cooking utensils, pillows, sheets, summer clothing, towels, and a million other things that were on the list that Madame (our housekeeper) had made up. The tension mounted.

Finally, one morning, the truck from Nagymaros arrived. This was an exceptionally interesting antique truck of pre-World War I vintage driven by Mr. Julius Wiesel, the Nagymaros entrepreneur. He was accompanied by three strong young Schwabs (later eminent members of the Waffen SS). Mr. Wiesel himself was a very large hairy freckled fat man in a faded tank top and baggy trousers, who was sweating profusely, his red chest hair glistening, even before helping to move our cases onto the truck. In fact, Mr. Wiesel did not help, but he made a lot of noise urging his helpers to hurry. When they all disappeared inside the house, I could not contain my interest in motorised vehicles and slipped out unnoticed by my nanny. The truck had very few distinguishing marks apart from a slight list to one side. I climbed into the cab and tried various buttons, but nothing happened. I went on with my survey outside and found two large old-fashioned unstreamlined headlights up front. They looked at me in a cross-eyed concentration. They had no glass in front of them, so I had no difficulty in removing two large light bulbs which I thought could be quite handy to me later.

Finally everything was loaded and covered with a tattered tarpaulin, securely lashed down, and after a few futile tries at cranking up the engine, Mr. Wiesel got behind the volant, and his helpers pushed until the truck began to roll down the hill. Mr. Wiesel ground it into gear, and after several violent explosions, the engine started. The helpers climbed aboard, and the whole contraption disappeared, dripping oil and enveloped in a cloud of black smoke. Mr. Wiesel's name was Julius, as was my uncle's and also our chauffeur's, and for a long time after, I was under the impression that everybody closely associated with the internal combustion engine was called Julius.

We had a leisurely breakfast because Mr. Wiesel could safely be given a couple of hours' advantage, and then we got into my father's black car. Of course, again I was up front with the chauffeur, while my grandmother, Madame, and the nanny sat in the back, with one of the maids facing them on a little folding seat.

My father had very wisely decided to follow us a couple of days later when all things were unpacked and in place.

Meanwhile, he stayed in our house, which was run after a fashion by the older of the maids during the summer season.

Soon after Vác, we saw Mr. Wiesel on the roadside; he and one of the helpers were applying a rather large black patch onto one of the red inner tubes, tools and a pump lying about them in the dust. The other two helpers were sitting on the other side of the road in the ditch among the cornflowers, enjoying the early summer sun. "No, thank you," Mr. Wiesel said, he needed no help and would be following us shortly. So we rolled on and arrived safely at the Takacs house in Nagymaros. The gates were opened and the car rolled onto a grassy area in the shade. Madame improvised a good lunch from a hamper, and I set about exploring the immediate surroundings. We did not worry at all about Mr. Wiesel until it got quite dark. But by nightfall, there was no sign of him, nor our bed things. Around ten o'clock, my nanny improvised a bed for me and I went soundly to sleep.

Mr. Wiesel's truck rolled in at 4 A.M., one of the assistants sitting on the front bumper with a carbide lamp. Of course, we all got up and heard the story of how after several blowouts they stopped at a roadside inn, and while they were having dinner, somebody stole the bulbs out of the headlights. That had slowed their progression to a crawl. Mr. Wiesel was rightly very angry and tired. They left the unpacking until the next day and departed. I quietly slipped out into the privy and dropped the two beautiful bulbs into the dark hole. Though my nanny suspected my guilt, nothing was ever proved.

And so the wonderful "first summer in Nagymaros on the bank of the Danube" began. As soon as my father arrived, he decreed that both of us should sleep on couches on the veranda. This he considered a healthy toughening-up experience for me. I did not mind as long as he was there also, but found it very frightening by myself. So in spite of his orders, I persuaded my nanny to let me into the house when we were alone. The Takacs were wonderful people who had a son, Jani, at that time 19 years old. In addition to his parents, his old grandmother, Horvath néni, also lived with them. The main brick house was long and narrow and was located at right angles to the street, two of its shuttered windows facing the brick-paved sidewalk. It had been built by Mr. Takacs, a professional mason. The veranda, facing south, extended the entire length of the house and was wide and very pleasant. Between it and a well-kept narrow walk, beautiful rose bushes grew, supported by white-washed posts on top of which were different-coloured glass globe ornaments reflecting the sun. The outdoor privy was located at the end of the house. The path went on along a little flower garden to the foot of the vineyard, where the summer kitchen was located at right angles to the main house, forming a kind of square. Next to the summer kitchen was the entrance to a wine cellar which went deep under the mountain, and beyond this and in line with the summer kitchen were the stables. The farmyard included a small orchard and formed a two-acre square bordering on Catfish Valley. The whole yard sloped towards the Danube and a well. The farm wagons and animals all entered on this lower side through a gate. At the bottom of the property was a thick row of lilac bushes which completely hid a narrow concrete catchment trench (much favoured later in cowboys and Indians games).

Between the wine cellar and the stables, a garden gate led to a series of stone steps which took you to the top of the vineyard, several hundred feet up. Here was a beautiful old mulberry tree, under which, facing the river, was an old stone bench overgrown with moss. In front of that, an old millstone formed a rough table. This became a favourite afternoon spot for my nanny and me. Under and around the millstone, perhaps because of the many fallen berries, one could find the most beautiful large vineyard snails. The tree itself was quite hazardous, particularly when the berries were ripe, because they left indelible marks on one's clothing.

The wine cellar and a narrow strip of land right in the middle of the property did not belong to the Takacs family, but to a widowed, friendly old Swab called Gress Bacsi, who resisted all efforts to buy him out. His resistance was reinforced by his love of his wines. Though he lived in quite a different part of the village, I can never remember a day when he was not in his cellar, puttering about among his barrels, filtering, filling up barrels, or burning sulfur sticks in the empty barrels to get rid of germs, all the while drawing off a gourd of wine from one or another of the barrels to sample. By late afternoon, he was usually quite pickled, but this only showed in a slight deepening of his already purple face and bulbous nose. He was a great friend of mine because he liked children and was always ready for a chat.

The neighbours to the south, behind the lilac bushes, turned out to be of little interest. The neighbours across the road were more so. In an elegant villa lived a Mr. Bock, the Hungarian representative to the International Court at The Hague. A portly fellow with a moustache, he looked every bit the Southern judge in an American novel and probably had a very similar mental makeup. He was rarely to be seen, but on those rare occasions, he always wore a crumpled white linen suit with a black tie and a boater. He had a son, George, who I was encouraged to make friends with, but with very little luck. The other George had a tree house, was three years older, and could not be bothered with me.

Immediately behind us were a garden and house in a similar arrangement to ours, also owned by a Swab farmer. That house in the summer was rented to a Jewish family, none of whose members we met for quite a long time because I was not encouraged to do so. Eventually, though, I became quite friendly with the little daughter, Marika. For many summers, however, this family was a source of constant irritation to us because they behaved in what was said to be a noisy and abandoned manner, partly perhaps because of their large numbers. Grandfather, grandmother, father, mother, daughter, and several aunts and uncles hustled and bustled around during the weekends. Their worst offence was their spring-operated record player, which they set up on a table in the garden just behind our brick wall. They had several quite scratchy records, but most of the time they played a fiercely patriotic nationalistic song, then very popular, and sung by a famous tenor: "You are beautiful, you are gorgeous, my country, my Hungary, more beautiful than the whole world." This continued on in a mushy and sentimental way. Even now, more than 50 years later, I can hear the tune wafting over the wall. The family itself is long gone, having been put into a cattle train in 1944 by their fellow Hungarian patriots and dispatched to a destination from which none of them ever came back.

Immediately above our house, the road narrowed, as I soon discovered, and ran uphill through Catfish Valley past about 20 more gardens and houses. There were only one or two buildings out of the ordinary. The first one, halfway up and on the opposite side from us, nestling right under the steeply rising hill, was a large villa, obviously unusual in design and stuccoed with trellised wood ornaments under heavily overhanging eaves. The view into its living room was quite unobstructed, and to my great fascination and puzzlement, I could clearly see two gigantic elephant tusks. Every visible corner of the huge veranda was also decorated with most unusual trophies. Whenever the door opened, a stocky individual emerged, with a shotgun slung on his shoulder. He wore a worn green loden coat and soft felt hat which was pulled down over his eyes so that the face was hardly showing. He peered in an unfriendly way at all children and never said a word to anybody. Briskly he trotted off up the valley in his plus fours with heavy hobnailed boots and with his Hungarian pointer on a leash. Much later, I found out that he was a Hungarian celebrity, Kalman Kittenberger, who had lived for many years in Kenya and was a well-known white hunter and wildlife writer. Today this house that I found so fascinating is a museum.

As my nanny and I walked on, we found that the houses were dropping behind, and the valley floor became a green meadow with honeybees buzzing and wild flowers and honeysuckle growing. The sun broke through only in a limited way because on both sides the hills rose quite steeply and were covered with chestnut trees. In fact, this place was known as the chestnut orchard. To the left, a small trail appeared to wind up to the crest through rocks and mossy ground, and except in the middle of summer, a small amount of surface water which came splashing down.

My nanny and I did not venture up the trail; instead, we used to carry an army horse blanket up to the meadow and throw it onto the tall grass. Well, as a matter of fact, we took the trail once. My nanny, a big-boned simple Moravian some forty years of age, was a great expert in mushrooms, and one early afternoon, after a particularly rainy period, when as everyone should know, the mushrooms just "mushroom", she decided that we should go looking for them on the hillside. Abandoning our horse blanket, we set off to climb the slippery path. I was more interested at that time in butterflies, having just acquired a butterfly net, but I went along without protesting. Anyway, I was getting tired of hunting butterflies, of which there was a most colourful and wonderful variety in the meadows. The mushrooms, too, were colourful and of many varieties. You had to be an expert to separate the edible ones from the poisonous ones. As I recall, the more colourful the mushroom, the more dangerous it was declared to be. There were hundreds of kinds: red ones, spotted ones, big umbrella types, small bulbous ones. We kept working our way up the mountain, with me running ahead and looking under the trees, and when I found a mushroom I was not sure about, I ran back to nanny. If she passed them, they went into the basket. Soon my basket began to get loaded with mushrooms. Her basket was empty because of her physical shortcomings. The climb was too much for her. She huffed and puffed as we went along.

The chestnut trees became fewer and fewer as we climbed higher on a rutted trail. Now we were surrounded by vineyards; never had we been so far from home. After about an hour, we arrived at a plateau where nothing grew but windswept grass on rock-strewn ground. There, for the first time, we looked back. The little valleys stretched below, running down towards the village. The houses were only little clots that grew denser the closer they got to the church. The Danube was a silver ribbon meandering around the big bend. We looked down at King Matthias' Castle in Visegrad below us, across the river.

Now we were tired. Putting down the baskets, we stretched out in the tall grass and fell asleep, the wind whispering softly in our ears and the bumblebees scurrying back and forth over us. When we woke up, it was getting cool, and the sun was fast dropping behind Dobogoko Mountain. Though we saw the village, we were no longer sure which way to go. Finally we set off across the plateau in what seemed the right direction. Suddenly we were in a pine forest, a thick dense forest, the ground strewn with pine needles which muffled all sound. It was strangely quiet, a little eerie. As we followed the trail, it got darker. The trail seemed to drop lower and lower, but then it twisted and went up again. We passed a charcoal burner's hut, but it was empty. It got darker and darker. It must be the trees above our heads, I thought, but soon we got to a clearing, and it was dark there, too. I looked at the sky—stars were beginning to show. We had to face it—we were lost, and night was falling quickly. I suddenly did not feel so brave, and for the first time that day, I reached for nanny's hand. Alas, she was no use at all; not only did she not know which way to go, she was just as scared as I was. I was also getting very hungry. We stumbled on in the darkness. There were some clouds on the horizon, above the trees, and through them the full moon had just begun to rise. The trees were closing in again on all sides. The trail went on winding seemingly in no direction; we stumbled on. I lost my mushrooms somewhere. Suddenly there was a big splashing noise ahead of us. I pulled up, clutching nanny. Now, as the moon freed itself from the clouds, it became a little lighter; in front of us, surrounded by bulrushes, was a small round lake.

The moonlight was reflected on the concentric waves created by the "thing" that caused the splash. It was very beautiful; I still remember the deep indigo colour of the water.

We were of course scared stiff. Yet through it all, I recognised the real beauty of the spot. Behind us, among the trees, an owl started hooting. There were more quick splashes, and a thousand frogs began to croak. After a while, I began to take courage and looked around. In front, a little way into the lake, there was a tiny island which appeared to float. On it sat, bathed in moonbeams, the largest and most glorious of bullfrogs, his throat throbbing. There was no doubt in my mind, based on some recently heard stories, that we had found an enchanted lake on which lived an enchanted Prince who at this moment had chosen to appear in the shape of a bullfrog. I was much relieved now that I knew what it was and could not appreciate the nanny's anxiety. The noises went on around us: the owl hooting periodically, the frogs jumping, the bullfrog calling, splashes, rustling in the bulrushes, and, I could swear, the rustle of four-legged animals in the forest. Above us, the moon kept appearing and disappearing.

We did not dare to go on and huddled in each other's arms leaning against a big tree. I know that I fell asleep, still hearing all the mysterious cries and noises. Then I remember a lantern coming nearer and nearer in the darkness, Mr. Takacs finding us and taking us off the mountain in the wagon. By the next day, I was not at all sure if it had all happened or if I had dreamed it. I still am not sure. I remember the lake, the clearing, the bulrushes, the frogs, the owl, the moon through the trees so very clearly as if it had happened yesterday. Yet, try as hard as I did in later years to find the spot, I never succeeded. Somehow, once I got into the pine forest, none of the trails that I took led me to the lake. And no matter who I asked many years later, no one seemed to know anything about the lake up in the mountain. Nor did any of the other mountain people ever hear about it. Yet I know, up to this day, that it is there; it has been there all this time, and I could find it again if only I took the right trail.

It was a wonderful impressionistic little world, with sunlit patches and summery smells and noises, butterflies of all colours, snails, curious insects, and flowers. On our blanket,

I learned reading and writing before my first year of school from an old-fashioned illustrated alphabet book where "F" was illustrated by a bad little boy who set fire to the house by carelessly playing with matches.

Not far from where we spread the blanket was a piece of land owned by Takacs Bacsi on which several pens were erected, surrounded by a high wire fence on wooden posts. These belonged to Jani, the young son of Takacs Bacsi. He kept several foxes and other small game in these pens, for what purpose I don't know—perhaps he was trying to tame them. If that was his aim, he did not succeed, at least not with the foxes I met, which were always restlessly pacing up and down with really foxy expressions on their faces. Jani was to become my only really good friend in those years. He was a handsome, strong, well-built young man, and he often took me with him when he was going to cut hay on one of the Takacs's outlying pieces of land. These were truly interesting expeditions. At the crack of dawn, I had to be up to assist Jani with harnessing the horse and loading the scythe and various forks and tools on the farm wagon. Soon we were rolling down from Catfish Valley towards the old brickworks, where we passed under the railway embankment through a concrete tunnel. Near the Danube, we came out onto the main highway, turned left, and followed the Danube for about three or four miles. When we were about level with the point of Szentendre Island, we turned left and crossed the railway again. As soon as we were past the tracks, we began to climb upwards. The road became more or less a track, with large rock outcroppings here and there. The noise of the wheels of the farm wagon became quite unbearable as it rumbled on. I was going up and down like a ping-pong ball on my plank seat and had to hang on for dear life. The mountains closed in on both sides as we climbed; the horse kept snorting, but needed no urging.

After about 20 minutes, we reached level ground, and a fair-sized field opened up. It was all covered with green hay. At the far side, the trail disappeared again in the thick forest. Here there was a separate little clearing covered with lush green grass. It was here that Jani pulled up, and we dismounted.

The horse was unhitched and tied to a tree on a long lead. In the back of the clearing, among some shrubs, there was a stone slab overgrown by moss, and in the middle a pipe stuck out, through which fresh ice-cold water was running from a deep well. This place was called the "King's Well" because apparently King Matthias used to water his horses here when on a hunt from his lofty castle. In any case, I tried it, and the water was fit for kings.

Now the sun was high, and Jani put together his scythe and quite methodically, with long swinging motions, seemingly effortlessly, began cutting a wide swath in the hay. I had nothing to do but watch and sit around in the shade. Once in a while, I moved the horse to another tree and then continued watching Jani. He went on row after row without looking around, his muscular arms swinging rhythmically. He usually wore a slightly faded black singlet. In two or three hours, when about half the hay was cut, he suddenly stopped and walked over. We sat down in the shade, and the lunch came out of the basket. It consisted of several green peppers, onions, two large slabs of double-smoked bacon, and gigantic slices of bread. There was a special way of holding the slab of bacon and the bread in one hand, alternately slicing each, spreading them with red-hot paprika, and then eating. All this was washed down with wine from a demijohn.

Afterwards, while I was lying on my back, Jani got out his sharpening stones and first began to beat the edge of the scythe on both sides. This part of the work done, he began to work the already sharp edge with the wet stone. Soon it was sharp enough to slice through a man, and Jani took up his position again where he had left it.

The sun was beginning to approach Visegrad Mountain by the time that all was cut and collected. Then the hay was loaded on the wagon, and here I made myself useful. Higher and higher I climbed, arranging the hay while Jani lifted gigantic forkfuls to my level. When all was loaded, we tied it down safely with a long pole and, hitching the horse back on, climbed aboard on top. Now this was quite a different trip than in the morning. The hay was springy, and the load smelt good from the hay and the sun. The wagon started rolling. At the end of the fields, we remembered the forest and had to lie flat as the branches of the trees scratched the top of our load. The horse went on without guidance. Soon we were back on the main highway, rolling home.

From the top of the wagon, the landscape was even more beautiful. The Danube was painted red by the sunset. There was a lot of activity, too, on the river. Passenger steamers were appearing in the river bend, tying up at Nagymaros and Visegrad. The *Beautiful Helene* was dodging them with her load of cars. When a car overtook us, the whole world was blotted out by the dust which took a long time to settle. It was beginning to get dark when we drove up to the Takacs' barn and Jani lowered me by my hands to the ground. My duties were finished as soon as I helped with the horse. The wagon was left to be unloaded later. Our veranda lights were on, and I could smell a good dinner.

This is how the first few summers passed in Nagymaros. Moving with Mr. Julius Wiesel in the spring, summers which were hot and sweet, then suddenly around August 20, the rains would start, and soon we would move back to Budapest.

Budapest, Tear of the Angels

"Budapest, pearl of the Danube,
Budapest, tear of the angels...."

Uncle Julius at the time was my favourite uncle, not only because he was the most romantic of my relations, but because of his habit of throwing me a shiny freshly minted silver five-pengo coin every time I bumped into him. Now today's child psychologists would no doubt disagree with his methods, but I assure you that it was a powerful gesture and one which I appreciated very much. So much so that, quite unashamedly,

41

I took to hanging around my grandparents' house every time Uncle Julius was expected.

My enthusiasm for Uncle Julius was somewhat tempered in the early thirties when one Christmas he bought me the most magnificent toy I have ever seen. This was a horse-drawn artillery battery complete with all equipment, including four minutely detailed howitzers that actually shot rubber projectiles in exactly the right trajectory. The officers, the soldiers, and the gunners were all beautifully moulded of lead and hand-painted in true regimental colours, each about two inches high. They were made in a famous Viennese toy factory which in fact even today is still doing a roaring business with its moulded lead figures in the uniforms of the historic regiments of the Austro-Hungarian Empire. Altogether, there were about 60 horses with the corresponding number of riders; there were trumpeters, regimental colour bearers, even a field kitchen. I spent the whole of Christmas Day setting up the artillery column in the proper marching order under my father's direction. When all set up, the column was about eight feet long and occupied most of the nursery floor. There were even camouflage hedges supplied with the set.

Even in those days of deflation, it was worth a great many dollars. The trouble was—and this became painfully obvious—that though Uncle Julius knew exactly how to please me, he did not have the money to pay for this largesse. This did not deter him, however; he simply charged it all to my father, figuring that he would not have the heart to take it away from me and would eventually settle the bill. My father, a man of great moral principles, was on this occasion utterly lacking in humour. He did not follow suit. When the fashionable toy shop Todor Kertesz phoned him to confirm the arrangement, he simply had the whole set packed up and returned it while I was out walking with Fräulein. It was years later that I got the full story, but in the meantime it was I who was punished, and not Uncle Julius, who was long hardened to the occasional setback.

The windows of the Todor Kertesz toy shop delighted generations of children, including myself, with their displays and elaborately set-up electric train models, and it was a sad day when, one day during the Great Depression, the shop simply boarded up its windows on the corner of the Servitan's square and closed down. The store's demise would indicate that there had to be many "Uncle Julius's" around at that time. But Budapest had other attractions remaining, even for an eight-year-old.

The great hotels of Budapest faced the Danube between the Chain Bridge and the Elizabeth Bridge and looked across at the Royal Palace. In front of the hotels were terrace cafés, before which on the upper Danube embankment stretched a promenade called the Corso. It was sunny here in the afternoons, and in the spring it was a pleasant meeting place for all. People sat on the terraces, and young men and women promenaded, greeting each other, chatting and flirting. This was where all the sartorial splendour of Budapest was displayed. Even as a child eating an ice cream, I enjoyed being part of it. And on outings with my father, I loved to visit the elegant shops, which contributed in no small way to the glamour of Budapest in the pre-war days.

My father's tailor was on the first floor of a building on Kossuth Lajos utca, a few minutes' walk from the National Casino, the club of the aristocracy. "Uncle" Knizek was a true Savile Row tailor, a famous cutter at a top Savile Row establishment, whom the magnates of Hungary had transplanted from London to save themselves the trouble of fittings during their annual visits to England. His shop was a wonderful place, with a huge counter where bolts of the best English and Scottish materials were spread out to be examined and selected. The walls were mahogany paneling covered with English hunting prints. You could not walk into the establishment without a proper introduction, and most clients were second- and third-generation customers.

All clients' cutting patterns, made of heavy English cotton, were hung permanently in a huge storage area next to the fitting room. Of course, to make sure, "Uncle" Knizek always took new measurements personally, and it was generally known that people had been told to go away and come back after losing some weight so that their measurements fit the patterns on file. Not that this happened frequently—almost everybody kept their measurements all their lives. The fitting room was a place of wonderful experiences. Cut-glass mirrors were all over. In the corner, surrounded by special mirrors, stood a full-size roan horse rigged up with a fine English saddle for fitting the tailor's famous riding breeches and hunting jackets to enhance the perfect seat of the horseman or cavalryman. "Uncle" Knizek was also the most renowned uniform tailor. As for his civilian clothes, only the best bespoke tailors of Savile Row could match them.

At Knizek's, unless a special hacking or hunting jacket was required, all you had to do was select the material; there was no discussion as to style. All suit jackets were natural-shouldered, three-buttoned, with the top buttonhole hand-stitched for a natural roll. "Uncle" Knizek went to London every year to keep up with Savile Row and to buy all the materials, cloth—tweeds, flannels in all colours except brown (which gentlemen never wore)—lining materials, buttons, and even thread. In fact, in 1939, foreseeing the war, he bought enough of everything to last him many years, and indeed until 1948 he still had pre-war English materials available.

Near Knizek, and also within walking distance, were world-famous shoemakers, Triznya, Csakany, and the "heavy-moustachioed" Mladencsics. But the most important shoemaker was Maestro Nyeste, in whose workshop the most exquisite leathers were fingered, smelled, and spread out over the counter before ordering a pair of shoes. In the back of the workshop, in a room completely filled with neat, labelled pigeonholes, were the lasts: exact replicas of the feet of most everybody who was anybody walking around in Budapest. Like Knizek's canvas cutting patterns, these lasts were a veritable who's who of the era. The shoes the Maestro made were tooled on these individual lasts and fitted to perfection when completed.

Within a quarter-mile of the elegant Kossuth Lajos utca, between Knizek and Nyeste, was the Habig Haberdasher, where not only were the finest Egyptian cotton and silk shirts and other underwear items hand-sewn to measure, but also Budapest's largest supply of heavy English silk ties and hand-blocked foulards was displayed. There were rows and rows of Italian Borsalino Antica Casa hats, while a good supply of English homburgs, bowler hats, and top hats stood imposingly on individual stands.

Hard by Habig's shop was the barber shop of Bernath and Toth, where at any moment of the day, a few cabinet ministers would be having their hair trimmed and sheared by such illustrious barbers as Mr. Kohler, who was the Regent's (Admiral Horthy's) personal and travelling barber, or their nails clipped by Manci, the corpulent manicurist whom everybody knew and who knew everything worth knowing. Manci was an authority on Madame Frieda's emporium, also a short walking distance away, where the gentlemen could relax after a day of fittings before returning to their houses for dinner. This was located in Magyar utca in a very elegant four-storey building with a classical facade, its windows heavily shuttered. A few steps led up to a heavy oak door, brass-studded with brass knobs centred on each of the double doors. This establishment lasted well into the Communist era before the ménage was re-educated and new employment found for many of the hostesses in the "Red Star" stocking factory. The building itself, without much alteration, became the "People's Republic Home" for retired actresses.

Kossuth Lajos utca, with its exclusive facilities, ended at the corner of Kecskemeti utca, where the small ochre-coloured Franciscan Church stood. On its wall, facing the street, was a memorial to the great Danube flood of 1838, with an arrow indicating the highest level that the floodwaters reached. A relief sculpture showed the baron Miklos Wesselenyi punting his wooden boat and plucking lucky citizens out of the flood.

45

Across from the church on the opposite corner could be seen around noon much of the fashionable population of Budapest on its way to shopping, clubs, or home for the important lunch and siesta. Many dashed into A.M. Kovacs' luxurious delicatessen located on the corner of the Archducal Palace on Esku ter. At this corner, unless weather made it impossible, stood at noon the imposing figure of my Uncle Feri, whose impeccably cut overcoat also came from "Uncle" Knizek, emphasising his still-slim figure. A careful observer could see that his right shoulder was slightly broader than the left. Few knew that this was due to many years of sabre fencing, during which career he became the Hungarian sabre champion ahead of many fine officers who coveted this honour. Uncle Feri, who was never in the army due to his age at the time of World War One, was only a lawyer.

It was Uncle Feri who introduced my father to Uncle Knizek before the first Great War, when my father was a young lieutenant. I myself had my first real Norfolk jacket fitted when my father brought me there at the age of six.

Many years later, in the Communist era, as part of my escaping clothes, Knizek made a last Harris tweed jacket for me. It still hangs in my closet today, and though a few buttons are missing, it still fits better on the shoulders than any other suit I ever had.

On the River

In those first years in Nagymaros, I met the Danube only on weekends or when my father spent a few weeks on holidays. He used to go down to the river front to a boat livery and rent a rather cumbersome skiff. When I was a few years older, perhaps in 1933, he decided to have a skiff built to his own specifications by one of the famous boat builders of Aquincum near Budapest, an ancient Roman settlement which was then dotted with hundreds of boathouses from which every weekend thousands of boats were launched into the river.

The usual Danube touring boat was based on the design of the classical racing skiff with two rolling seats, a seat for the cox, and a seat up front. They had keels and were built of wooden planks. The main difference was that they were a lot wider than a racing skiff, approximately 0.7 metres; the boat was also a little higher to withstand the rough storms on the river, and at the same time a little shorter, approximately 23 to 24 feet in length. Another difference was the elimination of the air space in the bow and stern to provide more accommodation. This frequently resulted in catastrophe because these boats could quickly become awash and there would be nothing to do but swim for it.

Our boat was finished and duly launched early in the spring, and for the next two months, I practised rowing with my father on the waters near Budapest. Then, when the holidays came, the boat was lashed to the deck of one of the packet steamers and duly delivered to the Nagymaros boathouse. This emporium was on the embankment, downriver from the ferry landing, and consisted of two boat sheds, where everybody's boats were kept on racks, and a large floating raft. On the raft was the office of the owner, a man called Antal Kmetty; the family were the owners of the hairdressing shop, and one of the daughters was Jani Takacs' future wife. Mr. Kmetty was bald-headed, olive-skinned with almond-shaped green eyes and rather full lips. Well, really, his name was not Kmetty. His real name was Naguli; he was Rumanian and had somehow married into the Kmetty family and assumed their name. Being Rumanian was a lot to live down in Nagymaros, and so Mr. Naguli-Kmetty spent his days sitting quite alone in his office on the floating part of the boathouse, doing his accounts or just meditating. Also located on the raft was a toilet with very elementary facilities emptying directly into the Danube and two dressing rooms, one for men and the other for women. In the changing rooms, there was a bench and a number of pegs on which one hung one's clothes. If one were foolish enough to bring any valuables, Mr. K would lock them up. In the pine partition between the changing rooms, there were a number of knotholes. By proceeding cautiously, one could take a peek through to the ladies' side. At the age of 11, I tried it and was rewarded with the first striptease of my life by a slim young woman who had a very nice suntan except on her boobs, which were flashing white with rich brown nipples. It was very exciting and much like a show.

As I grew older, the days in Nagymaros followed several routines. On days when my father had to go to Budapest, he got up very early and took my bike. By this time, I was the owner of a man-sized bike, a powder-blue IPAG. This was always shiny and clean because my father inspected it as he would a horse, running his fingers through the parts for specks of dust. He rode it down to Nagymaros station, where he padlocked it and took the train to Budapest. I got up around eight and after breakfast had to walk down to the railway station. I resented this walk very much, but I had to do it because I knew that my father would check with Mr. Kmetty regarding my activities. If I were not on the river by 11, there would be hell to pay later.

After I reclaimed my bike, I rode over to the boathouse. Not very fast, mind you, but with a little detour to the village square and to Galli's Confectionary for Italian ice cream, and also perhaps to the cigar store at the ferry station, where an unfriendly Schwab, again a wounded war veteran, was dispensing goods. I always had enough money for a few pocket books of the most awful kind. Finally I arrived at the boathouse, and leaning my bike against the building on the shady side, stopped in at the carpentry shop to call on the carpenter who did work on the boats and helped launch them into the water. He was always ready for a little chat and a little wisdom, smoking hand-rolled cigarettes while working with his plane on a snow-white piece of pine wood. Occasionally he would allow me to take a puff. From a little window he had in front of his workbench, we could see the raft; indeed, we had to watch it, because fraternising was not encouraged, and neither of us wanted to be caught by Mr. Kmetty. Sometimes I lingered until around noon, but eventually went off to explore the river.

There were several favourite spots, but when I went out alone, I usually went downriver. I would row halfway across and then let the current carry me perhaps to the point of Szentendre Island, where if the water was at a normal level, there was a nice sand beach. From here, one could see up as far as the big bend to Visegrad and Nagymaros and downriver to both the small and big Danubes. I would sit on the beach with legs spread, looking up and down river, observing the goings-on.

I was beginning to know the various steamers from their shape. Most of them were side-wheelers and had either one or two funnels. Because of this, once I had become familiar with their superstructures, I was able to recognise them miles away. The skimpiest of all was the *Tahi*, an old steam packet with hardly any superstructure and with one rather tall funnel. It was called a market wife's special because it usually travelled downriver at night stopping at each village, picking up farmers' wives who were carrying market produce in large baskets. The *Tahi* ended up every morning at the main Market Hall of Budapest, just downriver from Franz Joseph Bridge on the embankment. The most luxurious steamers were the Saints: two-funnel vessels named after Saint Imre, Saint Stephen, etc. These had five or six levels of superstructure with many decks with restaurants, and they were usually carrying English and American tourists from Vienna to Budapest. These seemed very glamorous as they swished by, and the music of their gypsy orchestras carried a long way over the water. The largest was the *Queen Elizabeth*—not named after the English Queen, but after the wife of the Emperor. Usually they arrived from upriver around 6 o'clock, and a few years later, as I will explain, my friends and I used to be ready, waiting for them near the station.

There were also some Yugoslav steamers on the river. They had a different shape and were extremely fast large passenger boats; in fact, they were referred to as the Yugoslav express steamers, and they would never stop in Hungarian territory, thus keeping up the old animosities. They just suddenly

49

appeared around the bend and steamed away at an unfriendly speed. Boats had personalities, and the Yugoslav express steamers were nasty, unfriendly, and bullies. They quickly disappeared, kicking up gigantic white-capped waves which would swamp you if you were caught unawares.

Around 2 o'clock in the afternoon, I usually rowed across from the island to the Nagymaros side and started the tedious upriver grind. Past shady banks, past the paper factory, I struggled, and finally reached the boathouse. If my father was expected back that day, I had to be at the station at 3:30. I tied my boat to the downriver end of the raft and hurried to the station. By the time I got up to the platform, half of Nagymaros' summer population (the children and mothers) was there waiting for the fathers. In fact, in local parlance, the train—a summer commuter—was called the "bull" train. Naturally, very few people in those days had their own cars, and all would commute by train. My father also preferred the train. He could not drive, and it just did not seem like a logical thing to be driven back and forth 40 miles a day each way.

When the train approached, everybody moved near the edge of the platform towards it. Only the two ever-present gendarmes showed no interest. They went on marching up and down, their rifles slung over their shoulders, the cock feathers on their shakos waving in the wind. The fathers (mine, too) descended from the hot train, and we went back to the boathouse or to Nemes' fruit store, where for his lunch, Father bought some fruit. In ten minutes, we were on the Danube, rowing upriver to some sandbars, where we would beach the boat and sit around in the sun, Father eating his fruit, then having a little nap, his face the colour of ripe peaches in the sun.

Five-thirtyish, we would ease the boat into the stream and drift downriver lazily. It was usually a very tranquil moment with little traffic, and the wind had died off. The trick was to get back to the boathouse before the big steamers from Vienna arrived about 6:30. Then we dressed and walked home pushing the bicycle which served to carry whatever loads there were:

his briefcase first, and then perhaps a watermelon. We always had to walk past Heininger's pub, and so it was natural that we should stop there so my father could have a glass of wine and a little chat. It was the closest equivalent in Hungary to the neighbourhood pub. The big open field in front of it was used to grow sunflowers. As we sat there looking at the unchanging view of Visegrad, the sunflowers turned their backs on us, directing their faces to the last rays of the sun.

Dangerous River Games

I was not the only boy out on the Danube. Others were also roaming about in their boats or hanging around Kmetty's livery. Inevitably we became companions, a select little group allowed out on the river on our own, unlike most of the children of the summer residents. We were a healthy lot of teenagers by now, proud of our suntanned muscular young bodies, risk-takers, maybe reckless.

In the mornings, we sat at the edge of the boat raft with our feet dangling in the smooth silky Danube, impatiently waiting for excitement. Often enough, suddenly in the bend downriver, five miles away, we found it: a heavy tugboat would come into our view, and behind her, maybe half a mile further back, towed by steel cables, would come eight large Danube freight barges, lashed together, their prows slicing the water. This was the moment for carefully timed action.

Moving very slowly upriver, the tug would cut across from the big Danube towards Visegrad, which took half an hour or more to reach. Then she would steam slowly past Visegrad and cut back to the other side again. This was the shortest route to navigate through the two large river bends.

We slipped into the river and began to swim diagonally across, all the time watching the direction of the tugboat. When the tug and the barges travelled in a straight line, the wire cables between them stretched about eight feet above the water level, kept taut by the hundreds of tons of weight of each barge. However, when the tugboat slowly swung to port towards Visegrad, the barges, not easily swayed, carried along on their previous course for some time. This reduced the distance between the barges and the tug, the cables slackened, and somewhere level with Solomon's Tower they usually actually touched water. That was the place and the moment for us.

Knowing the habits of the river, the tugs, and the barges, we were there, about 100 yards behind the tug and 150 yards in front of the barges when the cables came down. Quickly but carefully, on the look-out for split cables, and spacing ourselves about ten feet apart, we hung on. The water lapped against our bodies with the combined speed of the river and the tug, about eight miles an hour. Then slowly the barges began to follow their leader, and the cables began to rise. Soon they were as taut as ever, eight feet above the water. The only difference was that four boys were now hanging onto them, dangling above the water.

The helmsmen and the bargemen shook their fists, but there was nothing they could do. But we, at least in the first few exhilarating minutes, made faces and rude gestures, all the time hanging on with one hand.

In the first phase of this favourite game there were two hazards: one could miscalculate and miss the rendezvous altogether. In this case, there was no choice but to swim back to the Nagymaros side and spend most of the morning on a boring walk back to the boathouse The second hazard was that out of fear of being swept under the oncoming barges, one would grab the cable too close to the tugboat, in which case the tightening of the cables could result in the slicing off of an important body part. According to our group, you had to be awfully inexperienced or stupid to have this happen. But legend had it that a tough boy had had his arm sliced off below the elbow. He tightened his good hand like a tourniquet above the cut and, treading water, reached the shore and walked back to the village, where he collapsed. We never had proof of this story; none of us ever met him or anyone who knew him, but the rumour persisted, so perhaps he came from another village.

Standing on the rudder. The crowds were cheering us!

Once we had gotten onto the cables and had finished taunting the bargemen, a second interesting part of the journey began. Slowly the tug moved upriver and went past the Visegrad waterfront. We drew level with our Nagymaros boathouse and exchanged triumphant waves with our cronies. Ten more minutes, and we were opposite the free beach where there were often pretty girls. More waving.

At this point, we began to tire. Almost an hour had passed on the cable. The summer sun was beating down relentlessly. Still we did not let go. The first man off was a sissy. Teeth gnashing, we hung on some more. Suddenly we became aware again of the eight barges lashed together, covering almost 200 feet of water, eight razor-sharp noses slicing into the waves. It now seemed they were only a few yards away from us. With our cramped tired arms, it seemed impossible to swim fast enough to get out of their way. In the end, somebody yelled "Go!" and we plunged into the water, ice-cold on our naked bodies. But there was no time to think; we thrashed madly as the barges relentlessly drew closer, the bow waves parting, foaming and white in front of them. But we always succeeded and stopped swimming as soon as we were out of danger. Treading water, we watched the black hulls looming high over us slip by, little mongrel dogs yapping at us from the deck. In the sterns, there were little huts where the bargemen and their wives lived on board. The dogs ran right to the stern, yapping angrily, and as often as not got kicked in the ribs by their mistresses, usually active there hanging laundry out to dry, shelling peas, or peeling potatoes, and often dumping some slops on us for kicks.

Some days, no tugboat came around, and we restlessly looked for other activities. High among the possibilities ranked the Danube swim. This meant that one of us at a time dived in and completed around trip to Visegrad and back, a good three-quarters of a mile each way as the crow flies. But we were not flying; we were swimming the Australian crawl against current which was quite formidable in the middle and past it on the Visegrad side. When you managed to get back to the boathouse, your pals pulled you out, because you usually had no strength left. Of course, you were timed by the Visegrad church clock. There was no prize for the winner, but in any case, we were very closely matched, because the less combative had long ago dropped out of our group, exhausted. The river was our territory, and nobody could keep up with us.

But the last and most enjoyable river prank came at the end of the day. At around 6:30, the great Vienna double-funnelled passenger steamer came from upriver, her side paddles slowing as she turned in a great lazy arc towards the Visegrad landing wharf, where she had to dock first for navigational reasons.

All the summer people of Visegrad and many of the natives were waiting, promenading on the embankment. Hardly anybody ever got off here, but that didn't matter. This was the big event of the day. Excitement mounted as the huge steamer swung around into the current. The landing was an elegantly performed spectacle. The river pilot, standing next to the captain, eased the gigantic vessel along the floating landing dock. Ropes were thrown fore and aft. Then, at the very last moment, the pilot reversed the paddle wheels, and just as he rang the engine room down, the steamer eased its bulk alongside, and the great rudder swung in straight.

The ship's orchestra played afternoon-tea dance music, and elegant tourists lounged at the rails. They were English mainly, on a trip to Budapest along this most beautiful part of the Danube. To the people lining the landing stage, they seemed marvellously sophisticated, with cocktail glasses or delicate teacups. And for the tourists, the sight before them must have been truly arresting, with the mountains rising on both banks, the shadows of Mathias' Castle and King Solomon's Tower falling on the steamer, Nagymaros basking in the late afternoon sun, and to top it up, this exotic, colourfully dressed crowd talking excitedly in a strange tongue, waving and staring at them. This confrontation always reminded me of a drawing I had once seen of a bird and a goldfish in a bowl, each staring at the other, so close and yet in two unbridgeably separate worlds. And though the Visegrad crowd did not know it, they were the ones in the bowl.

We boys were there, too, though invisible under the floating landing dock. All four of us had swum across from Nagymaros around six and were hanging onto the understructure between the pontoons in the dank cool darkness. The boat blocked our last bit of light.

The underside of the overhanging stern of the boat was ten feet above the water level. The great rudder nestled under it, stationary. It must have been about ten feet long, its top surface, three or four inches wide. The rudder was now positioned horizontally under the stern, with a six-foot gap above it to its underside. A tall boy could just touch this, standing on the rudder's edge, reaching up with his arms. And that's exactly what we did, clambering up on the rudder one after the other and standing there shivering in the chill. Soon the steam whistle blew, there was ringing in the engine room, ropes were tossed, and the great paddle wheels turned again. The rudder swung to starboard and the ship slipped away, sideways and slowly, on its journey to Nagymaros.

The crowds waved from the landing at the retreating silhouettes of the beautiful people and the beautiful boat. Then, as the ship gained the river, four shivering boys could be seen standing on the rudder, moving with the rudder, walking with hands in reverse on the underside of the boat.

Then the crowds started cheering us. We had escaped from the glass bowl, even if only for a short ride.

By the time the boat left Nagymaros and had executed another beautiful big arc, we were lined up on Kmetty's boat dock, waving madly as the great paddle wheeler passed us on her way to Budapest, our raft creaking and protesting, rocking under us from her waves. When the last snatches of music and peals of laughter died away, we discovered that it was time to get out of the wet swimming trunks and, without even drying, into our shorts and to say goodnight to the river which was now reflecting the many lights of Visegrad. The clock in its tower was a glowing full moon, and not even our sharp young eyes could make out the time. Bells began to toll. Night descended on the river bend.

The Indian Camp

One day while four of us were camping on the beach at the tip of Szentendre Island, one of us noticed a thin column of smoke rising from a small island close to shore. This was unusual—nobody had ever been known to inhabit the small Berman Island, and we considered it our private territory. It had a nice big open meadow in the middle, completely surrounded by huge willow trees which ran right down to the water, overhanging the shores of the island. There was not much of a beach there, and it was not so good for sunbathing except in the late afternoon, but now someone was there.

There was nothing to do but investigate. This we naturally set out to do like Indian scouts in our usual stealthy way. After some hard swimming across the "large Danube," we arrived in the lee of our island. Noiselessly we came out of the water under the willow trees. Carefully crawling on our bellies, we reached higher ground, all the time keeping ourselves completely hidden. The smell of a campfire was now very strong. Parting the tall grass in front of us, at a given signal we carefully raised our heads. "I'll be damned," one of us said. "We must be dreaming." I could not say anything; I simply stared in utter amazement.

In the middle of our island, in the beautiful centre clearing, a big campfire was burning. Around it, arranged in a semi-circle, were about half a dozen buffalo-hide wigwams. A gigantic totem pole stood in front of the largest tent. Indians in full head-dresses and warrant sat in front, passing around the peace pipe. A large number of squaws, dressed in leather skirts with single-feather headbands around their foreheads, were busy preparing what looked like a festive meal. Lolling nearby were a number of children and dogs.

Luckily, we were downwind and so far undetected. We had seen scenes of this sort in the movies and in picture books, but this was real; buffalo hides flapped on the wigwams, and a number of war canoes were turned upside down on the embankment, hidden in the tall grass.

For a while, we quietly watched this unbelievable scene, uncertain whether we might be dreaming. After a whispered conference, we decided that there was nothing to do but attack. We crawled forward as far as possible undetected and then, with bloodcurdling war cries, ran to the Indians.

They were even more surprised than us. The chief dropped the peace pipe and then rose and greeted us peacefully with arms stretched high. To our great surprise, he addressed us in flawless Hungarian. All the braves gathered round, and we soon found out the story. The chief was Ervin Baktay, a world-famous explorer of the Far East and a Tibetan scholar. He and his associates had also travelled widely in America studying the Indian culture and were honorary chiefs of a Sioux tribe from whom they had got all their gear. They had decided to spend a summer's holiday on our island playing Indians.

We explained to them that they were squatting on what we considered our open range, and finally a delightful compromise was reached. We were all admitted to the tribe as honorary members and given all kinds of genuine Indian gear: feather bonnets, belts, jerkins, even Bowie knives and tomahawks. We were also invited to join in their meal, which was really, surprisingly, a very good goulash cooked by their women. This was the only allowance made for foreign culture in their Indian lifestyle.

Soon we were good friends and were invited to join them any time we wanted. The only condition—we must not spread the word. They did not want curious hordes. This was easily done because we were above talking to the other kids, anyhow. For the next three weeks, we spent all our spare time on the island with them, fishing and learning all the Indian skills.

It was a truly great experience. In the evenings, we sat at the campfire listening to the endless stories of the Chief about faraway Tibet: the Lama, his fabulous palace, and the monks with their prayer mills whirring in their hands. His explorations were connected with the tracking of the ancient Magyar nomadic tribes, and we learned more than we possibly could have in a year of school.

From the chief and his scientists, we also learned of the treachery of the white man towards the Indian, long before the Battle of Wounded Knee. We learned that the Indian was not a murderous savage—or even a noble savage—as we were told in school or read in John Fennimore Cooper, but that the Indian nations were peaceful nomadic people who believed that all land belonged to Manitou. They could not adjust to or understand the drive of the white man, who squeezed them into ever-smaller patches of land until their final defeat, then kept them in a captive existence almost like animals in a large zoo. We listened with all our attention and had no doubt that this suntanned silver-haired Hungarian chief was telling us the true story. He confirmed what we knew from *Winetou* by Karl May, the blind German writer who never travelled anywhere and was our favourite writer.

After three weeks, with our assistance, the Indians broke camp and pulled away in their canoes downriver. For many years after, they came back each summer, and we always called when we saw the first smoke of their campfire curling in the blue sky. But each year we had more and more new interests, and so gradually we spent less time with them. These were also times when liberal voices were dying in our country, and, though not consciously, we were less and less interested in stories of faraway lands.

Floods and the Gypsies

Once in a while, heavy rainy weather in faraway Austria caused considerable flooding at Nagymaros. The coming flood was announced in advance by a board mounted on the portside upper deck of the great Danube steamers coming down from Vienna. On this, every day, in big white numerals on a black background, was the water level at Gonyu, where the Danube entered Hungary. We were well versed in reading this information and could predict the exact time and magnitude of the high water which would reach us at Nagymaros. When a really big one was coming, we knew it a day ahead.

It was heralded by muddy, dirty water. The current speeded up, and everything that was floating but anchored to the embankment began to rise rapidly. The floating raft of the boathouse began to rise, its anchoring cables straining. The connecting bridge became horizontal instead of sloping, and the steamboat landing stages began to rise as well. Soon the ferry landing was under water and the ferry system suspended. *Szep Ilonka*, the graceful little propeller-driven steamer that usually scurried back and forth providing car ferry service from Visegrad, was tied up at a small landing stage.

Flotsam and jetsam began to float by, just as on Mark Twain's Mississippi. First, only small shrubs, trees, and wooden farm implements came by; later, as the water continued to rise, bloated and water-logged domestic animals began arriving. Our imaginations were fired by the sinister and dangerous events upriver that must have precipitated this evidence of disaster. By now, the water had reached the lower embankment, which we negotiated on our bicycles with the water up to the axles, sending up huge sprays as we pedaled.

That was the time when the gypsies usually put in their appearance. Where they came from, nobody knew—they were the wandering kind, barefoot, colourfully dressed with bandannas, and dark-skinned with flashing white teeth. The lice were crawling visibly in their long dark hair. First, only a few of their men arrived, but soon there was a whole tribe, with a convoy of caravans drawn by skinny old nags which were tethered under some trees on the upper levels of the still dry embankment.

A disproportionate number of small "purde"—gypsy children—disgorged noisily from the caravans and started their usual activities, which included running, screaming, pushing, engaging in all kinds of unsavoury and precocious activities, and periodically hunting the lice in each other's heads. The very young ones were completely naked, those slightly older had a few rags covering them, but not very decently; I have seen 12- to 13-year-old girls whose gorgeous prematurely ripe bodies were almost completely revealed to the eyes. All the purde defecated when and where the urge came, without the slightest embarrassment, even arrogantly.

The older women, also in unbelievably colourful rags, rushed around, started building fires, and unloaded huge cauldrons. The younger women also worked, carrying one or sometimes two babies on their bosoms, suckling them when they cried. The men looked fierce, with big droopy moustaches, and were usually dressed in pants rolled up above their ankles and shirts that were never washed. All in all, they were not at all like the romantic beautiful gypsies of the movies, but nevertheless romantic to us in a fearsome way.

All the gypsies were of a dark East Indian colouring with black hair, dark eyes, and teeth as white and perfect as dentures. In each tribe, there were also one or two children, sometimes beautiful little girls, with white skin, blue eyes, and blonde hair. Our grandmothers warned us that the wandering gypsies snatched and kidnapped children in the villages and then disappeared. They warned us, but we did not quite believe them, and also considered ourselves beyond the kidnapping age. Nevertheless, we watched the activities of the tribe from a safe distance, well towards the Danube, because it was known that gypsies could not swim, but ran fast.

The men took down from the tops of the caravans long poles equipped with grappling hooks and waded knee-deep into the water just below our boathouse. When a particularly large dead pig would arrive with the flood waters, they would hook it and drag it out of the water and up the embankment. After that, it was women's work.

If they did not get a pig, a couple of large hens would surely float by, or a goat; it made no difference, it all ended up on their spits. If they were upwind, the smell was atrocious, but this did not disturb them once the fishing part was over. All of them sat in the shade while the feast was prepared. Eating these cadavers would surely have killed anybody else, but obviously the gypsies had developed resistance. Once the meal was ready, all dug in, the children, too; out came the bottles of wine from raffia-covered demijohns, and the resultant intoxication ended in a night-long tribal orgy. But this we never observed; even a tough lot of kids wanted to be far away once the light faded.

Normally these kinds of gypsies were not permitted into a village; they were chased away by the cocky, cock-feathered gendarmes, but at flood time the gendarmes seemed to ignore them. A sure sign of the passing of the peak of the flood was the departure of the tribe. One morning when we arrived on the embankment, there would be no trace of the gypsy caravans, only burnt-out campfires. That evening, the Vienna steamer would carry the news on its blackboard that the waters were receding upriver, and sure enough, the next day the only reminder of the floods was the general debris left on the beaches by the receding waters.

In fairness to the gypsies, it must be said that there were many more gypsies that were not nomadic and therefore more, though not altogether, respectable and respected. One lot, the most prosperous, were the gypsy horse-traders—"Lokupec" in the slang of the times. These gypsies were dying out fast in my early childhood, although I still recall seeing some at village markets. They were prosperously dressed like wealthy farmers, in dark jackets with heavy gold watch chains on which bear teeth and other ornaments dangled, in riding breeches and polished black boots. Their hats were pulled low over their flashing eyes, waxed moustaches, and pot bellies. Only their dark skins and gypsy features gave them away.

At the village markets, these gypsies were busy selling and buying horses, but as I recall, selling mostly. What they did not know about horses was not worth knowing, according to my father, a keen horseman. He knew them from his childhood and prided himself that he could not be taken in by them. Of course, race horses and blood-line breeding horses could be bought at auction from more reputable hands and were also traded directly from the vast estates and stud farms, but before World War One, practically every estate owner dealt also with the crafty gypsy operators.

After the war, their business narrowed down to small farmers, and eventually the motor car put them out of business. This new merchandise they never learned to trade—though curiously enough, a new generation of Kupec (traders) grew up with very similar tricks and wiles, particularly in the used-car business in Hungary.

My father entertained me with many good horse-trading stories while sitting in the shade at the New World. Their banco tricks included such ploys as patting the tired lethargic horse on the back in front of the prospective buyer, then sliding a hand towards the tail while extolling its virtues. Towards the end of the pat, with one swift motion, the trader slipped a live kernel of black pepper up the unsuspecting horse's sphincter. As the gypsy groom then began to walk the horse around on its lead, the beast began such a convincing head-raising, high-stepping, full-blooded prance that the deal was usually consummated by the traditional handshake before the secret storm subsided.

As I said, this breed of gypsies died out slowly, but they died hard, and they died laughing.

Apart from this now nearly defunct breed of gypsies, there were also the music-making varieties. Of these, every Hungarian village, even the smallest, had at least one full band playing in the local pubs in the evening. The orchestra leader was the *primas* who decided which songs to play, wandered to the tables, and was the contact with the merry-making groups. His second was the *bracsas*, also playing a violin-like instrument. Always there was one man playing the Nagybogo, which roughly translates as "the great boomer," the bass violin. And often there was one musician playing the ancient Hungarian cimbalom, a stringed instrument played with two special long hammers. Good cimbalom players often entertained solo. Some orchestras had over 20 members, and there were even all-child orchestras, the child players being called "rajko." In some parts of the country, there were famous legendary *primas*, so romantic, wild, and handsome that ladies of historic noble families were said to have run away with them.

Nagymaros had at least six such orchestras, none very famous, but they were hard at it in the evenings in all the pubs, and if you came home late in your boat on the quiet Danube, you could hear their music over the soft splashing of the water, the booming sound of the bass violin carrying the furthest.

All the gypsies lived in one area, in a narrow steep valley that wound its way up towards the high plateau starting somewhere above the public school. It was the poorest part of town: little thatch-roofed adobe huts huddled together. The place had no name; it was simply known as the gypsy quarter. These gypsies were not nomadic; they had been settled for generations. Yet as much as possible they avoided school, the army, and any kind of registration, and generally defied all attempts to turn them into ordinary citizens.

It was not dangerous to visit the gypsy quarter, although one proceeded there carefully and never alone. It was also not advisable to linger. The routine was to take the route up to the mountain through their valley, looking at the sights from the corner of your eye. And the sights were interesting. The number of children, of course, was unbelievable, and they came out of the little huts, aggressively begging as soon as they saw you. Many of them from the age of two upwards had tiny violins, and all of a sudden one was surrounded by them, all of them furiously but rather inefficiently sawing away on their tiny instruments. It was difficult to get rid of them without a bakshish.

The old men usually sat on their haunches on the porches smoking evil-smelling pipes. In fact, there was a bitter acrid smell in the whole valley. The men were usually asleep in the daytime, having played all night, except for those who had never mastered music-making. This group was usually away at the brickworks, laying adobe bricks, the third traditional activity of the non-nomadic gypsies; they were the lowest rung of the ladder.

Many adolescent girls were hanging about, some of them quite beautiful. Their main occupation in the late summer was berry-picking on the mountainside. There were many delicious berries to pick there: blackberries, raspberries, and the queen of them all, the delicious wild strawberries. Most other times, they did not do anything other than pleasure their men, who had legendary prowess. The occasional more ambitious girl descended into the village and became a maid in one of the little hotels.

All in all, the place had an exotic, sexy atmosphere, but other than visually, contact was never made there. The gypsies lived according to their own code and never accepted the rules of the community. They lived on its outskirts, tolerated but not accepted. This did not bother them, and as far as I could see, they lived quite happily.

Some years later, when the German eagle spread its huge wings over most of Europe, many met their fate together with the Jews, a little-known fact. Hitler could not tolerate such unclean, non-law-abiding "subhumans," and they were hunted down by his legions, particularly the truly nomadic ones, and shipped with the Jews to the death factories, an ironic fate for the only truly "Aryan" race of central Europe.

In 1936, however, we knew nothing of what was to come. I had heard that in Germany there were big changes, and a man called Hitler was in power—but it did not matter on the Danube, and anyhow most of my Schwab friends belonged to the Hitler Youth (which at that time was underground). Each had a little swastika-decorated armband and began to dress in knee-high white German socks and the famous brown shirt. But even they did not take this too seriously.

The summers were lazy, and there was so much swimming and sunbathing to do—who had time to think of politics? Yet now, when I think back, gradually from 1933 onward, more and more signs of the impending storm were gathering on the horizon.

[III] Hitler's Terror

And so we woke up on the day in 1941 when we first heard that Count Teleky had been found dead in his suite in the Prime Minister's palace in Buda. The rumour, never quite cleared up, was that the prime minister—an honourable man—committed suicide when ordered by Hitler to renege on the just-concluded "everlasting peace and friendship" treaty that had been negotiated with Yugoslavia, our southern neighbour. Other rumours had it that he told the German ambassador who came to him with an ultimatum late at night that Hungary would honour its commitment to the Yugoslavs and resist the German Army if, *en route* to conquest in Greece, it tried to cut through Hungary, whereupon the ambassador shot him on the spot.

Whichever story is true, the next day the German Army started to roll through Hungary unresisted. To respect Hungarian "neutrality," the Wehrmacht moved through the country on a strictly confined route. Together with thousands of other Budapest residents, my friends and I watched the German Army from the upper embankment of the Danube in Buda as it advanced along the cobblestoned lower embankment beneath us.

Directed by German military police, they proceeded at 20 kilometres an hour in endless formation. Motorised infantry first, soldiers looking rigidly forward as if they were not on the Danube embankment in one of the most beautiful cities in Europe. Formation after formation, field artillery followed by flat transports with tanks piggybacked, motorcycle troops, more infantry units. People went home for lunch, for dinner, only to find on return to their watch posts that the German legions were still on the march, flowing south with the Danube. I was there between the Margaret Bridge and the Chain Bridge when the last artillery piece rolled by and the traffic director folded his signal disk, kick-started his motorcycle, and rode off with the end of the column.

Wedged between the wonderful summers in Nagymaros, the school years had almost passed. Four years of elementary school in the Lutheran Diocesan School were followed by my years at the Lutheran Classical Gymnasium. All this time, the distant kettle drums were audible; Hitler, the leader of the drummers, kept turning up the volume. Austria joined the orchestra in 1938, and the Czech crisis followed the same year. At school, the students came under the influence of these outside events, and a polarisation developed. There were the ultra-right, the centrists, and the unconcerned. I floated.

Certainly none of us worried. Our parents, too, in most cases were certain that the questionable happenings beyond, but close to, our borders would not spill over into neutral Hungary. Hitler gave us pieces from dismembered Czechoslovakia and made the Rumanians move over a bit so that we got back parts of Transylvania, which had been robbed from us, every Hungarian felt, after the First World War. One could not really be completely against this benefactor. True, his screaming and shouting could not be ignored, and he seemed to be particularly tough on non-Aryans, but then again "maybe he had a point." Anyhow, none of this affected us.

While we were growing up against this background, most of us had an outstandingly pleasant adolescence. With the long pants came the dancing lessons and theatre nights. We began to dress like adults and wear suits. All of us went on skiing trips together, and a small inner circle under the guidance of the arts teacher, a Mr. Oppell, went on yearly "cultural trips" to Italy.

Then in 1939, when I was 16 years old, World War II broke out. It was not unexpected, after all the German screaming and sabre-rattling—but now the atmosphere was more frightening, or so it suddenly seemed. This time Hitler had gone too far; no sooner had he attacked Poland than England and France declared war. Russia and Germany now were allies, a scary combination, and Poland fell before the Western allied armies could distribute gas masks to the troops. Hungary of course remained neutral, just like Sweden, Norway, Holland, and Belgium, and the projected speedy end to the conflict promised to return us to peace.

Three weeks after the Polish invasion, an influx of Polish refugees poured over the Carpathians into our neutral country. On our daily strolls on the autumnal Corso, my friends and I noticed the magnificent motor cars in which it seemed to us that the cream of society had escaped from Poland. They were lined up at the entrances of the elegant Danube hotels. Never before had we seen such fantastic cars—huge Packards, Cadillacs, Hispano-Suizas, and Minervas with the tops down in the splendid September weather. Beautiful Polish ladies alighted out of these cars, and bellhops carried pigskin suitcases. To our eyes, it was a concentration of opulence never before seen in Budapest. Unfortunately, in a few weeks, the owners' cash began to run out, their cars disappeared, and in no time at all they had left the hotels and become absorbed into the great masses.

Next came the phony war, with the Allies and the Germans eyeing each other across the Maginot line. This gave us a chance to see Italy once more in the spring of 1940. But no sooner had we returned from this Easter holiday than Hitler moved again. France fell in no more time than Poland. It was true that this time Holland and Belgium were gobbled up in the German advance, but Hungary was again lucky in its neutrality.

Then in 1941, we saw the German might on our own territory as the Nazis moved through our country to Yugoslavia and thence to Greece. It was an awesome spectacle to see that disciplined, matter-of-fact professional army stream through our city like a termite column on the move. By the end of the three-day march, we had a new prime minister who ordered the Hungarian Army to go into Yugoslavia behind the Germans for the spoils. By that time, Yugoslavia had collapsed. The war had lasted three days, but it had delayed Hitler's timetable by several weeks.

Although Hungary was still officially neutral, the war now began to affect us. There was plenty of food in Hungary, but hardly any gasoline, and the government shortly ordered strict rationing. At the same time, all privately owned cars were grounded, except for those belonging to people whose activities were considered economically important. These were issued triangular windshield stickers with the capital letter E in various colours in the centre. My father's E was blue, which meant that his use of his car was restricted to business hours on weekdays only. Others, for instance Uncle Julius, had their E in a colour which allowed unlimited use. All other cars went onto concrete blocks in garages.

Early in 1940, my father had allowed himself to be persuaded to buy me a small Matra motorcycle, a very nifty fire-engine red French-made machine of only one hundred ccm, but an exact small-scale version of a full-size motor bike. Soon I was spending my time racing up and down the Hill of the Roses, riding full throttle on the highway to Nagymaros, banking sharply in the turns, and in every way imitating the mannerisms of motorcycle racers.

As I rode my bike around town, I soon noticed that there was a particular group of young men who belonged to a closed fraternity headquartered in an espresso bar called the Paradiso. This was located beyond the row of Danube hotels facing Petofi Park and the Danube. At all times of the day, its terrace was populated by members of this group, while their great bikes, 500-ccm BMWs and other large shiny machines, were parked in front. This superior element would certainly not pay any attention to a 16-year-old puttering around on a tiny Matra bike, but my plans were to graduate from this level as soon as possible. And because of gasoline rationing, it seemed that this moment might come sooner than I had thought likely.

Before the war, motorcycles were not glamorous; they were the mode of locomotion of the lower middle classes, who for a weekend trip packed mother and children into the sidecars of venerable old machines and with goggles and dust coats, puttered away into the countryside. At that time the romantic vehicles were the sports motorcars—the BMWs, Bugattis, Lancias, and Alfa Romeos. But with the advent of rationing, some of their owners began to switch over to the best and largest of the sports motorcycles. The fashionable and trendy thing was now to ride around on these "magnificent machines."

Now in the spring of 1941, my father agreed to buy one. He had lost his personal transportation with the new restrictions, and at the same times taxis were scarce, with sometimes an hour passing before a taxi you had ordered turned up at the door. But under the new law, motorcycles were unaffected; the gasoline rationing for them was satisfactory. As a result, with some careful counselling from me, my father came to the conclusion that a motorcycle with a sidecar would be his best solution. I could drive him around in the evenings if he needed to go downtown, and we could take trips to our vineyards on the Balaton.

As luck would have it, in a villa close by ours lived a very attractive girl I had met while buzzing around on the Matra. Her father and two uncles owned a car and motorcycle dealership known as the Bruck Brothers Dealership. Several times, Ili took me down to see the beautiful English motorcycles that they had on display. At that time, Germany was certainly ahead of England in motorcycle design, having just brought out the magnificent 500-ccm horizontal twin-cylinder BMW, but in Budapest the conservative belief that British was best still had currency. The Bruck Brothers showroom was filled with gorgeous 250-ccm Velocettes and larger BSA motorcycles, but far more interesting to me was the 1939-manufactured

Rudge Whitworth sports racing motorcycle, of which only one example had been imported to Hungary from Coventry, England. It had a single 500-ccm vertical-cylinder engine with internal oil circulation, a most advanced transmission, and hydraulic suspension. But beyond all the technicalities, for me, the design was the most important feature. The Rudge was a panther gathering its haunches. And it was black, just like a panther, with gold trim and the Rudge logo on its gas tank. It was the Rolls Royce of motor cycles and the only one of its kind in Hungary, sitting right there at Bruck Brothers. There were many BMW 500s in Budapest; any time at the Paradiso, you could see four or five. My father agreed to visit Bruck Brothers with me.

Elite of the Paradiso

The principal display was the Velocettes and other small bikes, all glimmering with show-room polish. Father walked through this row of machines. He did not know anything about motorcycles, but he realised that these were not like the really heavy motorcycles he saw on the streets. He remarked that they looked quite flimsy to him. Then his eyes alighted on the Rudge, off by itself, but modestly illuminated. "Now that looks like a good sturdy machine," he remarked to Mr. Bruck. "You wouldn't want to buy this motor.... it's a very heavy machine," I interjected and implied (perhaps said) that it might also be slow and lumbering. "That's exactly what I want," said my father. It was thus that in half an hour I became the registered owner of one of the fastest motorcycles in Budapest, and the only brand-new 1939 Rudge.

Of course, Father ordered a sidecar. The negotiations were protracted. Mr. Bruck showed various designs from a coach maker. In these I was uninterested, save for making sure that the Rudge was fastened to the sidecar with three wing nuts only. I knew that I could never make it into the Paradiso with a sidecar. Of course, anyone could see that putting a sidecar on the Rudge was like putting a cart behind a race horse. Mr. Bruck certainly knew this, but he was not going to spoil the sale of his only Rudge motorcycle, which was twice as valuable as any other machine in his showroom.

I passed the driver's test, received my license, and drove the bike home to the Hill of the Roses. After a few weeks of practice during which I discovered the secret of speeding with a sidecar, particularly enjoying fast turns, I was ready to pick up my father one evening at the Belvaros café for his first ride in the sidecar. He was wearing his grey homburg and fur-collared coat. He settled in, the convertible roof closed over him, and I kick-started the motorcycle. The Rudge was roaring as we whipped across Margaret Bridge, then with a sharp right turn I started climbing up Zarda utca towards the top. Halfway up, after a steep straight run, Zarda utca made a sudden right turn, flattened out, and instantly made a 90-degree left turn. This was the spot I had been training for. After first groaning under the strain of the right-hand turn, the sidecar, now in an exhilarating left-hand turn, rose into the air, bearing my father aloft. After pulling out of the turn, the sidecar wheel slammed down on the road again with a tremendous bump.

Five minutes later, I pulled up in front of our garage. I opened the roof of the sidecar. Father emerged with his dignity intact, but he was furious. He ordered me to have an electric horn installed in the sidecar so that he could communicate with me if I got carried away again. Then he walked into the house, and I rolled the motorcycle into the garage. Next day I had the horn installed by Mr. Bruck, but Father never rode in the sidecar again. Shortly I loosened the three wing nuts and disengaged my Rudge. From that day on, the sidecar sat in the garage, leaning to one side.

Well, I made it into the Paradiso. Parking curbside during the noon-hour promenade in Vig utca with the motor quietly kicking over was like fly casting for salmon in well-stocked waters. In no time, the Rudge took its rightful place in front of the Paradiso with the big BMWs, Nortons, BSAs, and one water-cooled Scott, plus all the lesser machines. I was in seventh heaven, surrounded, I thought, by the most exclusive circle in Budapest: young army officers, university students, sons of landowners. The average age was about 25, but I was a part of it, although a junior. They were fearless bikers, and I tried to keep up. We drove eight abreast down Andrassy Boulevard, only to take off in eight different directions should the police give chase.

Meanwhile, Hitler presented his bill to Hungary for having returned territories lost in the first-war treaties to Czechoslovakia, Rumania, and Yugoslavia. Part of his price was that Hungary must pass anti-Jewish laws similar to the Nuremberg laws of Germany. The two houses of Parliament enacted these without much hesitation, then proceeded in the Hungarian manner to procrastinate. But the ranks of all non-Aryans in the army were taken away, and in the future those affected by the laws would not be able to serve in the army. Moreover, non-Aryans could not marry or otherwise consort with those of pure blood. But citizenship was not taken away, as it had been in Germany.

Summer came; we drove our bikes to Balaton Almadi for the holidays. Hitler now caught up with his long-delayed timetable and without warning attacked Russia with all the German might. From now on, events speeded up. Hungary remained neutral for a while, but after a bombing attack on the ancient north Hungarian town of Kassa—perpetrated either by the Russians or the Germans in Russian disguise, depending on which rumours you believed—Hungary entered the war against the Soviets but remained neutral towards Great Britain.

The Germans, with the Hungarians in tow, were advancing towards Moscow on a wide front when Japan attacked Pearl Harbour, bringing the United States into the war. Cheekily Hungary immediately declared war on the U.S. and Britain. "Now they are quaking in their boots," said my father sarcastically. But to my group, the great disaster was that the premiere of *Gone with the Wind* was cancelled, the film canned pending the outcome of the war. We had lost our tickets for which we had already paid. By Christmas 1941, the drive on Moscow had faltered, and the German and Hungarian armies were retreating in front of fresh Siberian Russian troops.

It was difficult to follow the events, to study, and to participate in the thrills of winter motorcycling. We raced on frozen lakes and also towed skiers at high speed, executing sudden turns, an activity called skijoring. The war was far away, and most of our circle had deferrals from military service.

One day in late spring, when I was near to graduation, there was a police raid on the Danube promenade. Sitting on the Paradiso terrace, we heard of strange disturbances on the Corso. We raced with our bikes to the Hangli Café and, dismounting, walked through the police cordon. We watched as plain-clothed detectives stopped all military-aged men, particularly if they had Semitic features. A few days later, we heard that they had been summoned to the army, thrown into labour battalions, and shipped to the Russian front. We did not worry about this overly long. It was not our business.

Miraculously passing my exams, I matriculated. I planned to leave in a few weeks for Nagybánya, a famous artists' colony in Transylvania, which had been recently restored to Hungary. I planned to ride there on my Rudge and spend the summer finding out if I was really blessed with the talent and devotion to become an artist. The next few weeks were spent riding around and polishing, greasing, and oiling my beautiful machine. She looked better than the day I took delivery. Her two beautiful chrome exhaust pipes ended in a 45-degree cut and were coated on the inside with red paint. From these I always carefully removed the film of exhaust smoke so that the red inside shone as brightly as the rest of my Rudge. Every day, I spent a couple of hours working on the motor.

As I was busy with this activity one morning, I saw through the garage doors two Hungarian soldiers marching in my direction. "Are you George Eber?" one of them asked as they reached the garage. Without waiting for an answer, he thrust a summons into my hand. In essence, this announced that the Army was seizing the motorcycle. "We'll drive our truck down the ramp and take it now to the Army motor pool," declared the soldier.

While they went for the truck, I ran up to the house, where I found my father watching the events from the window. "Do something," I cried. "They are taking the Rudge." My father did not answer. "Try to stop them before it is gone," I pleaded. Finally my father said, "There is nothing we can do. The war is on." And so they loaded the motorcycle and drove off with it in their camouflaged army truck; the sidecar went with it. By the next week, Hitler's great summer offensive had started, and with the Hungarian Second Army, my sensitive racing machine must have dragged that hateful sidecar in the great advance towards the Don and Stalingrad.

Only many years later did I find out that through his army connections, my father had arranged to have my motorcycle conscripted. Sure I would kill myself, he decided that this was the only way to get me dismounted.

So I took the train to Transylvania, and in the company of masters, teachers, and young artists, tried to console myself for the loss of the Rudge, the most treasured possession of my youth. By the end of the summer, my father had agreed that I should become an artist—on the condition that I get a university degree first. I applied to and was accepted by the faculty of economics and political science of the Palatine Joseph Technical and Economic Sciences University, and began serious studies.

By Christmas, the great Russian offensive had broken through the German left flank where the Hungarian Second Army stood. The defences collapsed, and by early Christmas, Stalingrad was completely surrounded by the Russian armies.

The bulk of the disorganised Hungarian Second Army arrived back by the spring of 1943, leaving behind, along with my Rudge, much of their ordnance, but as I and many others in Buda found out, they brought back something else; looking in the mirror one morning, I found that my eyeballs were a yellow colour. Together with thousands, I had become infected with the hepatitis that came with the soldiers. It was referred to as the Ukrainian disease. By spring, I had recovered and was looking forward to the summer of 1943.

The summer started well. In July, I travelled to Transylvania to spend a few weeks at a famous spa called Tusnád Fürdö. It nestled high among fragrant pine forests, a typical 19th-century resort with small Swiss country-style hotels, tree-lined promenades between well-kept flowerbeds, and a Transylvanian bandshell. Here a real *fin de siècle* lifestyle was enjoying a revival in the middle of a war which was still far away, so far, in fact, that we could all forget about it. I joined Father there and settled down for a few weeks in an atmosphere redolent of the Austro-Hungarian monarchy. Swimming and sunbathing in the mornings, or long walks up the mountain on well-kept marked trails; then, in the afternoon, when it became a little cooler, dressed in light beige pants, silk jackets, and white and brown wing-tipped shoes polished to the limit, we took walks along the promenade. One listened to the military band in the grandstand, greeted acquaintances in the time-honoured manner of such spas, then gathered in the shade and on sun-dappled terraces for an afternoon tea dance.

The resort was located in territory that in the upheavals after the peace settlement that followed the First World War (in Hungary referred to as the "Injustice of Trianon") had been taken away from Hungary and attached to Rumania, a bounty for this country's loyalty to the Entente. In 1938, after the Munich agreement between Chamberlain and Hitler, part of the territory—including the venerable old Hungarian cities of Kolozsvár and Nagyvárad—was reattached to Hungary. This was Hitler's bribe to the Hungarians, who were now expected to aid the Nazi war effort, as in fact they somewhat half-heartedly did.

The days passed like petals falling from a flower. There was much, so much, to do In the golden sunshine, but we were far away from busy Budapest, and if you did not listen to the radio or read the two-day-old newspapers, and no one did, the scene could have been Marienbad in the days of the Emperor. Most of the guest families came from Nagyvárad or Kolozsvár, well-dressed, elegant ladies with good-looking children. Many of the families were Jews, fierce Hungarian patriots who had actively resisted the colonising efforts of the Rumanians for twenty years and who in 1938 were deliriously happy to be liberated and reattached to Hungary. When the war came, and with it in 1941 the first tentative efforts to introduce the Nuremberg laws in Hungary, the patriots of Nagyvárad and Kolozsvár were convinced that these could not apply to them, so undeniably faithful to the Hungarian crown had they been during the Rumanian "occupation."

It did not take me long at the pool to get to know a group of lively teenaged girls, all suntanned, healthy, and friendly. Among them was a short-haired, olive-skinned girl called Baby Ritter. While her parents were involved in endless bridge games, we found an old, hand-cranked gramophone and a bunch of scratchy records and sat in the darker parts of the hotel lobby listening interminably to "Miss Otis regrets" and American ragtime music. My father, who always kept himself aloof from the crowds, had found a few gentlemen of like disposition with whom to discuss the war and the future in the cafés.

Suddenly posters appeared everywhere announcing that Mihály Borcsa de Kolozsvár, the government commissioner for the Transylvanian territories, was arriving the next afternoon to take the waters. The ukase from the police was direct: all guests not able to satisfy the 1941 Jewish laws were to leave forthwith; the spa had to be free of Jewish elements. By next morning, my father and I were the only remnants of the holiday crowd left at the pool. Baby Ritter was gone with her parents, too, but not before giving me her address in Nagyvárad.

In the afternoon, the Commissioner arrived at the nearly deserted resort in a big open 12-cylinder German Horch touring car with motorcycle outriders and an aide-de-camp who jumped to open the door. A retinue of uniformed men followed in two motorcars. They requisitioned an elegant villa, and gendarmes began to patrol around the promenade and the hotels.

The holiday atmosphere vanished, and even I could feel the cold wind blowing down from the east. A few days later, our time was up, and we departed. My father and I said goodbye for the summer. He went back to Budapest, and I left for Nagybánya, the artists' colony and art school, which I had attended the year before.

The colony was founded by a group of Hungarian painters who had been part of the Barbizon School in France and found the atmosphere of Nagybánya, a charming old mining town, to their liking. They had put down roots here around the turn of the century, and a generation of world-class painters emerged from this tightly knit community. Here the lighting was exceptionally good for *plein air* painters. The skies were always clear, the light reflecting the mesmerising waters of the river Szamos. There was a park with ancient oak trees, a stone bridge, and the nearby mountain harboured an ancient gold mine, its peak named for "Dénes the Thief." This was the legendary highwayman who used to sweep down from his redoubt to raid the king's gold shipments centuries ago. High and far away in the distance, the always-snowy peaks of the Rozsály glittered on clear days. It was to this active and hard-working colony of artists that I came the first summer after matriculation, hoping to follow in the footsteps of Van Gogh and Gauguin. I had talent, good talent, my teachers said, but did not like the torment, the forge which makes steel out of iron.

Now my second season was to start. The train wound around the final bend to the small railway station and with grinding, clanging, huffing, and puffing, came to a stop. Carriage doors were thrown open, and passengers passed down luggage to the platform.

I took a horse-drawn carriage to my lodgings, dropped off my gear, and walked over to the shady porch of Agricola néni—Aunt Agricola—where the younger artists used to take their lunch. Everybody knew me here from last year, and I settled down to lunch, which consisted of a huge plate of bean soup with smoked pork ribs, carrots, and dumplings floating in it and topped up by a pint of sour cream. Agricola néni sliced off an inch-thick helping of peasant bread from a tire-sized round loaf. The conversation started up noisily. I had arrived two weeks late because of the holiday with my father, and there was a lot of catching up to do. A roly-poly longhaired painter in flip-flops and canvas pants called "Sleka" was holding court.

At the end of the rough-hewn wooden table sat a girl who did not particularly look like an artist. She wore a plain blue cotton dress, and she was quietly eating her soup, her long ash-blonde hair partially falling over her high forehead. I will never forget the picture that she made sitting there. She did not take part in the conversation, but once raised her eyes and glanced briefly at me. The eyes were blue-grey and seemed to suggest intellect. Her name was Éva Hochteil, and she was the daughter of a country doctor from Erdöszáda, a community near Nagyvárad where Baby Ritter lived. They went to high school together, and now Éva was visiting a cousin in Nagybánya. We became constant companions that summer. I am afraid I was a little superficial for this serious, wonderful girl, but that summer we spent every free minute together, walking hand in hand in the park, or along the towpath of the Szamos river, with me carrying my inevitable painter's gear. Half a century later, I remember how one beautiful day we sat on the river bank under the weaving, weeping willow branches, reading together in English Thornton Wilder's *The Bridge of San Luis Rey*. This is the famous story of twelve people whom fate brought together on a bridge just at the moment the bridge was about to collapse. Only many years later did this book appear staggeringly relevant to our lives that summer. We ate cheese and drank wine and kissed in the lazy afternoon. Suddenly, on the other side of the river, a company of Hussars rode down the embankment, dismounted, took off their uniforms, carefully folded them into piles, and placing their swords alongside, rode their horses naked into the stream, splashing and glittering in the water. We watched as both men and horses enjoyed a cool bath.

The summer passed quickly, too quickly. Soon Éva went home to Erdöszáda, and I returned to Budapest to university. The night I disembarked from a ratty old taxi at our front door, and just as I stepped out, the air-raid sirens started shrilly wailing. The Hill of the Roses where we lived was suddenly pitch dark, although the raid was obviously a complete surprise to the air defences of Budapest. In checkerboard fashion, the lights were going on and off in all the districts of Budapest as the first bombing of the war began. Apparently no one knew how to extinguish the lights. The sky was filled with ominous rumbling as heavy bombers flew overhead, even as the city lights still went on and off in a crazy pattern. I heard the whistling of bombs and then suddenly a tremendous explosion, really close by.

A stray bomb had hit the villa of the well-known writer Istvan Zilahy and had torn away a corner of the house, together with the life of a young woman house guest. Immediately after the explosion, the all-clear sounded. By the time I walked the few hundred yards to the Zilahy villa, ambulances and volunteers were at work in the rubble. The war was nearing the Hill of the Roses.

This was not immediately evident when the 1943-44 academic year started at the Faculty of Economics and Political

Science of the Palatine Joseph Technical University. My main purpose in pursuing these studies was to obtain a deferral from military service, which after the disastrous performance of the Second Hungarian Army in the Don basin in 1942 was decidedly the preferred course of action. The army, with Commander Janyi at its head, ran straight from Stalingrad to the outskirts of Budapest—as the crow flies, 2000 kilometres; this was facilitated by the expedient abandonment of all materiel and equipment, including probably my beloved motorcycle. The Russians achieved the first breakthrough at the battle of the Don Bend by concentrating on the Hungarian sector, the weakest element in the fighting strength of the Germans and their vassals.

In Budapest, at the ancient faculty building in Szerb utca in the older quarter of Pest, life went on little disturbed by this rout. Lectures started at nine, and the more worldly wise, such as myself and my little group of friends, generally drifted away by 11 A.M. to gather for some serious discussion of the world situation in one of the old town's many pleasant, dimly illuminated espresso bars. Somebody by then had usually obtained an airmail copy of the *London Times*, *Manchester Guardian*, or *Zürcher Zeitung*, which even at this stage of the war could regularly be obtained at the good hotels and were even openly read in the cafés. The evening BBC broadcast, heralded by the booming sound of Beethoven's *Fifth*, these papers, and their editorials were our sources of information. After an hour or so of intense discussion during which all the while we smoked "Darling" cigarettes (the Hungarian version of Camels), the group broke up, some going home for lunch in the time-honoured manner, others like myself repairing to the Floris or Gerbeaud confectioners on Vörösmarty Square, where light lunches were served and an international atmosphere prevailed. Going to Floris involved a couple of passes along the elegant part of Vig utca, where one could meet just about anybody in fashionable Budapest promenading before lunch. And at Floris once or twice a week, I used to meet my English teacher, Mr. King, a Hungarian, who for years had lived in the

U.S. and presumably had dual citizenship. He was a man of mystery, disappearing once or twice a year to Constantinople or some other exotic and neutral country to do some business of an unexplained nature. I used these lunches to practice my English conversation. Other glamorous people regularly joined our table, including a beautiful red-haired girl—Irish, and therefore neutral—and her balding freckled friend Kauders, who according to the grapevine was a member of the German secret service. My cousin, Andy Salusinszky, who lived in Stockholm, regularly directed journalist friends from the Swedish *Dagens Nyheter* newspaper there to listen to the current rumours.

After a couple of Martini Rossis and sandwiches, everybody departed, only to gather again late in the afternoon in one of the old traditional cafés for more of the same conversation and a game or two of billiards. One of my favourite cafés was the Stamboul; its big plate-glass windows, the lower parts protected from drafts by heavy maroon blankets suspended on brass rings from heavy brass rails, faced the Danube with a view over a snow-covered park on the Buda side of the Margaret Bridge. It was in this park that my cousin Johnnie and I had conducted our famous exchange years ago. In the winter, while the wind blew down the Danube and snowdrifts were shifting and building up outside, the Stamboul was a pleasant place to sit and contemplate life, fortified by undoubtedly the best hot chocolate in Budapest. The war was far away, and it was at my table here that I used to read long affectionate letters from Éva and wrote my—I am afraid—very inadequate answers.

The curriculum at the university had some interesting aspects, but largely it was strictly academic rather than a practical or intellectual exercise. Statistics, economics, accounting, the history of double-entry bookkeeping, including a list of names of a hundred or so pioneers in the field whose names I can still partially recount in cadence, were of the essence. For intellectual stimulus, my close friend, John Kolozs, a talented mathematician and linguist, started to translate the *Mariage Forcé* by Molière into Hungarian. A new translation was hardly necessary because all of Molière's plays had been translated several times already, but they were again in vogue in many of the good theatres of Budapest because they were seemingly non-political, but still full of relevance to the times. They satisfied our intellectual pretensions, too, with their humour, sarcasm, and the fact that they descended from the great French culture.

In *Mariage Forcé*, an old man is being forced to marry a young girl, although he has his doubts about the wisdom of the proposed May-December union. Under pressure from the bride's father, he turns to the Greek philosophers, who address him with philosophical eloquence, but with no straightforward advice, and the old man is left as unsure as ever. On his way to his betrothed, he meets a gypsy girl who listens to him and gives him a succinct answer: he will grow horns on his head. John asked me if I would design the stage sets, and our friend, Pista Horvath, who was to become famous later in the Hungarian theatre, was the director.

We decided to have the performance in contemporary clothing, and I started working on the stage sets. Right through Christmas and early in the New Year, this was the major occupation of our little group. A theatre had agreed to stage the performance in the spring. The set for the play was to have a fountain in the middle and five house-like structures in a semicircle behind the forbidding manor of the girl's father. The flats, designed to symbolise the four branches of philosophy, were to be lowered from the ceiling. The actors would stand behind their respective structures and come forth as required. It was a good idea and a good design. I still have the sketches.

The final dress rehearsal was on a rainy Saturday in March. After this, with the actors and stage hands, we had a few drinks in a nearby pub, and then John and I went on foot across the Margaret Bridge to Buda. By this time, the rain had stopped, and using my umbrella as a cane, I briskly walked over the river. The city seemed peaceful and beautiful, with thousands of lights reflected in the fast-flowing water. At the bridge head, we considered a final drink at the Stamboul Café, then decided to go to John's apartment instead for a cognac. I left from there around midnight, and only when I was halfway up the Hill of the Roses did I realise that I had left my umbrella, a fine English specimen, at John's apartment.

Excited by the coming first performance of our play, it took me a long time to fall asleep, and so it was almost noon when I woke up to find out that overnight the German armies had arrived in Budapest. Finally fed up with the Hungarians' half-hearted war effort and pendulum-like swings from right-wing to liberal governments, Hitler had invited Admiral Horthy for a friendly chat in his mountain retreat, the Berghof, and with Horthy in residence, without warning occupied Hungary with full force. Motorised troops and armour were entering the city. The war was *ante portas*, and evidently we could not hope to escape its final throes.

My immediate reaction was to go for my umbrella. When I arrived at John's little apartment that chilly day of March 19, there was no answer to my knock. Mrs. Schmidt, the caretaker, poked her head out from her door, drying the dishwater off her hands with a not-too-clean dishcloth. From her, I found out that, upon hearing the news, John had packed and left early in the morning by train for Szeged, where his family lived. Not one to give up a good umbrella, I tore a page out of my notebook and penned the following note: "Hi John, left my umbrella in your apartment. See you after the war, George." It was to be found there more than a year later when John returned from his trip to Auschwitz, Buchenwald, and the rest.

After this, I returned home to hear the news that the Germans, together with the commandeered Hungarian authorities, had begun to round up a prepared list of prominent hostages and other undesirables. From here on, things progressed rapidly.

The Final Solution

The German programme for the final solution in occupied lands had by now been honed to a very fine science. In short order, Eichmann and his administrative staff in the SS Death Head division proceeded to separate, earmark, isolate, and deport all racially unacceptable elements: anybody whose ancestry did not fit the Nuremberg laws, that is, all persons not possessing two Christian parents and at least two Aryan grandparents. In Hungary, this comprised about a million people, and for good measure and to show impartiality, Hitler also threw in the gypsies, a so-called antisocial element.

To carry out the work in front of them—just as with cattle at the slaughterhouse—the Death Head had now to misguide their victims systematically so as to make them walk conveniently and obediently to the point where no return was possible. First, they instructed the leaders of each community to form a so-called "Jewish council" from among their elders. The SS henceforth would give their instructions only through the individual Jewish councils.

In Hungary, only one-third of the people affected by this program were of the Jewish faith, but since 1941 the authorities had kept records of all who could not prove their so-called purity. There were totally assimilated Christian families, some intermarried with the aristocracy or gentry, whose children until 1941 had not the vaguest suspicion that these laws could apply to them. But the first order coming through the Jewish council made it clear: all people designated Jews by the Nuremberg laws henceforth had to wear the yellow star. They were, however, assured that this was really an administrative act without any danger.

Needless to say, this converted, assimilated, and often Christian-born population now found itself at the bottom of the totem pole as far as the newly created Jewish councils were concerned. The councils had pitifully small room for manoeuvre, and Christians affected by the Nazi laws were not their priority. Nor, sad to say, were they a priority for the

Christian churches, which displayed no vigour in defence of their flock.

Suddenly, all over town, yellow stars appeared by the thousands, and people were soon attempting to adjust to the dictates of the new regime. However, almost immediately new steps were taken to register, separate, and concentrate these people in designated ghettos, usually the old original Jewish districts. In each dwelling unit, more and more people were concentrated, until each room had at least ten inhabitants. This was explained as a measure to give more living room to those who were fighting for the war effort; it held, of course, no danger for the Jews. But as soon as these people, now concentrated in crowded quarters, began organising their new life, a further step was taken: ten-foot-high palisades were erected all over the country to seal in the residents of the ghettos. This was represented as an administrative effort with no danger to the inhabitants concerned. Stories were circulated about the schools, hospitals, and theatrical and musical life in such exemplary ghettos as Teresienstadt in Czechoslovakia. People wanted to believe, and therefore they did.

Similarly, some of the Hungarian population wanted to pacify its conscience and believed the unbelievable, that their neighbours, benefactors, and friends who suddenly had been so attacked were in fact safe. But not everyone was so naive. Authorities cooperated, often enthusiastically, and there were many who felt that the Jews were only getting what they deserved, "having lived in such luxury in the midst of the war." That was the Nazi position. The gendarmes (the federal police force) were enthusiastic, the municipal police only partially so, and the army less so, but undeniably without their active help and participation, the Germans would have faced an impossible task.

It was known by now that the Russian front was advancing in Poland and on the Rumanian border, and therefore the time for the final solution was short. And so in April the deportation began, first in the east, close to the advancing front in the Hungarian part of Transylvania, and from here the rumours spread through all the ghettos and to Budapest. As a final deception, suddenly thousands of postcards showing a pine-covered hillside descending to a crystal-clear lake, all labelled "Waldsee" and postmarked with the Waldsee postal stamp, were received by the relatives of those already transported. These described enthusiastically their treatment at this location. Still people wanted to believe and bought up all available maps of Austria and Germany, where they found hundreds of communities with the name "Waldsee." About this time, too, there was a rumour that only people from the former Rumanian territory, now close to the front, were being resettled. Slowly, hopefully, people were shuffling along towards the slaughterhouse.

Call Up

Of course, I did not think that these events could have any effect on my own life. After all, my father was a highly decorated retired army officer, a powerful businessman, with connections to the highest political levels and powerful friends even in the German establishment. It had turned out, of course, when the 1941 anti-Jewish laws were promulgated, that some of our ancestry, particularly on my mother's side of the family, was not without serious blemish, but we were part of Hungarian society and enjoyed its privileges. These laws would not touch us. My father was entitled to wear the King's uniform, and every month the War Ministry faithfully delivered his well-deserved military pension. Had I not boarded at the prestigious Lutheran boarding school together with the cream of the sons of the Protestant gentry, including two nephews of Admiral Horthy's wife, the Purgly boys? So we went on, navigating through rumours of outrage and the Germans' systematic tightening of the screws. My father was still dashing in his army uniform, his decorations glittering, his sword at his side, and was saluted with respect even by the occupying Wehrmacht officers.

I still dropped in at Floris, but my luncheon companions, including Mr. King, had vanished from our luncheon table and apparently from the streets. I met many acquaintances furtively sneaking around corners with the Star of David on their chest, while the columns of the occupying forces and those of the Hungarian Army marched about town. Yes, the Hungarian Army, whatever may have been on the minds of its senior officers, including the supreme commander, accepted its role as a satellite force for Hitler's regime and went about the Nazis' dirty business.

In addition to the fighting forces, the army, since 1941, had organised within its cadres units of an unarmed labour force. The conscripted members of this force, all of military age, were persons who could not satisfy the requirements of the Nuremberg laws. In 1941-42, these labour battalions, dressed in civilian clothes with a yellow armband to indicate their despised status, were dragged into Russia behind the advancing army and were treated with much cruelty by their commanders; many vanished forever in the frozen vastnesses of Russia. After Stalingrad in 1943, when with the first signs of defeat the pendulum began to swing against the Nazi policies, the Regent appointed a more liberal government, and the fate of these conscripts improved. In fact, in a gesture typical of the Hungarian caste system, they were now divided into two segments: the Jewish Jews and the non-Jewish, or Christian, Jews. The division was signified by yellow armbands for the battalions of the Jewish faith and white armbands for the others. The battalions with white armbands were better treated and were assigned better duties, but generally both groups were treated by the Hungarian Army command as only "nearly" human. It was not a desirable position to be in, even in a white-armbanded unit, and all potential conscripts used whatever influence they had to stay out. But with the country now occupied by the Germans, the perceived wisdom was that, white armband or yellow armband, the protection of the Hungarian Army was better than being hunted down by the German SS or being put into a ghetto, and so when the conscription papers arrived for my year of 1923, with the order to report at the army barracks at Jaszberény on a given date in late April, with much hesitation I complied. I did not want to go, nor did my classmates and friends, and some acquaintances went underground with fake papers. But my father was firmly convinced that the army would defend its white-banded troops against the Germans.

So, on the appointed day, I went to the railway station to commence a journey into uncertainty. I was equipped with the best waterproof marching boots that Master Nyeste could procure in one week, and clad in a butternut-coloured, calf-length soft leather flying coat that my Uncle Julius, a distinguished fighter pilot in the first war, had donated for this occasion.

On the platform of the great western railway station, there was a tremendous crowd of similarly outfitted people, among them some of my oldest friends from the Lutheran elementary school and the Fasor gymnasium. Pali Fabo was there, one of my oldest cronies, a skating and skiing partner and a fabulous horseman. With a few equally close friends, we formed a little group, and right then and there decided to try and stick together in the coming days.

After much delay, we boarded the special train of third-class coaches, and with typical jerks and clangour, enveloped in puffs of smoke, the train left for Jaszberény. It was here that I discovered the wisdom of the old Hungarian saying, "You never know how many people go to Hatvan until you get on the train for Hatvan." Well, this train went to Jaszberény, though inevitably through Hatvan, a small railway junction exactly "hatvan" (sixty) kilometres from Budapest. As even the least informed of us had heard, Hatvan was the railway junction where in the last weeks, the administrative head of the county of Pest, in collaboration with the infamous Gendarme Colonel Zöldi, had cast his nets, raiding the passing trains to winkle out those leaving eastward trying to escape the German noose. Anyone caught was thrown into the local ghetto. We were apprehensive: would our train pass through safely? It did, and in the early afternoon, we pulled into Jaszberény.

With the White Arm Bands

The military camp was at the outskirts of town, surrounded by a barbed-wire fence with a guardhouse and military guard at the gate and inside, 20 or 30 low-slung barracks on either side of a straight road. Altogether, it seemed to us to be rather similar to Aldershot (of which we had heard): clean, well-kept, with a lot of uniformed men and labour conscripts lining the shaded road. A sergeant ordered the trainload of us to one of the furthest barracks. As we went off, I noticed a group of officers standing on a terrace in front of a low building. In the middle stood a very dapper-looking colonel with light-blue collar tabs, tapping the palm of his hand with a riding crop as he contemplated the ragtag crowd.

The barracks to which we had been assigned filled up quickly, and my little group, which had been holding back until all the bunks were occupied, was ordered to settle in the next empty building. This manoeuvre, only half-planned, resulted in us having uncrowded, you could say privileged, accommodation and was the starting shot of the tortuous "pinball game" all of us now were to play, although at the time I don't believe that any of us knew of a game by that name. No matter what effort and skill or influence we could muster, none could determine how the ball would roll. Calculated risk, instinctive moves might save our lives—or not. The jackpot, not yet evident, was survival.

The lights came on at 8:30 with a beautiful bugle call. Within 24 hours, we fell into the routine of military establishments everywhere in the world. Our separate little group did everything possible to be inconspicuous. Meanwhile, the army began, barrack by barrack, to form the motley mob into companies 200 strong, some units with all yellow armbands, others all white, each with a commanding officer, sergeants major, sergeants, and a couple of corporals.

The newly formed units were to leave the camp within the week. By this time, Pali and I had befriended a couple of sergeants and from them obtained information on the larger plan. It seemed that the units had to clear the camp to make room for further recruits, newly called up and due to arrive in a month's time. We learned that some of our units were to be dispatched to the eastern war zone, while others were to be billeted on nearby large estates.

Pali and I had made friends among the kitchen staff and every morning regularly visited the kitchen, where in gigantic cauldrons the main meal of the day was in preparation. In the Hungarian Army, there was never any shortage of food, except in the front line, but day after day the food was the same: boiled beef with delicious bouillon in which big beef marrow bones were also cooked. The best of the delicious marrow bones were traditionally the province of the duty officers, who came around 9 o'clock for their share. There was plenty left for the kitchen staff, and through the friendship of the cooks, Pali and I were also served gigantic portions on slabs of toasted army bread; we were also allowed to cart away the rest of the marrow bones for our little barrack group.

After a week, there was nobody left in the camp but our little white-armbanded group; there were not enough of us to form a company. The weather was beautiful, and we were convinced of our wisdom in separating ourselves and thus becoming supernumerary. We had been assigned various light to tedious duties: Pali and I, because of our expertise with horses, along with a couple of friends, were assigned to work at the nearby army Lipizzaner Stud Station. At first, our job was to shovel coal slag onto the exercise rink, where dashing young officers were riding the Lipizzaners. Soon Pali and I talked ourselves into the task of assisting the stallions in their daily duty of covering the breeding mares. These magnificent creatures were brought to the stud and presented as they came into heat by the neighbouring estates and farmers. The stallions were walked by the tail end of the mares as they stood in line, and when a stallion indicated interest in one of them, both were taken to a small rink, where two soldiers held the mare's halter. Pali and I first covered the mare with a specially fitted padded blanket and then led the stallion forth and guided him to penetrate. This was a wonder-filled task, the thoroughbred stallions were beautiful in their excitement, nostrils flaring, eyes rolling. The actual act lasted only a minute, after which we led the trembling lather-covered stallions on a long line for a half-hour walk around the edges of the exercise rink to calm them down. For the moment, the Lipizzaners and we were both having an excellent war.

All the horses were taken out each day from the stables to exercise or to perform their duties, and then the cool beautiful whitewashed stables stood empty. The stalls were immediately and impeccably cleaned; just the light pleasant smell of horse manure lingered on. The clean-up was accomplished with military efficiency by the permanent staff of the stud farm; only the swarms of horse flies buzzing about waiting for the return of their horse customers defeated their efforts, and because my duties with the stallions required only a couple of hours, I was assigned the important task of catching flies in the empty stables. The sergeant gave me a bucket which I had to fill during the day with flies and then report to him with a full bucket before falling out. The first few days, I went about this task with enthusiasm, using huge fly swatters and filling the bucket brim-full with flies in about two hours. The rest of the time I spent dozing in the cool shade of the stable and chatting with the sergeant's lady who cooked the meals for the stud soldiers. She kindly passed on to me some choice bits from her kitchen and then, with a little persuasion, allowed me to store my day's full bucket in the army's large walk-in refrigerator. After this, fly-catching was simplified. At the end of every day, before reporting to the sergeant, I removed my bucket. Once the sergeant was satisfied, I slipped the bucket back into the refrigerator and joined my comrades on the return trip to the camp. After a plentiful dinner, our group was free until lights out. We had passes to go into town, and we spent the evenings playing cards or just chatting, occasionally going into Jaszberény to the movies.

Our group, in addition to Pali and myself, consisted of three or four old cronies from high school or university. This was the core, and in addition there were a few other new friends, among them a tough aggressive young man called George Ligeti and also Erwin Leichter, a wiry bespectacled blond wavy-haired boy whose mother was the owner of a well-known brothel in Vig utca in Budapest. She and her common-law husband, known in the Budapest underworld as "the careful Johnny Ament," together ran not only their first-class brothel in Budapest with selected, inspected, and able staff, but also a second, very profitable enterprise which supplied country brothels with staff on a six-week rotation basis. Erwin Leichter himself had studied classical music and was an established piano player who earned his pocket money playing jazz piano in his mother's establishment, where he was the spoiled favourite of the girls. We were fascinated by the stories that Erwin told us about his interesting life in Vig utca, but we did not suspect at that point the importance for us of this network which encircled most of the country, including the faraway Transylvanian areas. One evening we all went to the local bordello, where we were royally treated as friends and comrades of Mrs. Leichter's only son, who, unfortunately for him, descended from a Jewish accountant, who, among other things, attended to the complicated double or triple bookkeeping that lay at the heart of the business.

The weeks passed pleasantly, and we almost believed our good fortune would last to the end, that is, to the end of the war, which even according to controlled news emanating from the radio of Mrs. Nagy, the sergeant's wife, could not be very far away. The ball was still wandering aimlessly among the obstacles on the pinball machine.

One afternoon, we had special duty. With a couple of soldiers in charge, we had to load up three horse-drawn farm wagons with thousands of freshly baked loaves of army bread from the camp bakery. It turned out that the colonel, whom so far we had seen only from a forbidding distance, was not without human compassion: we had to deliver the shipment to the enclosed Jaszberény ghetto, where it was received with enthusiasm. It was, however, a depressing reminder of how things were in the outside world away from our Shangri-la barracks. On the return trip, Ligeti, an ice-cream enthusiast, slipped from our empty wagon and bought us all dripping chocolate ice creams from the local Italian Gelateria.

It was at dinnertime that evening that we received orders to be ready at 6 A.M. with our gear to move out from camp in the morning. At 5:30 A.M., after drinking steaming hot coffee from our army-issue canisters, we were ready. The same three wagons and the same soldiers rattled down the main camp road, and in minutes we were rolling out through the gates into the countryside. Here the soil was sandy, and in a few minutes our wagons branched off onto a track where the wheels sank deep into the sand. An hour later, after slow progress, we arrived at a large flat exercise field surrounded by farms. On this temporary parade ground, in quadrangle formation, we saw about 20 of the companies that had previously been assembled at our camp and which were now billeted at the neighbouring estates. The companies were at ease, with the company commanders and their staff walking around and organising the formations.

Flawed Ball

Everybody had his gear in front of him. We dismounted from the wagons and, forming up in a semblance of military order, marched to a gap in the quadrangle, where we, too, placed our gear in front of us and sat down on the dewy ground. It was still chilly, but the sun was beginning to climb, and it soon began to warm up. Nothing happened for some time. Then the master sergeant and his staff arrived and set up chairs and a large table in the middle of the field; then, in typical army manner, there was a further long wait, until finally over a hill came the colonel and his adjutant, both in pale-green twill summer uniforms, riding two fine non-government-issue horses. They rode to the middle of the quadrangle, dismounted, and threw their reins to a soldier. Now most of those present in the battalions had no military background, but I with a military father and Pali who had ridden all his life could appreciate the way the colonel sat on his fine horse

95

and were impressed. Colonel Zentay was a former Hussar, currently wearing the tab colours of the successor to the cavalry, a light armoured regiment. Now we were ordered to stand at attention. We thought we were an almost Napoleonic sight, perhaps at Waterloo after the battle was lost.

Now we were ordered to stand at ease, and for the next hour or so, the commanders of the different battalions reported to the table, and a complicated shuffling procedure followed. Three men from company X were ordered to join company Y, after which two men with their gear were transferred to Company X from Company Y, and so on. All these transfers were duly recorded by the clerks and orders of transfers cut. The Colonel did not participate in this procedure; he stood apart with his adjutant, looking disinterested, although occasionally, when something sparked his interest, he uttered peppery comments. A strange fellow carrying a huge backpack with all sorts of attachments passed through his field of vision. The Colonel noticed him and waved him over. "What is that thing you are carrying on top of your backpack?" "Sir, it is my inflatable rubber washbasin," answered the man. "What!" said the Colonel in a stentorian voice. "To war with an inflatable rubber basin? Are you also carrying an inflatable vagina?" After this military witticism, events dragged on hour after hour as we patiently sat, hoping again to be left unassigned.

But boredom set in. From a farmhouse behind us, the smell of freshly baked bread wafted over the martial field. George Ligeti and I were the first to notice this, and soon Ligeti, who had already emerged as a keen and ingenious provisioner, slipped away to investigate with the view of obtaining a "lángos"—something like a pizza, and a traditional delicacy of country ovens prepared out of leftover dough at the end of a baking session. After a while, Ligeti returned from his foray to the homestead beyond the hill and reported that in an hour he was to pick up a huge lángos specially made to order for us.

The day dragged on; the unpredictable switching around of personnel continued, and because none of us had yet received orders, we began to hope that we would be able to remain together. At the appointed time, Ligeti went back to the farm to pick up our lángos. He was a long time away, but eventually he came back with the lángos and it was delicious—the bottom was nice and crusty, with bits of ash baked into the dough. But he told me that we had almost lost our custom-made lángos to a delegation of older fellows from another company who obviously also possessed good olfactory equipment. To keep control of our prize, he had had to fight them, and this he had done with youth and vigour.

We had eaten the lángos, but although we didn't know it, Ligeti had shot a fatally flawed ball on the pinball machine. With unexpected suddenness, our group was called out and split up with lightning speed. My sweet friend Pali was thrown in one direction, most of the others in another, and those who were left, myself, Ligeti with the remnants of his lángos, Erwin Leichter, Pali Rona, and a few others were assigned to another white-band company. I immediately found friends: the company clerk, Laci Bartok, the former European single-scull rowing champion, had been the head coach at my rowing club. Another friend, George Segal, had been a classmate at school, and he received me with open arms. George's father was in the movie business and owned his own small movie theatre next to the big German UFA Urania theatre on Rakoczi utca, and George had often smuggled us into his family theatre for the best shows. But unfortunately, the company also had in its most influential inner circle two older men, veterans of the Russian front, one of whom now sported a black eye, while his friend had a big bruise on his neck. These two glowered unforgivingly at Ligeti, who was still holding a few pieces of the lángos, and muttered threats of revenge in a most unfortunate manner. Stronger and younger, at the time we paid no attention.

We fell in with the company which was commanded by second Lieutenant Dr. Rasko and had been bivouacking for the last three weeks at the nearby Gosztonyi estate, to which we now returned. Naturally, by now, company members had formed a certain loyal unity. There is no doubt that as newcomers, we were outsiders, and of course because of the lángos we had stirred up bad feeling in certain quarters.

The Gosztonyi estate was a beautiful farm on a gentle knoll, with a tree-lined drive leading to the old curia (manor house) which was surrounded by more ancient trees. We, however, did not head in this direction, but to an area behind the stables, where a large partially open building used for drying corn after the harvest served as headquarters for the Dr. Rasko company. Of course, as newcomers, we were allocated a rather windy section in the open building. Nevertheless, by nightfall, Ligeti and I had found a protected corner, and as we found out next day, the routine was not arduous in this beautiful place. A small brook was chattering behind our building, and the young scion of the Gosztonyi clan rode out from the stables early in the morning every day, jumping fences and galloping around and eyeing us from a distance. Thanks to the kindness of the company commander, only very light activities were prescribed, apart from the usual cleaning and washing activities.

Three days after our arrival, orders came down that eleven men were to leave by railway next morning for the easternmost part of Transylvania. They were to go way up in the Carpathian Mountains near Csikszereda in the Marosszék district, presumably to assist in the building of some fortifications in a military zone not very far from the advancing Russian armies. Of course, for dispatch to this faraway place, the company automatically made a list of the most expendable company members, and this included our little group of newcomers. As soon as I heard the bad news, I raced to the company office, and Laci Bartok took my name off the list. But when I returned to our corner in the barn, I found Ligeti tearfully packing his belongings and in deep depression on account of my "desertion." I rushed back to Laci Bartok hoping to get Ligeti off the list, too. But this was denied; on account of his fight over the lángos, Ligeti was considered a pariah. So with a lot of misgivings, I had my name put back on the list, and a "lucky man" was allowed to stay with the company instead of me.

Everybody was convinced that ours was a dangerous assignment. We would now be cast out from the safety of the company and would embark on a journey towards the fighting line and the retreating German and Hungarian armies. The pinball was spinning.

The orders were cut, and next morning we were marched out of the compound. The entire company lined up on the grass verge to wave goodbye to the little group of warriors marching *moritori* towards our unknown fate. Dr. Rasko in his impeccable field uniform was standing there with a good-looking young man, unknown to me at the time, whom I had seen a couple of times around the company offices. Laci Bartok came over and shook hands and embraced me. As we moved forward, the last person I saw was George Segal waving at me with tears on his cheeks. It was a gloomy send-off. I had a premonition that I would never see them again, and only on the hard benches of the rattling train, with the neat villages of the great Hungarian plains rolling by, did our mood improve. We began to speculate about how it would be high in the mountains with quaint wooden Transylvanian churches nestling among the tall pines, fresh mountain streams rushing towards rocky waterfalls, and snowy mountain peaks glistening in the sunshine. Such is the optimism of youth.

The mountains were still a long way away when darkness fell. We spent the night on the hard benches of the Hungarian State Railway, stopping occasionally at empty and deserted stations. The following morning the train pulled into a major station; the sign over the electrically illuminated clock announced it as "Nagyvárad." On the platform, farmers, soldiers, and city folk were hustling and bustling. The railway restaurant came into view, its illuminated interior, with a crowd of people at the tables, inviting. We decided to get off, stretch our legs, and have a bite to eat. I suddenly remembered that I had friends in this town. "Hey, George," I said to Ligeti, "I know some pretty girls here; maybe if thetrain stops long enough, we can phone." I was thinking of fun-loving friendly Baby Ritter from Tusnád Fürdö and sweet beautiful Éva Hochteil from Erdöszáda, just on the outskirts of the town. There were many other trains at other platforms, and it looked like a long stop.

We moved off along the platform towards the "Resti" and noticed a couple of gendarmes with their rifles slung on their shoulders, standing quietly near the entrance, scrutinising the crowds as only Hungarian gendarmes could, casting penetrating glances from under their cockfeathered black gendarme hats. The senior gendarme looked at us and called us over with an imperceptible movement of his head. "Papers," he said. I dug out our official orders, which he scrutinised slowly. "Follow me," was the next brief communication. We fell in and walked with them along the platform, not really apprehensive because our papers were in order, but aware of the fact that we were in a territory where civilian administration was suspended. The war was near.

Shortly we were ushered into the gendarme post in the station building. More studies of our documents followed, and then the steel ball on the pinball machine trembled, hesitated, and rocketed through the levers. Suddenly the gendarme tore our papers in half, threw them in the garbage bin. "You won't need these any more. You are to follow us."

We headed out to the main street, escorted by two gendarmes amid the morning traffic. We noticed people casting careful glances in our direction. After about 15 minutes, we arrived at a high solid wooden fence where several more gendarmes stood by a wide open gate. On the other side was a schoolyard, with the school building hard against the fence. More gendarmes were coming and going through the school entrance, which was guarded by two more gendarmes with bayonets fixed. We were marched across the yard to what looked like a gym storage building. Here we were handed over to a German SS Sturmführer in black uniform with the death-head insignia with the skull and crossbones hanging on a silver chain from his neck. Here the ball stopped rolling and fell into the trap. We had arrived in the Nagyvárad ghetto.

In the Ghetto

The SS man had Nordic blond hair, rosy pink cheeks, and a misleading smile. He stood us down and took the first in line into the storage building. George Ligeti and I, as was our custom on principle, waited at the end of the line, hoping to find out what was up. After about ten minutes, the first man interrogated came out, and the next one was called. We found out that a pretty rough questioning happened inside and that any valuables that were found on the person after a few threats and a cursory search were confiscated. As time passed, we sat down on the yard floor. George and I each had a roll of hundred-pengo bills in our pockets for emergencies, and in an unobserved moment, we dug the money into the ground where we sat. After we ourselves had been searched and released, we sat down again and dug out the money.

The SS man never reappeared, and we were escorted through various streets crowded with people of all ages and conditions. The streets were lined with three- and four-storey apartment buildings with courtyards which were also crowded and disorderly. After a few blocks, the buildings became smaller, with gardens, which were also crowded with people. The fences around the houses, which in Hungary surrounded all private properties, were torn down, and people walked at will across the once-neat gardens. Finally we came to a large house with a wide drive-through portal. Inside the house was a covered patio overlooking a large brick-paved courtyard with fruit trees around the edges. A multitude of people were sitting, walking, and talking in this area, a well-dressed crowd of men and women of all ages. We stopped in the middle of the yard and were immediately surrounded by curious questioners. We found out that we were in the large garden terrace of the Baksi Restaurant, once an old established Nagyvárad eating place. It also turned out that none of the people in this building were from Nagyvárad, but were people like us, caught in the net that the gendarmes had spread, and whose status was unclear. They hoped to be released. The rest of the ghetto, however, contained the local Jews, 27,000 of them, whose status according to the mad laws of the Germans was clear enough. At that moment, their interpretation of their situation was that with luck, this place would be their home for the duration of the war, and they began to settle in. The entire ghetto has been set up only a few weeks earlier. The administrative centre was the former Jewish gymnasium (high school), where the gendarmes had their headquarters, along with some offices of the SS. The area around the gymnasium had, of course, always been a Jewish district, the first ring around the school being residences and apartments of the less affluent. This was surrounded by concentric circles of garden housing of ever-increasing prosperity. This whole area was now surrounded by an eight-foot-high solid fence, the Gentile minority once living in the area having been moved out into evacuated Jewish residences, while the Jews from all of Nagyvárad were forcibly moved into this new enclave. Here there was no industrial activity, no shops, no cafés, no schools; however, there was a small hospital that Béla Zsolt had set up, which later was to become quite famous. The biggest problem was that the population density had increased by a factor of five, so that where one family had lived in comfort, now six had to live. People moved in with friends and relatives, and somehow all found accommodation. The density was so high that seventy percent of all the people were constantly outside moving around trying to reconcile themselves to the new circumstances. There was a solution to the density problem— the Hungarian and German authorities were already working on it—but few of the residents knew about it, and if they knew, they kept it to themselves.

The interior of the ghetto had been divided, for reasons not very clear at the time, into eight districts of about 3,500 people each, and of course, not surprisingly, the eight districts were roughly representative of the social strata of the Nagyvárad Jewish community. Its prominent elders had been drafted into the German-organised Jewish council of Nagyvárad, which had offices side by side with the gendarmes. Their main role was to keep the population unaware of the German plans and to relay messages and instructions. The ghetto was not yet permanently sealed off, and certain influential people on both sides of the fence had a limited authorised freedom of movement.

The interior rooms of the Baksi Restaurant were filled choc a bloc, and we had to settle in on what was once the partially open covered dining patio of the restaurant, which had large windows opening onto the yard. It was under these windows that George Ligeti and I, Paul Rona, Doni Donnenberg, Erwin Leichter, and the rest of our group spread our blankets. Having settled in, George and I began to investigate the immediate area and discovered a door opening onto a steep ladder-type stair into the attic. The attic had vast rafters rising to a peak, with heavy wooden crossbeams. We climbed up to the beam level, and where the rafters met the beam in the little triangular recess, we hid most of our cash, leaving just enough for small expenses.

By this time it was late afternoon, and the low rays of the sun barely filtered through the clay roof tiles. We casually returned and began to meet the residents of the Baksi. I discovered two gentlemen in elegant army captain's uniforms (though without sidearms). Introducing myself, I found out that they were reserve army officers from Szeged, Dezsö Patzauer and Lipót Löw, the son of the world famous Szeged Rabbi, Emmanuel Löw, both of whom were classmates of my father at the Piarist Gymnasium in Szeged. They told me that they had been travelling with orders towards the Carpathian Mountains, just like us, and were taken off the train by the gendarmes only a week earlier. They had already sent messages to the Szeged army command and expected to be released shortly. They explained that a type of curfew was in effect and that after dark people were not supposed to move from their own district, but that this was not too rigorously enforced. The locals had all brought in food supplies for a month, but people in the Baksi who had been caught empty-handed could arrange for certain foods to be brought in from outside for a price. Messages went back and forth to the outside world, but it was not advisable to send letters through the mail; only letters sent by courier were likely to arrive. We had a couple of pounds of double-smoked bacon and salami as well as bread in our knapsacks, so after a satisfactory meal, we decided to bed down early. By nine o'clock all was quiet. We slept until the sun came up.

But by 6 A.M., even we could not go on sleeping. People were moving all around us, talking, arguing. We decided to leave our noisy crowded quarters and investigate as much of the ghetto as we could. Walking through the archway, we set out towards some quite elegant houses on a tree-lined street. Everywhere people were coming and going, standing, sitting, talking. After walking for a while, we reached the houses we had set out for, and as we were passing, we saw in the backyard under the shade of some fruit trees a group of young girls sitting on garden benches around a table. We cut across the lawn, doing what was natural even in those frightening circumstances, and approached them.

In the middle of the circle, surrounded by half a dozen other girls, sat Baby Ritter, my light-hearted friend from Tusnád Fürdö, her short black hair bobbing as she held court. She looked up and ran to me. "What are you doing here?" she said right away. "I don't know myself, but it's wonderful to see you, the only person I know in Nagyvárad except your classmate Éva Hochteil from Erdöszáda, my love from Nagybánya." "You come back in the afternoon and bring some of your friends, and then well have time to talk," Baby said.

I promised, and we hurried beck to the Baksi to organise outside provisioning and a message system. Erwin Leichter had the best idea. "I'll get a message out to the local brothel, where my mother's exchange students will find a way to get messages to our families." So George and I and the others scribbled short S.O.S. notes. I wrote to my father asking him to get me out any way he could. By early afternoon, our letters were in the hands of a young lady on her way to Budapest on the night train after having done her tour of duty for the war effort.

In the afternoon, George, Doni, and I left for Baby's house in our cleanest shirts. In spite of the circumstances, we were greeted with coffee with whipped cream and a delicious kuglehupf. How this was possible, I don't know. Several of Baby's friends from the morning were also there. After a second cup of coffee and more cake, Baby and I sat on the steps to the veranda, and she told me that the house belonged to her uncle, her mother's younger brother, and that her family and the families of the other girls had moved in when they were forced from their own homes. The four mothers were friends and bridge partners. At this moment, we could not see them because they had just been released from the "Brewery." When I questioned Baby, she finally told me that the Brewery, just inside the walls of the ghetto with its own railway siding, was the inquisition headquarters of the Hungarian gendarmes. This organisation, Baby told me, made sure that no Jews were transferred into German hands before any hidden jewellery and money were beaten out of them. From a prepared list, they took the women of the wealthier families for questioning about hidden assets. Threats were followed by beatings, while a radio blared throughout the huge factory and beyond. The least cooperative women and also the good-looking ones were taken to the machine. With tears pouring down her face, Baby told me that the machine was a low-voltage electric generator which was used on the women after they had been ordered to strip and spread their legs wide over a table. Then, for the amusement of the gendarmes, they were jolted with electric currents through electrodes inserted inside their bodies. The women's screams could not be heard over the radio's blaring, which, even as we sat there, was unrelenting. There was no escape from the noise. Baby's mother had just returned from this treatment and had collapsed upstairs in the house. In spite of the humiliation and pain, she had given up only some of her personal jewellery.

By now, Baby was weeping on my shoulder. "All this has happened because my mother was not a good wife; it is God's punishment—for her sins, her lovers, her bridge games." No reassurance could help her. After a while, she calmed down a little, and I remembered her promise to talk about Éva, and I asked. She dried her tears and told me to wait a minute, and she went into the house. After a while, she came back carrying half a dozen rough photographic proofs of 8- x 11-inch size and put them on the steps. There on the steps was a series of life-size portraits of Éva, serious, with her long dark blonde hair falling in that unforgettable way over her high forehead. The pictures were not finished and not very well developed, and there were a few footprints faintly visible on the paper. "I managed to save them from our house," said Baby, "but Éva and her entire family have already been transported east with a concentration of suburban families." Baby and I held each other, seeing Éva in our minds for a long time.

I promised to be back the next day and departed, and for the next while, I came every day when I could, to talk about life, our holiday at Tusnád Fürdö, about Éva, and about Baby herself. And Baby talked about guilt, about her mother and her family and the bad lives which they must all have led to find themselves in this position. Baby knew that I was taking steps to get out of the ghetto, and we said that we hoped that we would all meet when it was all over, but in reality, Baby had no hope for herself. She knew what was coming. I was the lifeline that could survive and remember all that she told me.

As the days passed, our little group roamed all over, meeting more people, hearing more stories. It was a Dantesque scene of despair and fear. We knew that we were in desperate trouble, but the life force of the young kept us hopeful.

One day, a gendarme arrived and took the two army reserve officers and myself out of the Baksi to gendarme headquarters. Here they were handed over to an officer who had come to claim them and marched off, saved. I had to wait in the school corridor. Suddenly a door opened from the anteroom of Colonel Ferenczy, the Commander of the Ghetto, and out came Mr. Szücs, chief of detectives of the criminal division of the Budapest police and an old acquaintance of my father. I was ordered into a small room by a gendarme officer for interrogation by detective Szücs. It turned out that my father, in making efforts trying to get me out of the ghetto, had arranged to have Mr. Szücs try to serve a summons on me from the criminal court in Budapest so that he could take me into custody and take me back to Budapest. Of course this was refused by the colonel, but he was allowed to interrogate me. The interrogation was a sham, but he brought the message from my father that he was well and, if this did not succeed, he would find other ways to get me out. I was depressed by the departure of the two Szeged officers and the lack of success with the summons, but knowing that Father was taking action buoyed up my spirits, and I sent him a note through Szücs.

That afternoon, Ligeti and I found an abandoned Orthodox synagogue and rabbinical school. In the basement of the building, there was a huge concrete bath with pale-green algae floating on top of the water. It was a warm day in May, and we jumped in and swam a few laps, splashing around, forgetting about the holy men whose ritual bath it was, and who most probably were already traveling east.

The same afternoon, Baby's mother, having recovered, joined us at our afternoon tea in their garden; she looked just the same as she had in Tusnád Fürdö.

Escape from the Boxcar

The next day, the gendarmes completely sealed the ghetto, and in the morning the deportations started. The first district was surrounded before dawn by the gendarmes, and all 3500 of its residents were jam-packed into boxcars and shipped off to Auschwitz.

All day, wild rumours spread, some probably instigated by the Germans: "No more groups will be taken," "The Russians are near the mountain paths," "They will have no time to take more people." And indeed there seemed to be a pause (caused by lack of available empty freight cars).

That night, two young Poles, beaten to within an inch of their lives, were tossed into the Baksi courtyard. They had escaped from Auschwitz, and after having crossed the Carpathian Mountains, hiding in the forests, they came to within 100 metres of their goal, the Rumanian border (and safety, since the Rumanians did not participate in the deportations). There they had been caught by the gendarmes. After interrogation, because now "administratively" they belonged to the Germans, they were dumped into our yard, the catch-all of the ghetto. That night we heard their stories of the death camps—Auschwitz, Treblinka, and Sobibor—where all of us could be headed, and I realised that help had to come soon, or the pinball game would be up.

When next morning I approached the district and the ghetto house where 15 members of the Ritter family had been living, I did so with deep foreboding. The garden was empty, the back door open. I went up to the porch and for the first time entered the house. By then, I knew the worst. Their district had been evacuated early that morning. In the kitchen and the living room was every sign of a hasty departure: dishes with half-eaten breakfast; a milk jug knocked over, drained of its contents; knives and forks scattered all over. Suitcases partially filled, gaping open, an umbrella on top of a winter coat. Underneath an overturned kitchen chair, the scattered pictures of beautiful Éva from art school. And deadly, ghostly silence. They were gone, the scene frozen at the moment of their departure. I picked up one of the photos and took it back to the Baksi.

In the next ten days, more and more districts were transported. Soon the Brewery radio was eerily silent; there was no one left to be tortured.

During this time, as I later found out, my father called on Count Zsigmond Csaky, a retired Field Marshall of the Gendarmes, father of a former Hungarian Foreign Minister. The General owed my father a favour from many years before when they had been comrades, and he was shocked to hear of my predicament. He promised to send his aide-de-camp, a gendarme Colonel, to save me. The Colonel did indeed come to get me, but was misled to believe that I had already been transported.

By now there was nobody left in the ghetto but those in the hospital, supposedly infected by the plague, and we in the Baksi courtyard. Illogically our confidence rose. After all, we were only a few hundred in the Baksi, not enough for a train load. The trains used freight cars of the Hungarian State Railway, stencilled before the first war with the phrases: "For Mobilisation" and "4 horses or 8 men," the last referring to the maximum capacity. When used for transporting the Jews, these same cars had 75 people forced into each of them, along with their belongings, a milk bucket full of water, and some loaves of bread. Each of these cars had full-height sliding doors on either side and four vent openings, one by one-and-a-half feet, with wooden drop panels. These were positioned high up, two to each side, one for each horse. Some cars had steel bars built into the window openings, others did not, but in all cases, the outside wooden drop panels were screwed or nailed down. A train consisted of 45 to 50 boxcars, capable of transporting a total load of 3500 persons, or a complete ghetto district. Now that we were so few, we would be saved.

Late in May, Nagyvárad was bombed by a heavy concentration of English Wellington night bombers. We sat in the yard listening to the explosions of the cluster bombs and the racket of anti-aircraft guns, and it seemed to us that some bombs fell on the railway yards. This, we decided, would make transportation even more difficult. It was a warm night, and when the all clear sounded, we went to sleep rather soundly.

Orders were barked out in the dark. Ligeti and I got up, rolling our blankets and putting on our coats, while the gendarmes pushed through the Baksi courtyard, roaring, "Everybody out!" Chairs fell over, people tripped. "Move, Move!" We were the first out in the yard in the chilly morning. It was 5 A.M. "Form a column!" We were up front; old people were chased out of the building. Mr. Fried, the agronomist, fell in last with his wife, clutching his all-important catheter. George and I had forgotten our money in the attic, but it was now too late. "March, one, two!" We were marched to the high school and into the auditorium. The yard was empty, except for a gigantic pile of confiscated winter coats, fur coats among then. A mountain of coats three storeys high! In the auditorium, we sat down. Outside, it was getting light. We could see the gendarmes with their bayonets fixed, fidgeting at the double doors. We dropped our gear and sat on some benches; I knew that the time to escape from Nagyvárad was gone. We were on our way, like everyone else. I was depressed, my mind finally registering the hopelessness. Time passed; some people fell asleep, some just walked around. At about 8 in the morning, a policeman came around, asking for volunteers to go into town to clear the ruins from last night's bombing. Ligeti, always ready to play another shot on the pinball machine, jumped up, ready to go. "Come on, let's go," he said. "At least we can buy some ice cream, maybe." I was too depressed. "Leave me alone, you idiot," I said.

Ligeti and several others, though none from our group, went off. Although he did not know it, he had set another ball spinning through the pinball gates. I sat lethargically penning a postcard farewell to my father, telling him that we were off. A policeman came around, took it from me, and for 50 pengos agreed to drop it in the mail. A message in a bottle in the ocean, who knew if it would arrive.

There was little noise in the auditorium, just a low murmur of voices, until the gendarmes came in and ordered us to pick up our gear and get out. No sign of Ligeti. Without him, we marched off towards the Brewery, to the railway siding, where a freight train was already being filled from a long line of people, three or four abreast: single people, families, children, old people. We stood at the end of the train, near the caboose, with a gendarme sitting on its steps. Other gendarmes moved about, processing people into the boxcars. This was not easy because the car floors were high up. Young people went first, helping the others; old people were pushed in from below. When 75 people were counted in, the water can and some bread were squeezed in after them. The gendarmes pushed the sliding doors in place, shot the bolt, closed the padlock, ticked off the shipping documents. Next! next! Where is Ligeti? Next car, next car! Now it was the turn of the Baksi group. Still no sign of Ligeti. Up we went to the forward part of the boxcar. We were all there, Pali Rona, Doni Donnenberg, Erwin Leichter, a few powerful young fellows from Mateszalka, Stephen Gipsz, a medical student, the whole group except Ligeti. Well—we'd have to meet him when we got there, wherever that might be. Meanwhile, more and more people were being pressed into our car. We tried to hold the corner for ourselves so we had a little more breathing space, but it became clear that this was not possible. By the time 75 people were in, there was no room for sitting down, no room for breathing. We were pushed closer, closer, as more people were shoved in with us. A pretty blonde with cornflower-blue eyes stood next to me. Where she came from, I didn't know; she was alone. An old couple was also beside us. Tighter, tighter the crowd became. The door was slid shut; we could hear the padlock being fastened on the outside.

Inside it was dark; the only light came through the cracks. All four vent openings were shuttered. It was 12 noon, and the train was ready; we could hear the gendarmes and the train crew outside. Then silence; nothing happened. The temperature rose as the sun beat down on the tin roof. The old boxcar creaked from the weight of its cargo. Families kept together. People fainted standing up. After a couple of hours, the train started with jarring and clanging and moved through a few switches, and then, clanging and shrieking, stopped again. By now, we were a mass of sweaty, parched humanity. The hours passed, the old lady not far from me fainted; on closer examination, it was found that she had died, standing on her feet, held up by the crowd. Somehow they lowered her to the floor, out of the way against the wall.

The water can was empty. More starts and jarring stops. We could see that it was getting dark outside. Now it was even darker inside. It must have been around 9 P.M. when the train finally gathered speed and got underway. The old boxcars, built under the rule of the Emperor King Francis Joseph, swayed on the badly undulating tracks. Some time passed, and the boys from Mateszalka, who knew the area quite well, said that we were heading north to Debrecen and beyond, to the border. In the movement of the crowd in the dark, the blonde girl was pushed closer to me until we were rhythmically rubbing against each other, and in this desperate situation we did the only thing that for a few moments could transport us away from here, away into Nirvana.

I notice that some of my friends had worked their way over to the left front vent opening. The powerful boys from Mateszalka had succeeded in forcing the nails that held the wooden shutter, and with a bang the shutter opened, dropping down on its hinges. As I worked my way in that direction, a wiry fellow with a build like a jockey yelled: "Help me up! Help me up! I will jump." The train was gathering speed in a long curve, the car tilting to the right. Up he went, and I pushed him out. But after hanging onto the outside, the wind rushing by, he lost heart, climbed back in, and dropped on the floor exhausted. It looked as if this would not work. The telegraph poles flew by one after the other, dangerously close. "Let me try," I said. With the help of the Szalkans, I climbed up and out and hung onto the opening with my right arm. The train was still accelerating. The only chance was to jump as soon as a pole whizzed by and before the next one came up. The face of the Szalkan was in the opening. "Call," I asked him. He understood. "Now," he yelled. A pole went by. I was not ready. "Now," he yelled. And once again, "Now." And with the third "Now!" I let go, flying feet first into a ditch full of swamp water.

Jump Now! May 1994

I landed on my arse after a 100-foot slide along the slippery ground, my upper body thrown forward. There I sat in the water among the reeds, motionless, as the train rattled by with its desperate cargo.

The caboose came last, its sliding door open, the gendarmes playing cards in the light of a hanging lantern. Swaying and rattling, it passed by me, the red light in the back diminishing as the train went on. I straightened up and climbed back up to the tracks which were reflecting the red light on their shiny surfaces.

The stars were glittering in the clear May sky. The air was clean and fresh. I took a deep breath, then squatted on a wooden tie between the rails, pushed down my pants, and did what I had wanted to do for the last 12 hours. I had a really good solid young bowel movement.

Safe Landing?

The train rattled on and grew smaller and smaller, but suddenly, my God! they had stopped the train! In fact, it was travelling in a long curve around me, and the sound seemed stationary. It took some moments for me to realise this, and I was not going to give up my suddenly regained freedom. Quickly buttoning up my flannel pants, I took off at right angles to the tracks. In a minute, I was hip-deep in the swamp, with the ghostly whistle of the train diminishing. Finally there was silence, with only the frogs jumping and calling.

I was free! But not home free.

Short-Lived Freedom

I must have jumped around midnight, and for several hours, I kept wading aimlessly in the swamp, with no idea of my geographic location, trying to put together a plan. For the fateful train journey, I had luckily dressed in my good flannel pants and one of Knizek's excellently cut rust-brown tweed jackets, so except for my heavy boots, I could pass for a civilian.

For identification, I had the Royal Hungarian Railway pass, a perk for all military officers and civil servants and their children up to the age of 21, which I always carried with me. This was an impressive document: in passport format, with a black leather cover, with the crest of the Royal Railway tooled on its face in gold print. Inside, on the left page, my picture was affixed with metal eyelets and sealed with the embossing seal of the Railway. Underneath, the text read, "Issued for John Eber, Royal Hungarian Army Captain, ret. (Son of: George Francis Eber)." The pass had been issued in January 1940 and revalidated yearly with a special stamp of the railway. It had last been validated in January 1944. All my other gear I had left behind in the train, but the pass was in a waterproof sleeve in my inside pocket. I felt sure that, combined with a bit of typical army-brat arrogance, this prestigious document would carry me through the gendarme post in Debrecen onto the first train to Budapest. That is, if I made it as far as Debrecen. For where was Debrecen, and how was I to get there? All I knew was that it must be to the north somewhere.

A plan began to emerge. When daylight came, I would start off on the country roads heading north, away from populated areas. So far, so good, but I was still hip-high in algae-covered swamp water and alone, very alone but for the croaking of frogs all around me. Slowly the dawn began to break.

About a mile away on a slight hill, surrounded by acacia trees, a farm homestead began to take shape. The water carried the noise of a cock crowing from behind the stables. I realised that soon it would be full daylight and that I would be standing exposed in the swamp. As it got lighter, I noticed nearby on a slight elevation a clump of bushes which would give me cover until I could orient myself. I started to wade towards it, and then in the morning haze, strung out on the horizon, I noticed five or six ghostly figures moving towards me. I froze, thinking that my freedom had been short-lived. The gendarmes must have noticed my escape, and I was already being hunted down. If I could only get into the bushes.... But the shadows also froze and vanished from sight. Every minute it was getting lighter. Now one figure re-emerged—strange behaviour for a search party. We looked at each other's hazy images for a while, and then other figures appeared and started to move towards me. I took some tentative steps toward the clump of bushes, but suddenly the hazy figures became clearly recognisable.

We met up at the bushes. The mysterious figures were the two boys from Mateszalka, Pali Rona, Donnenberg, and Erwin Leichter. They had jumped from the train after me but arranged to meet up along the railway tracks and had wandered around all night. They saw my shape in the hazy light and, like me, thought that they had been caught. Now we were all sitting under the bushes, happy to be together. The farm came to life. An old farmer brought a horse from the stable, hitched it to a farm wagon, and started down the road. He passed us without a glance, not half a mile away, the dust rising behind the wagon. Our spirits soared; we had escaped, and we had found each other.

We began to assess our situation. We all agreed that we had to get to Debrecen, which the older boy from Mateszalka insisted was no more than 50 kilometres away. I wanted to go alone as I had previously decided, hiding in the daytime, moving on the mountain ridges at night. All of us together, I felt, would attract attention, and I suggested that we split up into small groups. I would go alone. I knew I had a chance that way. As we debated the matter, the farm came to full life with animal noises, and a thin wisp of smoke emerging from the chimney. Farther down the road in the valley, the outlines of a small village took shape. We all agreed that we could not hide for a whole day in our present location, close to the road and fields which we now also began to discern. But the group did not favor splitting up. "You got us out of the train," someone said, "now stay with us." I found myself in the unwanted position of leader. My hand hesitated on the pinball machine lever. The ball neared the paddle. I shot at it, and the paddle sent it sideways, and the game went on. By now it was around 8 in the morning. "All right," I said. "We'll go together."

The Szalkan had an idea of our location, and we decided to get out on the road together and march steadily through the villages on the shortest way to Debrecen, pretending to be a carefree group of summer students on a hiking trip. I had strong misgivings, and now in retrospect I can see that our chances were poor. But how do you calculate the odds on the pinball machine? I am here to tell the story. Who knows what would have happened had I played the ball another way?

"Let's clean up a bit and get underway." Ten minutes later, our ragtag group emerged on the dusty rutted road, walking rather than marching, but with steady speed to the north.

By the time we reached the first village half an hour later, the farmers were all out in the fields working, and the village was deserted. The road wound its way between the shuttered houses with their gable ends facing the road, their porches running alongside the houses towards the barnyard. A few hens scratched away, the odd cat stretched out on the top of the wooden sill on the porch watched us. Near the church facing the village green, a group of older women set on wooden benches, shelling peas from a large basket. From under their babushkas, they cast surreptitious glances at the strange phenomenon we presented. When we drew abreast, in the traditional Hungarian village way, I sang out, "Praised be the Lord," and the answer came hesitatingly, "For now and forever amen." We kept on without hesitation, past the church and the village school, from where, through the open windows, we could hear the noises of children at class. Soon we reached the end of the village. I looked back, but nobody came after us.

The road kept rising, and soon we were surrounded by trees, and we walked for some time on a forested stretch. After a while, the trees fell away, and we approached another village, which we negotiated with similar success. We began to feel a little more secure.

We approached another farmstead with its characteristic outbuildings and its "Gemes Kut"—a tall stork-like water-lifting device that stood beside all country water wells in Hungary. By now we were really hungry, and I decided to go in and buy some food. The farmer and family were out in the fields; only the old grandmother was at work in the summer kitchen. Soon we were sitting under the well structure with pitchers of fresh milk, smoked bacon, and huge slabs of bread. We stayed only a short while and exchanged only a few words, but the old woman was friendly enough: she complained about the "terror bombers" which had flown overhead two nights ago and to distant rumbling had dropped their cargo in the area of Nagyvárad. I got my group up, and thanking her for the food, we set out again on the road.

I began to feel confident; it seemed that we were causing little curiosity. More villages and fields went by. We must have covered about 20 miles when a larger village loomed up ahead. I considered walking around the village over the hills rising on one side, but trying to make time and having successfully negotiated four or five villages, I led the way into the village.

By this time, it was late in the day; the farmers were coming home from the fields for supper, which as we could see from the smoke rising from all the chimneys, was now being prepared. School was out, and the children were very much in evidence behind the fences and on the village green. In the village centre, past the church, a few municipal buildings huddled off the main road, and a group of villagers stood around reading a poster nailed to the wooden gates of the village office. We walked on as usual. A few glances were cast in our direction, I could feel more than see, but we kept our distance and went on. Soon we were out of the village, back on the empty road, the hills rising sharply on our right side. The sun began to die, and the trees cast long shadows across the road. We could smell the freshly cut hay from the fields to the left. I began to look for a place on the wooded hillside to settle down for the night.

The road took a turn, and on our right a large meadow, still sun-dappled, rose gently to meet the bordering forest. While the field was still lit by the last rays of the sun, the forest loomed dark above. My eyes surveyed the edge of the forest as I looked for a suitable spot. Something glistened.

Soon two figures emerged, moving fast down the hill from the tree edge in our direction. Soon we could discern that they were uniformed soldiers; it was their fixed bayonets that I had seen glittering in the setting sun. We walked on as casually as possible, pretending to be on our

119

lawful way. They emerged from the roadside ditch, and one figure positioned himself in the middle of the road facing us, the other remaining on the side with his World War I Mannlicher rifle off his shoulder and the bayonet pointing in our direction. They were old soldiers, not suitable for front-line duty, with old-style uniforms, their caps pushed back on their suntanned foreheads. Both had drooping moustaches. The one in the centre of the road was a sergeant, the other a corporal. Campaign ribbons were sewn onto the chests of their ill-fitting uniforms.

When we drew abreast, the sergeant said slowly, "Now what do we have here?" I approached him smiling, but I knew that our short-lived freedom was at an end after less than a day.

The master sergeant listened to my story kindly enough. Then he said, "I have to take you fellows back to the village to the village clerk. He'll sort you out." So we turned around, and with him in the lead and the corporal bringing up the rear, we started back to the village.

The film rolled backwards; we passed the trees and fields, now deserted, and descended into the village. I joined the sergeant up ahead and found that he was quite willing to chat. He and the corporal were village farmers and had been soldiers in the Great War of 1914-18. They had been called up for air defence duty. This consisted of sitting on top of the hill in a little wooden structure with their binoculars and reporting any approaching planes on an ancient field telephone which they had set up. There were similar posts all over in the area now that the air war seemed to be closer. There had been three air raids around Nagyvárad, and everybody was tense because even the simple farmers realised that the war was now at hand. Even the sheepdogs were nervous, and every time a formation flew by miles up in the sky, they herded the sheep together under the shade of large trees.

While I was chattering amiably with this veteran of the Great War, we suddenly arrived back in the village. In front of the municipal building, high on a wooden pole, a single yellow light, the moths circling around it crazily, illuminated the area in the gathering dusk. A large number of villagers were gathered there: farmers, their wives with black kerchiefs tied over their heads, and children. As we halted in front of the doors of the administrative building, the crowd gathered around us, and it seemed to me that they spoke in an agitated way. I was close to the door and saw the poster which I had noticed earlier on our way through. "Warning from the village clerk," it said in large print. "By order of the Royal Hungarian Army Command, Eastern Transylvanian War Zone ..." and it went on in the jargon of a military command ukase, warning all villagers that a new phase of the war had started with terror bombings. All must now be on the alert for spies and saboteurs who might be parachuted into the district.

The hostile glances and murmuring intensified, and we began to feel extremely uncomfortable. Suddenly a wiry army captain came out of the offices with a clerk in civilian clothes in tow. Being the spokesman, I addressed him respectfully in the military manner and began to explain our story. We were summer students on a field trip returning via Debrecen to Budapest.

He cut me off with a hysterical outburst. "I have served three years of the war on the Russian front. I know your kind of stories—you are nothing but spies—saboteurs, dropped in from the planes two days ago. You are in civilian clothes behind the front. We'll make short process with you. We'll hang you all before the day is over."

We had dropped from the frying pan into the fire. The crowd was threateningly close, and the captain began to open the holster of his sidearm. The trap seemed to close around us, but before I could gather my wits to answer the attack, the ring of people around us opened up, and a gendarme patrol pushed their bicycles through. They were impeccably uniformed, as gendarmes always were: their green cockfeathers glistening on the top of their black hats, their whistles on a green braided line stretching across their tunics, their rifles held to their shoulders by a green-faced roll at the end of their shoulder strap, their gendarme swords attached to the front wheel of their bicycles, cavalry style.

The older one of the two, his black waxed moustache pointing forward in a traditional manner, came towards us with a steady motion. "I heard you," he said to the captain with authority. "There will be no hanging here." The captain looked at him, but was quiet. "We represent the law here and we will deal with this." Then to us: "Follow me quick step," and so, with one gendarme in front and the other behind, we marched through the hostile crowd.

By now it was completely dark, the one yellow lamp on the post casting deep shadows. Never had I imagined that I could be relieved to be in the hands of the gendarmes. Their post was just a few steps down from the municipal offices, and they ushered us into a large guardroom with tables and benches and a wooden cupboard against one wall. The gendarmes leaned the rifles against a wooden rack and made us stand to attention against the wall. Now in a quiet not unfriendly voice, the gendarme sergeant said, "Now I want to hear the real story from you."

Without hesitation, I started to tell our story again. "Not you," the gendarme barked. He started walking in front of us, looking at the faces of my companions. "You," he said, stopping in front of the older Szalkan. "I want to hear it from you." I was beginning to feel my short-lived relief slipping away. The Szalkan was not prepared, but he stuck to the story. The sergeant let him finish, then he strolled to the rifle rack, lifted off his 18-pound well-oiled Mannlicher rifle, and casually holding it vertically with the barrel pointing to the ceiling, walked back to the Szalkan and held the stock about three feet above his feet. We were standing at attention immobile, but I watched from the corner of my eye as he dropped the heavy rifle onto the Szalkan's toe. He went down howling. The gendarme said,

"Now will I get the story, or shall I hand you over to the captain to deal with." So by and by we told the whole true story, starting with how we left the Jaszberény command with orders to go by train to the Carpathian Mountains. How the gendarmes took our papers at the Nagyvárad station, our detention in the ghetto, the train, and our escape. All through this procedure, the sergeant never raised his voice. Now he said, "You can all sit down on the bench while I go and get my orders," and he left us guarded by his second.

The sergeant went over to the adjoining duty office, and I could hear him crank up the old-fashioned phone, but could not hear the conversation. There were several calls, and time passed. Meanwhile we managed to remove the Szalkan's boot. His toe was swollen and looked a mess, but no bones seemed to be broken. The sergeant came back. We could hear the voices of many gendarmes in the guardroom. He called in a man who brought in a typewriter and put a large printed form in triplicate into the machine. The sergeant questioned us formally. Our names, the designation of our labour unit, company number, etc. Then followed the description of how we got into the gendarmes' hands. Then he dictated, "Designation: return prisoners under guard by train in the morning to Nagyvárad ghetto command. At the same time have three typewriters returned to Nagyvárad, to be carried by said prisoners." All this took some time, after which other gendarmes were sent to complete the documentation. Administration was one of their fortes.

The sergeant ordered some food to be brought in for us and told us to rest as well as we could, because our transport would start at 5 in the morning. Then he left. Dinner was brought in, and we were left on our own in the guardroom after a heavy bolt was shot in place from the outside. It was then that I first looked around; all the windows were heavily barred. We ate the meal that came from the village pub, but we did not talk much. I looked at my little crew—they were exhausted. Pali Rona, who was very good looking, with features reminiscent of Robert Taylor; the two Szalkans, tough country boys; Doni Donnenberg, huge, with the arms and fists of a bear, who used to work in his father's bakery; and our little wiry-haired musician from the brothel, Frank Leichter, all were disheartened and exhausted. At 9 P.M., the lights went out, and there was nothing to do but settle down on the wooden benches for a restless night's sleep. I was trying to figure out the next step, but couldn't think of a useful move. Finally I fell asleep with the others. The ball was resting in a trap.

In the early hours of the morning, I woke up to the noise of the door opening. The gendarmes pushed in a group of people, 10 or 12 men, and shut the bolt again. The men found room on the wooden benches and tables. Light came soon, and I saw that our companions were young village gypsies.

The gypsies were friendly and explained that they had been dragged out of the gypsy quarters which were usually located at the edge of Hungarian villages, where they lived in huts made of bricks formed out of clay mud mixed with straw and then dried. Brick-making was the main trade of the gypsies, other than making music, and they lived a life of work, drinking, and loving—a life similar, we thought, to that of the black slave workers on a Southern plantation. They were not quite slaves, but had a restricted existence.

Hitler considered them "subhumans" and an antisocial element, and the gendarmes were instructed to gather as many of them as they could and ship them east with the deportation trains. We told them our story, and we tried to cheer each other up. The time passed with talk. At five in the morning, we were all given steaming hot coffee and then lined up outside. Our two gendarmes from the day before stood beside us. Three farm wagons had been requisitioned and were waiting for us. Sitting up front were three elderly farmers who regarded us indifferently.

We climbed up onto the first wagon, the gypsies taking the other two. The gendarmes handed up three broken-down typewriters, and the little convoy started up, the horses flicking their tails in the harness at some early-rising flies. Our gendarmes got onto their bicycles and rode alongside us, and we were underway.

We travelled for about an hour on the dusty road, passing through several small villages, until we reached a small railway station. By this time, the sun was up, and we began to feel better in its warmth. For quite a long time, we had been able to hear the puffing and wheezing of a locomotive blowing steam as it idled. After a final bend in the road, a long train of familiar boxcars came into view, halted on a track. The other track was empty. As we drove by the train, from every boxcar came a murmur, with no individual voices audible. Here and there, through barred windows, hands were reaching out, and behind them were anxious eyes. Some of the windows had no bars, but had barbed wire nailed across them, others had wooden flaps screwed tight. We could not take our eyes away. Not long ago, we could never have thought that we would ever see such a train from the outside.

At the end of the train was a large caboose, with a machine gun mounted on its top, its door open, and in front a group of waiting gendarmes with an old railway flagman. This was where our wagons stopped. We were ordered to dismount, and our gendarmes went forward across the empty track. The signal lamp on the arm of the semaphore glowed red. The wagons turned around and left without a backward glance. Perhaps the farmers were in a hurry to get back to work. A master sergeant detached himself from the waiting group. Our sergeant made his report. "Twelve gypsies for transportation. Six escapees to be escorted back to Nagyvárad." The master sergeant looked us over and said, "We might as well take them also, they will be going the same way anyhow." We stood frozen, holding our breath. Our gendarme said,

"I would, but my orders are clear; we have to take them back. And we have to deliver the typewriters, anyhow." The master sergeant struggled and then barked an order. Two gendarmes opened the sliding door of the last boxcar. Inside we could see people jammed together, looking with frightened eyes into the sudden light. The gypsies were marched to the door and disappeared into the maw of the Germans' final solution.

The door was slammed shut and padlocked, and the gendarmes climbed into the caboose. The signal man waved his flag, and with much clanging in its effort to get underway, the train started. The engineman waved from the locomotive. The gendarmes waved from the caboose and began to diminish in size as the train gathered speed. Standing on the platform, we gazed after it. In a little while, it had disappeared beyond the bend, and there was total silence except for the buzzing flies.

With a quick movement of its leading wires, the semaphore lifted its arm, and a green light glowed. The signalman returned to the station office, and in a while we heard the signal bell ringing, and a small milk-run train rattled in from the direction in which the other had disappeared. We clambered aboard along with our two gendarmes, who left their bicycles behind. The train had wooden benches, most of them occupied by sleeping farmers, but we found places and settled in. The wagon had the smell of onion, garlic, and cheap tobacco, but it seemed like first-class comfort compared to the alternative.

The sun was at its highest point when, after innumerable stops, we pulled into the main station of Nagyvárad, back where we had arrived for the first time almost exactly a month before. However, the station was not the same. It had taken several direct hits from American bombers. Its roof was gaping open, beams and joist hanging at crazy angles. The station platform was nevertheless a beehive of activity, with soldiers and farmers moving about in every direction.

*We stand behind the gendarmes, their cockfeathers waving,
as the gypsies are loaded onto the departing train.*

The gendarme offices were partially boarded up, but still functional. We halted in front, carrying the typewriters. One of the gendarmes went inside and came out with three sets of handcuffs and, handcuffing us together in pairs, deposited the typewriters on our handcuffed hands, leaving our free hands to balance them. Through the partially ruined ticketing office we emerged onto the station square and started marching down the main street. Pedestrians stopped in their tracks. "Look at the terrorist spies!" "Look at them carrying their spy radios!" These were the covered typewriters we were balancing on our arms. Our gendarmes marched on both sides of us, stone-faced. Eventually we pulled up at the ghetto's huge gate set in the plywood palisade. The outside guard box was empty.

The pedestrian door set in the gate opened, and we were back in the large schoolyard where a month earlier the blond SS man with the death-head insignia had received us. But now the whole ghetto was empty; it stood like an eerie abandoned movie set. The high-school building which had been the combined SS and gendarme headquarters also seemed largely empty—gone were the officers in the black SS uniforms with their silver piping, and most of the gendarmes were gone, too, with only a few lower ranks idling about. A large number of municipal policemen were also evident. These we had never seen before.

Our escorts took the typewriters from us and disappeared inside. Having done the paperwork, they returned with a young gendarme, removed our handcuffs, and formally handed us over. New gendarmes led us to a low building inside the school quadrangle which adjoined the gymnasium where people had been gathered before the final transport. This, too, was empty. The low building turned out to be the gym storage, which the gendarmes told us would be our temporary quarters. We were to settle in and stay within the schoolyard area. He did not seem to be interested in us and retreated to his office. The gigantic pile of winter coats was still in the middle of the yard.

We had no inclination to venture far on this first evening. We were tired from all the tension of the last few days and settled down on some leather-lined horsehair-stuffed gym mats for the night. There was eerie silence, broken only by moans coming from an adjoining small lockup.

Tiger Rag

Early in the morning, soon after we came out into the yard, a captain of the municipal police walked over to us from the school building. He came straight in my direction, introduced himself as Dr. K., and shook hands. He said that breakfast would be brought in for us and asked me to come to his office afterwards. Having gone through so many ups and downs lately, I could not figure out this polite, almost friendly behaviour. After breakfast, I anxiously climbed the stone steps to the school.

Where once there had been eight gendarme guards standing at either side of the door, Schmeissers at the ready, now there was only a rosy-cheeked roly-poly police sergeant with a large moustache. He directed me to the second floor, and as I climbed up stairs worn by generations of students, I could see a few police officers carrying files. There were also a few gendarmes packing papers into cardboard boxes. Dr. K.'s name was affixed to the door of the large corner office where Colonel Ferenczy, the General Commander, used to issue his orders. I knocked and was asked in. Dr. K. sat at a large scuffed yellow oak desk, and he waved me to a chair. At the moment, he was busy with a small machine, filling empty paper cigarette shells from a large tin of yellow Virginia tobacco. He filled a cylindrical hinged pod with his tobacco, snapped it shut, and inserted its end into the empty cigarette shell. Pumping a wooden rod on the other end, he pushed the tobacco into the paper cylinder. These machines were quite popular at the time, and a skilled operator could make near-perfect cigarettes, saving a lot of money by bypassing the excise taxes of the tobacco monopoly. He had about 20 cigarettes ready on the desk. He finished the last one and packed away the paraphernalia. He offered me one of his products and lit one for himself. Watching him at work with this charming innocent machine, I suddenly felt inexplicably an overwhelming sense of relief. He was the first official of whom I was not afraid, and my instinct proved right.

In Hungary, there were two uniformed police forces: the so-called "common" municipal police, who were responsible for law and order in the major towns, and the gendarmes, who were state police responsible for the country areas, the villages, and the guarding of railway stations, bridges, and communications equipment. The gendarmes were a disciplined, well-trained force, but rougher than the police, and were generally feared. Their officers were elegant, almost like their military counterparts, but considered lower on the pecking order by the army officers, partly because they never saw battle but kept tough order on the home front.

The "common" municipal police were normally concerned with policing traffic in the cities and with minor and major crime, including white-collar crime, and in addition to their uniformed men, had a large force of plainclothes specialists. The municipal police kept the central registry of all citizens, who had to report to them every time they moved, filling in reports with copious detail. The registry contained all vital statistics on the citizenry, including (since 1941) their racial status. All police officers had to have a law degree and therefore had the predicate Dr. (Juris) affixed to their names. After the German occupation, it was the duty of these police to collect the Jews and deliver them into the ghetto. Except for the Budapest ghetto, the ghettos were administered by the gendarmes. The "common" police were generally more humane, but they, too, carried out the orders of the government, which since the occupation was totally subservient to the German command. As it turned out, Dr. K. was a thoroughly decent police officer, upset by the events he was caught up in.

He told me that he knew the details of our case, detested the gendarmes, and knew that we had been illegally detained and taken off the train in Nagyvárad by the gendarmes. He said, "You are members of the armed forces, and I will see that you get back there." He explained to me that the gendarmes, having done their dirty job and completely emptied the Nagyvárad ghetto, had now been ordered to hand it over to the police. Today the gendarmes were to move on to another nearby detention centre filled with Jews collected from the villages and small towns and were to hand over the Nagyvárad ghetto formally to him and his policemen. He told me to stick to our part of the schoolyard and generally to keep a low profile until the gendarmes left. He promised to come over with further news and instructions the next day.

In the meantime, he gave us some newspapers, which we read sitting on some gym benches in the shade of the mulberry trees at the edge of the schoolyard. I discovered that the moans I heard the night before from the small lockup had come from a man in his early 30s who was now also sitting under the mulberry trees. He told me that he was caught hiding in the ghetto after the last transport and hoped to escape by pretending to be mad. He had a large jar of cream called "Barbasol" which religious Jews who were not bearded used instead of shaving on the Sabbath. This was a very strong chemical, and every time a gendarme or a policeman was seen, he started moaning and rubbing the cream all over his face in thick blobs. This did not seem to create much interest, but his skin became flaming red.

Early in the afternoon, our compound was surrounded by armed police. The time had come for the gendarmes to hand over the ghetto, and Dr. K., the police captain, took no chances with our safety. Sure enough, the gendarmes tried to take us, but the police did not let them. After the last gendarme left, the police guard withdrew, and the man locked up next to us was released into my care. I had to promise that none of us would try to escape. For this, I was responsible to the captain. Now we were free to roam through the whole empty, evacuated ghetto. We immediately began to wander, but first I went back to the Baksi building, where I climbed up in the attic and found Ligeti's and my bankrolls intact, just where we had left them.

It is difficult to describe the eerie feeling as we roamed through this giant Kafkaesque movie set. Everywhere we saw the remnants of human habitation. It was as if a giant flood or volcanic eruption had made all living things run away at the same moment. Everywhere personal items were scattered, children's toys, books, toilet bags, clothing. The gendarmes had done a thorough job. We went building by building, street by street, all day long. Once in a while, we heard movement in an attic of a building, a sound like rats scurrying, but while we assumed that people had been hiding there ever since the transportations, we never saw anyone.

A quarantine hospital was located in one small building. Signs all around it read: "Bubonic plague: do not approach," and we could see people through the windows. After the war, we found out that the ingenuous journalist, Bela Zsolt, with the aid of a doctor, had managed to fool the Germans and the gendarmes into believing that all in the hospital had been contaminated with the dread disease. He and some thirty others survived in quarantine until the Russians' arrival.

When we returned from our depressing tour, we started to look around in the various storage rooms opening from the courtyard of the school, the base of our operations. Somewhere in the school, Erwin Leichter had found an upright piano, a harmonium as it was also called, and we set this up outside in front of our quarters next to the huge pile of winter overcoats.

In the middle of the life-threatening events that involved us, we had found ourselves a protected quiet home, and we began to settle in. It is proof of the resilience of youth that we managed to blot out everything that happened to us and around us, and in the eye of the storm, we began to live as if we were safe forever. The paddles of the pinball machine were standing still.

*Erwin Leichter plays the Tiger Rag in the vacated ghetto.
Only the mountain of coats belonging to those who had
disappeared in the transports dulled the reverberations.*

George F. Eber

Eric Leichter survived the war but died six months into the peace in a traffic accident in Budapest.

As the day ended, a full moon began to rise above the roof of the school. The mulberry trees on our side of the yard cast purple shadows. Sitting at the edge of the coat mountain, we surrounded the upright piano, and tentatively at first, Erwin Leichter began to play. In no time, he had warmed up, gathered rhythm, and was playing the *Tiger Rag*, the piano shaking from the unusual treatment. The rhythm grew, and the sound bounced back from all sides. Only the massive mountain of coats belonging to people who had disappeared in the transports dulled the reverberations. In the manner of the entertainment in Budapest's most popular brothels, Erwin played mostly American ragtime music. The moon made quite a long trip up the sky by the time we decided to go to sleep. Everybody went inside, including our newly acquired friend with the shaving cream, and because of my personal responsibility to the captain for the group, I slept on a gym mat laid across the threshold of the double door. I slept lightly those days and woke up immediately when our friend, his face shining with red splotches, tried to climb over me and run away. I could not let him go for the sake of the group. Next day, the gendarmes came back to claim him from the police and took him away, back into the machine.

Our life went on. Our meals were brought in by the policemen from a nearby restaurant, and so were newspapers, while the mail was still carried back and forth by the "heavy physical labourers" as they were called at that time, the girls of the bordello. So we had newspapers in the morning with our coffee and during the days made sorties into the creaking buildings of the nearby sections of the ghetto, We could feel the presence of the former inhabitants.

At night, we gathered around the piano, and Erwin played bordello music. He kept going back to the *Tiger*.

Back with the Army

One sunny morning early in June, I was having my second mug of coffee, sitting on a deck chair under the mulberry tree, when looking up, I saw the captain rushing towards me in some excitement. "The Americans and the British just started the invasion," he said. "Come and listen to my radio." All day long, we listened to the German Liedremacht reports, which were pretty non-informative. First, they announced that the attack was dying on the beaches, then that for strategic reasons they had allowed the Allied forces to obtain a foothold. By the end of the day, the Germans reported that they were controlling the invasion on all beaches and that they were glad that the Allies had managed to land in force because now the German panzer armies would be able to destroy the whole invading army in a giant battle (it's good they came, we'll get rid of them).

Being trained to decode the German army reports, the captain and I understood them to mean that a total rout had occurred in Normandy and that Germany was on the point of collapse. This, as it turned out, was a little over-optimistic, but in any event, it made me turn back to the pinball game. I tentatively touched the levers: "Captain," I said, "the time has come for us to get out of here and back to the army— what can you do for us?" Whatever it might be, I suggested, it would not be forgotten when accounts were settled after the war, and to strengthen my point, I discreetly handed over a couple of thousand pengos. The captain, who was a really honest, well-meaning, but underpaid Hungarian official, agreed that the time had come to take action and promised to think overnight about the best approach.

The next morning, he came with further news of German victories on the beaches. It seemed that the Germans were luring the Allies into an ever-widening noose. The fools of the Allies under the command of this idiot, Eisenhower ("who by the way was of German descent himself"), were landing more and more troops, tanks, and artillery in endless waves. Whole divisions were forming up everywhere, and the Germans had to take new positions so that the whole invading force had enough room to walk into the trap. In other words, the Germans were taken by surprise. Having analysed this, the broader situation, the captain now told me to get my group ready, because he was going to march us over to the Nagyvárad Horse Artillery regiment and make it their responsibility to get us back to our own army units.

By noon, we were ready with our meagre belongings, and after a final call on the Captain, during which we exchanged more war news and analysis of the situation, we said farewell to each other. As I shook hands with this good man, I thought I detected real concern.

Downstairs, a police sergeant and four armoured policemen surrounded us. The gates of the ghetto opened, and once more the pinball rolled. After a short march, we arrived at the massive entrance to the artillery barracks. This consisted of a stone archway with the regimental coat of arms carved in stone over heavy oak doors. The outside guard opened a small door at the side of the big entrance gate, and we marched in and were ordered to stop in front of the guardhouse, an impressive barrack structure on the side of the road leading into the barrack square. The policemen waited with us while the guard went inside to report. Shortly, a typical moustachioed red-faced sergeant of the guard appeared, approached the police sergeant, received our papers from him, took us over, and dismissed the police. Then he looked us over in the manner with which a superior being looks at creeping insects and issued a stentorian order: "Put all the things in your pockets on the ground in front of you. Remove belts, bootlaces, and put them on the ground likewise. And hurry up, we don't have all day." This meant, of course, that he was going to throw us into the guardhouse lockup. Not an auspicious reception. We bent down and, having already emptied our pockets, started unlacing our boots as slowly as possible.

Suddenly the huge entrance doors of the barracks parted, and a gigantic open command car, a 12-cylinder German Horch, drove through the archway. In addition to the driver, I could see an adjutant in the front seat and an artillery colonel ramrod-straight in the back. As they were about to roll by the guardhouse, the sergeant and the soldiers of the guard at stiff attention, our motley crew drew the Colonel's attention, and he stopped the car. The driver rushed to open the rear door, and the Colonel stepped out, his riding boots gleaming, his uniform fitted to perfection on his spare frame. "What have we got here, Sergeant?" he said in a quiet voice. "I beg to report to the Colonel, a bunch of Jews, escapees."

This was the moment, I knew, when I had to start the pinball rolling. Straightening up, I marched toward the Colonel, stopping at a respectful distance, and said, "I beg to report, Colonel, Sir, we are not 'escaped Jews,' but a white-band detachment that was travelling under military orders and has been illegally detained by the gendarmes." The Colonel called me closer and listened with serious interest, and in a few sentences I sketched for him the events of the last six weeks and introduced myself and my group. In telling our story, I managed to point out that I myself was the son of a highly decorated army officer in retirement. The Colonel listened quietly to my words; he then called the sergeant of the guard, and in a loud voice that everybody within fifty yards could hear, he said, "These are not escapees, these are honourable Hungarian men. Give them back their belongings and feed them at the guardhouse until further orders."

"And you, son," he turned to me, "you follow me." He turned and started walking away. The adjutant and I followed. A minute later, the Colonel guided me into his first-floor office. I was behaving a little awkwardly, being used to the frying-pan-to-fire sequence. Here, I seemed to have fallen from the frying pan into paradise. The office was very large, and although it had a huge desk with an old-fashioned desk lamp, the rest of it was more like a drawing room in the National Casino, the club of the aristocracy: heavy dark leather-upholstered armchairs, a beautiful Oriental carpet, and on the walls, English-type prints depicting beautiful horses. Over the sideboard, in glass-faced cabinets, antique duelling pistols were shining. On the sideboard, various dully gleaming silver trophies surrounded a beautiful wooden cigar box from "The Thousand and One Nights." I was fully aware that with my dirty clothing and uncared-for hair, I did not fit into this elegant room, so different from Colonel Zenday's matter-of-fact field offices at the Jaszberény camp.

But the Colonel did not allow me any hesitation. "Sit down, son," he said, "let's hear your story in all its detail, but first I'll have some food brought for us so that we are relaxed and not disturbed." So saying, he pressed a button, and instantly his batman appeared, dressed in a mess steward's uniform. Sandwiches and mineral water were ordered by the Colonel, and then, rather haltingly at first, I explained my family background and my father's service and, warming to it, I began my detailed account. By now, I realised that the Colonel, although he was a demigod to his regiment, had little detailed knowledge of what the gendarmes and the SS were up to just a few miles away. Two hours and many questions later, I finished the description of the terrible fate of the Nagyvárad ghetto, our miraculous escape, and the roller coaster of emotions we had lived through in this frightening pinball game. "You can say that your escape was miraculous," said the Colonel, as he offered me a delicious-smelling Puerto Rican cigar from his cigar box, handing me a bone-handled cigar cutter and a large bowl full of club holders and wooden matches, "but it took a lot of guts, too, to fight your way out. I wonder how many of my soldiers would have it in them under similar circumstances. Now let's talk about the future and about the war."

I had little to offer in wisdom, and I was aware that the Colonel knew that the Axis was collapsing. Surrounded by the aroma of delicious cigars though we were, I realised as we sat there, me a shabby looking young man just fished out of a vortex, and he an impeccable gentleman of the old school, that we were really not conversing. My role now was to listen to his monologue. Time passed. Finally the Colonel said, "Enough! Now, let's see what we can do for you. You are back in the army, and I will send you wherever you all want to go, under military orders with armed guards, to make sure that you arrive safely." And so we went down to the guardroom, where he chatted with my friends and asked again where we wanted to go.

I first considered Budapest, but in the end, we decided to go back to where we started, to the Jaszberény command. The Szalkans decided to play their pinball game independently and asked to be sent to their home town, Mateszalka. The colonel wished us Godspeed, shook hands, and walked back to his office. Only a short while later, the adjutant returned with our orders cut, and our two groups, each furnished with two guards with bayonets fixed, began to march out of the barracks. As I looked back, I saw the Colonel in front of the stables, ready to put a huge stallion through its exercises. He raised his riding crop, stretching a final salute, and rode off. I thought I would never see him again, this man who gave me back my faith in humanity as represented by the Hungarian army. Little did I know.

At the station, we said tearful farewells to our Szalkan comrades, and half an hour later, we were in the wooden-bench-class wagon of a slow-moving milk-run train. But the train, however slowly, was going westward, away from the approaching Russians, closer to Budapest. We felt unreasonably secure as we bounced sleepily through the night.

Early in the morning, at a small station whose name I have forgotten, we changed trains, and around 9 o'clock arrived in Jaszberény. It took our guards another half hour to deliver us to the gates of the Jaszberény barracks. The gates opened, and we marched in.

A great silence received us. The whole gigantic camp appeared deserted. We marched past the camp offices and along the central road. There was no one in sight, except halfway down the road, a single figure standing quietly in the shade of a tree. The guards sat us down and went to report at the office, and the "solitary figure" sauntered over. He was somewhat familiar. He introduced himself as Jani Vago. Then I remembered who he was. He was one of the Rasko company from the Gosztonyi estate, from where our group along with George Ligeti had marched sadly away, while the whole company including my dear friend, George Segal, who had tears in his eyes, stood waving us goodbye. That's where I had seen Jani, standing beside Doctor Rasko, our commander.

"Where are Dr. Rasko and the company?" I asked. "Oh," Jani said, "they received orders of transfer to Bor in Yugoslavia." He told me that it was known that this was a bad assignment and that he had been left behind because Dr. Rasko had made him report sick and had him sent to the camp hospital. "This saved me from Yugoslavia," Jani said. "All the others are gone. In fact, everybody has left the camp and the surrounding areas. I have been alone here for two weeks. As far as you are concerned, we thought you were gone forever. We heard about Nagyvárad."

Now Colonel Zentay, followed by his adjutant, appeared on the office porch and motioned to me to approach. The guards that brought us from Nagyvárad departed for the mess hall, after which they would return to their station. The pinball game had stopped for the time being. The ball rested in the starting slot.

I climbed up to the porch, where Colonel Zentay and some other officers stood, and in my best military style, reported: "Colonel Sir, I beg to report that George Eber and seven others on special assignment to Transylvania from the company of Dr. Rasko have returned and are awaiting your orders." Zentay smiled and said, "Well, surely there must be more to report, so come on upstairs and let's hear it." I followed him and found myself back in his office.

Zentay seated us, and I started again with my whole story, from background to the more recent adventures. The Colonel and the officers listened seriously, asking much the same questions as had the artillery colonel in Nagyvárad. No food or cigars were offered, but Colonel Zentay said, "Now you will have to stay here until we get a half company together, and then I will give you an assignment. Until then, I am happy to have you back; rest and enjoy the time. I will try to assign you to a detail not far from Budapest. In the mean time, are you or any of your company bridge players? I and the major here have no partners at present and would enjoy a good game in the evenings."

So we settled into the old barracks, had all the food and leisure we wanted, and occasionally ventured into Jaszberény to our old haunts. This included Erwin Leichter's mother's local emporium, but the atmosphere was not the same. So many of my closest friends were missing, and the only news we had from the company in Bor was that they were having a very difficult time of it, working in the copper mines.

The Colonel got his bridge game: Pali Rona and Erwin were assigned. The days flew, the main event from time to time being the appearance of some new comrades from Budapest. Apparently no major call-ups were expected, but people who until now had managed to remain outside the army got conscripted and ended up with us. These included 40ish lawyers, an eye surgeon, and an assistant professor at the university, as well as a few people who got transferred from military hospitals. They were a superior, highly educated group, and before they heard our story, considered us as a bunch of kids. After they heard it, our stocks rose.

From them, we heard that the deportations from the country ghettos were over and that the Regent, Admiral Horthy, in one of his typical pendulum movements, had dismissed Sztojay, the radical Nazi prime minister appointed the previous March. Now a liberal, General Lakatos, had been appointed in his stead. He had to proceed very carefully so as not to upset the occupying German forces, but imperceptibly he kept easing the situation of the Jews in the Budapest ghetto. His ultimate aim was not to hand these people over for final solution. At the same time, the government again began casting around for ways to get out of the war with the army, the civil service, and even the government intact. It was a naive hope considering their past sins and the advancing Russian steamroller which was now beginning to cross the Carpathian Mountains towards Transylvania while another army group was circling at the "soft underbelly" of Europe—the Balkans—and was attacking Rumania. One of the new arrivals, a balding, good-looking, but slightly chubby young lawyer, George Racz, whose family owned a small hotel on Lake Balaton, became a good friend and helped us to analyse the big picture.

There was news from my family also. My father had gone to a country town called Szentes with my future step-mother, Eta, and was staying at her family's house, planning to spend the summer there. My uncles and aunts on my mother's side were all well in Budapest. Pista Salusinszky and Marika, his sister, two cousins who were devoted and serious Communists, were active in a special underground movement.

Before the German occupation, Marika and I had gone out together, mostly on highly intellectual expeditions: theatre, museums, and the opera. The Wagner Cycle came to Budapest with the famous Swedish tenor, Svanholmset, and the four parts of the cycle followed each other at monthly intervals. Not only did we attend ail the performances, which I really enjoyed, but before each performance,

Marika played on her piano again and again all the musical themes that are found throughout the composition, until I could eventually recognise from a subtle motif played over the main tune that the giants Fafnir and Fasit were about to appear lumbering from behind some great rocks. Marika was a true bluestocking, and I was attracted to her in spite of the necessary intellectual *tour de force*. She had always been a little aloof, but now, having heard of my odyssey, she wrote that it seemed that despite our political and intellectual differences, our friendship might become meaningful after all.

Time went by, and our newly found friend, George Racz, joined the Colonel's bridge game. Other new faces arrived in Jaszbereny and joined our group. Three young fellows from a village somewhere northeast of us appeared: Samuel Feder, an 18-year-old boy, came first, then a sickly-looking chap named Pavel, who arrived with Weisz, a muscular young man from the same village.

Just about then, a new reserve officer arrived, and we found out that he would command our company, now about to be formed. Various sergeants joined us, and we knew that our departure could not be far away. Then one day, Colonel Zentay called me and George Racz to his office and said that he wanted to give us a safe destination, but that he would have to form a short company and dispatch it under the command of the second lieutenant. He had two destinations available: the first, Budapest; the second, a small village in the Matra mountains, not too far northeast of Budapest. The American air force had recently started bombing Budapest in earnest, and the duty there would be mostly cleaning up after the raids. On the other hand, the assignment in Matraderecske, a charming small village, would be to work in a brick factory. He gave me the choice. Here I was at the pinball machine again. I did not hesitate, but played the ball in the direction of the Matra village.

Summer Idyll!

And so, after a brief inspection by our Colonel, two days later our company, 80 men strong, led by the corpulent second lieutenant and flanked by a couple of gentle, big-moustachioed farmers with World War I decorations, now disguised as sergeants, went marching by the camp offices, out through the open gates towards the railway station. Zentay and a few others watched us sadly, and I could not make up my mind whether the Colonel was sad on account of sending our group again into the unknown or whether he simply hated losing a couple of really good bridge players.

Late on the same day, we arrived in Matraderecske by train, and a couple of waiting gendarmes led us to the brick works. The owner, Nicholas Bell, stood waiting on a small platform. We were lined up in front of him, and he made a short, alarming speech: "Men, you are here to help in the war effort, and you will have to work hard; any slacker, any saboteur will be severely punished. You may even be sent to the east to the front (work will get you better treatment). Dismissed." Nicholas Bell was not as dangerous as he sounded. The gendarmes left, and Mr. Bell led us to a long building, just completed with his own bricks. Inside were wooden bunks, all brand-new, smelling of freshly cut lumber. Nobody had ever lived there before.

This day started what I can only refer to as a pleasant working summer holiday in the midst of the most ferocious war in modern history. The work consisted of quarrying out clay from the mountainside and sending it to the brickworks on little gondola cars running on a narrow-gauge track. At the factory, a huge steam-driven machine, like a giant dough mixer, worked the clay until it became a smooth pliable paste. Then another machine pumped it through a brick-shaped opening, from which it appeared in endless ribbons like toothpaste coming out of the tube. As it flowed out onto a belt, a wire cutter cut the paste into brick-sized units. These were placed on wooden pallets and ferried to eight rows of open sheds, where they were air-dried and stacked up in long rows with air spaces all around under the shade of the overhanging roofs. Only when they were free of all moisture were they taken to the brick ovens, where they were fired and loaded in endless rows along the railway siding for shipment.

It was all outdoor work, and our lieutenant let us decide what part of the process we wanted to work on. The most difficult work, transferring the freshly formed bricks for drying and the loading and unloading of the brick ovens, was left to about 40 gypsy men and girls, a professional team from the village.

I immediately chose the job of counting and watching the bricks drying in the open sheds. Pali Hirsch, a well-known lawyer, joined me there. Pali Rona and the rest of the Nagyvárad team loaded the clay into the small gondola cars. Dr. Biro, the eye surgeon, and several other sports-loving intellectuals volunteered for quarry work. George Racz, with whom I shared a cosy corner in the bunkhouse, having come from a hotelier family, took over our field kitchen. He and I jointly employed Samuel Feder, a very sweet young boy, as our full-time helper. Johnnie Vago took on the job of counting the clay gondolas entering the works. Everybody enjoyed the work, the mountain air, and the beautiful summer days.

As long as the production process was not interrupted, Nicholas Bell left us alone. Occasionally, after the gypsies had explained the procedure, when the weather was too hot and the guys at the quarry wanted an hour's break in the shade, they would hide a fair-sized blob of rocky matter under the clay in the gondola car and send it down to the mixer. When it was dumped into the machine, the blob knocked out the mixing mechanism, and the whole process came to a halt until the foreman Imre Kovacs or Brer Nagy from the village and a mechanic took the machine apart and repaired it.

This interrupted our routine at the drying sheds, and Pali Hirsch and I would use the time to dig into one of our hidden depots behind the brick piles and prepare ourselves huge salami sandwiches. The gypsies were also idle during the repairs, and some of them spent the time chatting with Pali and me. The gypsy girls were quite beautiful and very friendly. Behind the drying sheds, a row of about six one-hole latrine booths were located, without doors to discourage idleness. While Pali Hirsch and I were lounging near our hidden "Pemmican" depots—Pali called them this after the depots that the famous Antarctic explorer Scott scattered all over the barren Antarctic—the gypsies came and went to the latrines, the girls also, chatting with us unabashed while sitting on the wooden thrones.

It turned out that Nicholas Bell was an old friend of my grandfather, so I was called to his office one day for a chat. He was quite a decent chap, trying to finish his season's production of bricks to ship to Germany before the advance of the Russian army became too menacing and he had to abandon the place. His family was already in Austria waiting for him. He was quite a handsome older man, with a real Hungarian country gentleman's moustache and always in a crinkled but clean summer linen suit. He also was an ardent bridge player, as was our commander, and very soon every night bridge games were going on out on the spacious veranda of the Bell mansion. Bell was an amateur astronomer and years before had built quite an excellent observatory whose structure towered above all the other buildings with the exception of the factory chimney. He told us he did not care how we lived or passed our time as long as the factory output was kept up and as long as there was the semblance of discipline whenever the local gendarme patrols made their not-too-frequent visits. This gave us quite a bit of leeway. Through Tejes (the Milk) Kovacs and "Brer" Nagy, we made friends with the villagers and had special dinners cooked for us which were served in the farmers' dining rooms on weekends.

By July, the German terror had abated considerably in Budapest, and we were able to organise weekend visits of wives and girlfriends, who arrived on the little branch train line laden with salamis, breads, and cold chickens. Marika

Salusinszky came on all the visiting days, and our romance was developing in a very satisfactory manner. On the banks of the little creek behind our barracks on a grassy knoll, overshadowed by the branches of willow trees, we had picnics. For dessert, George Racz used to make a delicious concoction, the main elements of which were several pounds of butter, sugar, and cooking chocolate and at least one bottle of cognac. This we ate from a large pot, each of us using our own spoons. After the meal in the summer heat, we all felt a little sleepy, and in groups of two, we meandered along the banks of the brook to find a more private hammock.

It was left to Samuel Feder to clear up the remnants of the picnic, which he did very efficiently, running around in the heat in his boxer underpants. Before he shipped out to Jaszberény from his village, his older sister lovingly but not very skilfully stitched his monogram on all his clothing. On his boxer underpants, the letter "F" happened to be near the front slit, while the letter "R" was definitely to the rear. George Racz declared that this was so arranged by the sister, who knew that our man Sam was a little slow-witted and just in case he should get mixed up with his functions.

On Mondays, after a visit, Pali and I would sit by our Pemmican depot, surrounded by all the newspapers brought by our friends from Budapest, and try to interpret to our gypsy friends the progress of the war. This was not easy, because we had first had to interpret the rather bland lies of the German Wehrmacht. Unfortunately visits had to be voluntarily limited to about every third weekend because we did not want to draw the gendarmes' attention to this highly illegal activity.

For the other weekends, to alleviate the monotony of living the camp, George Racz and I proposed scenic walks disguised as forced or punitive marches. Our commander agreed, and orders were cut for all-day marches. The favourite destination was Parad Furdo, a 19th-century spa, famous for its health-giving waters which were good both for bathing and drinking.

Leaving Matraderecske at a brisk speed, soon we entered a cool pine forest, through which a well-kept trail wound its way to Parad Furdo spa. The fallen needles of previous years dampened the noise of our marching boots, and to keep up a proper military tempo, we sang marching songs with modified lyrics. One of these predicted that we would remain in "slavery" until by miracle "Ravel," the puniest of the company, developed an erection. There was a sad refrain, "Never shall we be free." The all-time favourite was the Glengarry March, which we all were familiar with from the Empire movies of Sir Alexander Korda. This we whistled on our marches, and a lively time it was. Once the gendarmes followed us, and to the barked commands of our sergeant major, he was an old ham himself, we marched briskly to this eminently suitable tune. After ten minutes, apparently not enjoying this strange whistling, the gendarmes turned their bicycles around, and we continued on our way to Parad Furdo.

After about two hours of exhilarating walking, we arrived on the chestnut-tree-lined main promenade of the spa. Here the sergeant and his complement split off to the shaded terrace of a pub, while we, promising to report at 5 P.M., went off in a casual stroll to the local ice-cream parlour and confectioners, where on the terrace we drank hot chocolate topped up with heavy cream, followed by cakes and ice creams of the Italian gelato style.

Culture came next. We visited the famous local glassblowing works, where on a guided tour we watched exquisite figurines being formed by the artists. At 5 o'clock sharp, we reported to the pub, where a merry bunch of soldiers reluctantly joined us. The march back to Matraderecske was always considerably more undisciplined, and I remember that on one occasion, we had to support the sergeant major all the way. Fortunately it was dark when we arrived, the only light on Mr. Bell's veranda where the bridge players were hard at their game.

After these punitive marches, we always went to bed early to be ready in the morning to support the war effort. The war seemed to be progressing well—for the Allies. The Americans were now well into France and the Russians were pouring westward through Poland and across the Carpathian Alps. Not very far from us, across the Slovakian border, we heard that an uprising had started against the Germans and that partisans were hiding in the deep forests.

Towards the end of August, we were all invited by our gypsy friends to a wedding that was to be held not very far from us on the banks of the creek at the edge of the village gypsy quarters. We arrived just as the sun was going down, and a huge fiesta was underway. There were trestle tables laden with the finest village food—chickens, roast pork. There were barrels of wine and beer, with everybody drinking from huge glass mugs. The gypsies had strung up on the trees coloured paper lamps, similar to Japanese banners, and in the pleasant light of these, now that it was fully dark, the bride and bridegroom sat in the place of honour. Next to them was Mr. Bell, who, surrounded by colourfully dressed gypsy girls who did their best to entertain him, seemed to enjoy himself immensely. Not far off, in front of one of the gypsy houses in the light of a lantern, a wrinkled old gypsy woman sat studying her tarot cards and telling fortunes to all comers. The orchestra now drew closer, with their leader playing the violin. At least 30 more gypsy violinists surrounded him, and the cimbalom, a flat board with many strings, was played by an older man who ran his padded hammer-like batons over the strings with real virtuosity. The *bracsa* player was next to him, and from behind him rose the deep booming sound of the gigantic bass viola. They played the beautiful Hungarian gypsy songs.

Suddenly there was silence; everybody jumped up drinking health and happiness to the young gypsy couple. Then the orchestra altered its mood, and the young couple danced the wedding csardas. After that, everybody danced, the bright full swirling skirts of the girls contrasting with the high black boots, black pants, and white loose-sleeved shirts of the men. I saw Mr. Bell dancing with the bride, the sergeant twirling alone. The lanterns were swinging in the light wind, light and shadows were mixing, the wine flowed, and the dances went on endlessly, now fast, now slow.

Towards Germany: Into the American Terror Bombing

Our summer idyll came to an end a few days after the wedding. First, Mr. Bell drove away in his large convertible touring car, sitting next to his driver, the back of the car piled high with pigskin bags and a few precious objects wrapped in blankets. Perhaps he cast a wistful look at the summer's crop of bricks piled up on the platform at the siding. In the confusion of the end of the war, with refugees streaming westward and all trains used for military purposes, Nicholas Bell would never get his bricks to Austria. Our orders came the same day.

The news reaching us was not good. The Russians were now much closer, and from all of eastern Hungary, waves of refugees were pouring westward, mistakenly thinking they could escape the advancing army. All roads towards the west, towards Austria and Germany, were clogged, as well as the railways. At the same time that a wave of humanity was heading west, the roads and rails going east were also jammed. These carried the munitions trains and the trains loaded with the last reserves of the German army, the old men and young boys who were now to be thrown into the battle to stop the Russians before they reached the Motherland.

Our dream of surviving the war in Matraderecske had collapsed. Our orders were to go towards Austria with all haste. Because we were in the northernmost part of Hungary, our area was free of the refugees who in the south were a human flood moving in a westerly direction on both sides of the Danube. We packed up and said goodbye to our friends in the village, who were determined to stay close to home. Somehow our commander managed to commandeer a small locomotive, a number of boxcars, and a small passenger wagon for himself and the staff. These remnants of rolling stock had survived on our little branch line, away from the main lines. The whole village was at the station as we boarded. Johnnie Vago, George Racz, Samuel Feder, and the Nagyvárad crew scrambled in, and we got a boxcar all to ourselves. The train gathered speed, and the village and its inhabitants faded away.

For the next hour, we headed slowly in a northerly direction through narrow valleys and mountains. The going was slow. We sat on the floor in the open sliding door with our feet dangling out. Once again the future looked grim, but we tried to be cheerful. None of us wanted to go into the boiling cauldron of the collapsing Third Reich, but for the moment there seemed to be no balls to play.

After a while, we reached the Slovak border, and here the tracks branched off to the west and ran along the border. On the Slovak side, the mountains began to rise more steeply. They were covered with a pine forest that carne down almost to the railway, and as we slowly headed west, the forest got denser and denser. The mountains rose higher and higher. We knew that far to the north were the High Tatra Mountains, part of the Carpathian Mountains, famous for their resorts and beautiful scenery. But this was not where we were heading, and around noon, our train came to a sudden stop out on the open track. The locomotive blew its whistle, letting out a lot of steam. The engineer jumped off first. We all followed his example. Way down the track, the red light of a semaphore was glowing. We began to stretch our legs, and knowing that the train would not move while the semaphore was red, we walked to the edge of the deep forest, where a few felled fir trees offered a good place to sit down. Here we sat, smoking and chatting, enjoying the sun. The rest of the company followed suit; even the Commander and the staff were glad to get off the train.

As we sat there, half dozing, breathing in the pleasant smell of pine needles and resin of the trees, very slowly a figure emerged from the dark forest. He moved slowly, silently.

He wore the traditional clothes of a Slovak woodsman: soft moccasin-like shoes held by criss-crossed lacing reaching as far as his knees over his white halina pants (a kind of felt-like homespun material). He also wore a halina tunic and a wide-brimmed black round topped hat with an axe tucked into his black belt. He was followed by four to five other woodsmen who also emerged almost magically from the forest. They slowly came to our tree trunk and sat down with us. Cigarettes came out of their pouches, and speaking good Hungarian, they started talking in the slow measured way of the mountain men. I had seen their kind of woodsmen before, working in the forests, cutting trees, and stacking logs, when I was on holidays before the war in the Tatra Mountains.

They asked where we were going. We quite naturally admitted that we did not know where in Germany we would end up and that we did not like the direction. After much talking, the first of the Slovaks said in a low voice, "You don't have to go! Just as we came, we'll go one by one back into the deep forest from where we were watching you for awhile. One by one, you should saunter up the hill into the forest after us. There we'll wait for you and take you to our partisan camp, and you will be free; just join our fight against the Germans." He looked around and lit another cigarette. "I'll be leaving soon and you all (my little group); follow me, quickly." The endless pinball game started again. There was not much time for thinking. Finally I said, "We wish you success and appreciate your offer, but we will stay with our company." He finished his cigarette, and as mysteriously as they had arrived, they melted into the forest again. One minute they were there, the next they had disappeared. We were not yet ready to leave the security of the company to join a partisan group. That was a ball that was not played.

The light changed to green down the track, we all clambered back into the boxcars, and our journey resumed. After a while, the tracks changed direction, to the south, we could tell. Johnnie Vago, who also spent his summers in

Nagymaros (although we had never knew each other there) and I began to wonder if we were not going towards the Danube. Sitting again with our legs dangling in the door opening of the creaking boxcar, we watched the mountains recede and the landscape become more gentle. I suddenly saw the meadow where as a child I used to spend my days with Jani Takacs, watching him cut the hay. There was no doubt where we were heading. There among the trees, I could just see the King's Well zip by in the shade as the train swept westward in a curve. In a minute, we were rattling though the level crossing from which our hay-wagon used to roll down to the main road. Miraculously, we were back home.

The whole magnificent view of the Danube bend opened up in front of us. Past the paper factory, past the brick factory, the train began slowing down. I could see Csukavolgy rising to the chestnut grove. I could even clearly see Heininger bacsi's inn. It was like watching a favourite old film.

Johnnie and I were really excited when the train began to slow down. The surprises were not yet finished. The train stopped at the outer platform of the lower station where I used to arrive and depart (Johnnie's house was at the upper station). There were not many people on the platform. but one figure was standing there, leaning on his bicycle. As he stepped out of the shade, we could see him clearly: we both knew him. Incredibly, it was Jani Takacs.

The train came to a complete stop, and we jumped down and rushed to Jani. He was genuinely overjoyed. He was not in the army; as an only son of a major farmer, he had a special dispensation. He rushed to the station office and found out that because of the heavy traffic, the train would stay for a couple of hours. Johnnie got onto Jani's bicycle and rushed off to visit his parents, and Jani and I sat down and caught up with our recent history. The time passed quickly. Johnnie came back, and the train got ready to move on. We all climbed aboard again, and Jani Takacs stood on the step at the door and came with us all around the great Danube bend, all the way to Zebegeny, about 10 kilometres away. Here the train slowed down, and Jani jumped off and stood there waving to us until he disappeared out of our sight. I am sure that he never expected to see us alive again. The train followed the Danube west through Szob to a major railway junction called Ersekujvar, about 20 km from the river. Here beyond the large station, the tracks spread out in ten parallel lines, and on each of them a train was standing. It was clear that we were stuck, but night had fallen, and only next morning were we able to assess our situation.

The railway station was at the edge of the town on a high embankment. Two parallel main lines ran through it, to the west towards Bratislava and Vienna, and to the east towards Slovakia and Hungary. To the south were eight or ten sidings connected to the main lines by an elaborate network of merging tracks. Signalling and switching equipment sprouted everywhere. Our train was on the outermost track at the edge of the embankment. Next to it, on the next siding, was a much longer train filled with refugees, mostly women and children. I found out that all the trains on the sidings had low priorities as far as the war effort was concerned. On the two main lines, every ten minutes or so, a train would go through eastward full of soldiers and ammunition, while the westerly track carried an unending flow of trains with wounded soldiers or official German loot heading to the motherland.

The women in the neighbouring train told us that they had been waiting already for two days, but that the trains on the other eight or ten lines had higher priorities, and even these had been waiting for a long time, some of them as long as ten days, hoping that a gap in the traffic on the main line would allow them to move on.

It looked as if we would have a long stop on our siding, so we ventured forth to inspect the other trains. The locomotives of all the trains, including our little old engine, were continuously kept fired up, and the asthmatic snorts of the old steam engines were audible at all times. Johnnie and I walked around the refugee train and found next to it an official Hungarian army train full of horses. The soldiers on guard had put wooden ramps up to some of the boxcar doors and were cautiously walking the horses down to the platform level, where they were exercising them in pairs. The soldiers had horse artillery colours, and the horses were magnificent animals. I started to talk to the guards and found out that the train was actually carrying the complete complement of the Nagyvárad artillery regiment, whose colonel had been our saviour in the spring. The horses were being evacuated to Germany because Nagyvárad had already fallen to the advancing Russian armies. Attached to the end of the train were two parlour cars and a sleeping car for the officers, while the soldiers and grooms were traveling with the horses as per regulation: four horses and two grooms per boxcar. I wandered down to the passenger cars in front of which two guards were posted, bayonets fixed. I inquired about the Colonel, but found out that all the officers had got tired of waiting on the siding and, with the exception of the duty officers, were passing their time at the hotel in town.

I hoped to catch up with the Colonel later and continued the exploration. The remaining sidings contained various goods trains all waiting for clearance to resume their westward journey. Among them was an ammunition train, its huge locomotive spewing grey-white plumes.

The railway station, which was quite spacious, with huge waiting rooms and first- and second-class restaurants, had masses of people sitting with their luggage in every available corner on the dirty station floors. There must have been literally thousands of people. A long way down the railway platform, a huge sign indicated the entrance of the air-raid shelter. In front of it, cool and steady as ever, two gendarmes were surveying the crowds from under their black cockfeather-decorated shakos. Even though our commander and protector was not far, my recent experiences did not allow me to pass the two gendarmes, and with Johnnie reluctantly following, I retreated to the safety of our group.

It was beautiful autumn weather. Clear sky and sunshine, the leaves turning yellow. At the bottom of the embankment, a corn field had been harvested, and the stalks were piled into pyramid shapes at regular intervals. A tunnel ran under the embankment at a point under our track. Through it, a dusty country road meandered away through the corn fields towards a young forested area about two kilometres away. The trees had been planted in a perfectly square field of about 100 acres. The road skirted the little forest and disappeared beyond a small village which was hardly visible on the horizon. Only the church spire could clearly be seen beyond the trees.

The days passed slowly. We climbed down the grassy embankment into the cornfield and, propped up by the piles of corn stalks, we played endless poker games. There was the distant rumble of priority trains, but the only movement on the sidings was when the locomotives were shunted to the water tower to replenish their water supply to keep their steam up. From a distance, they looked like cows at a water trough.

Three days after our arrival, around noon on a beautiful September day, as my group watched the exercising of the magnificent horses of the artillery regiment, the air-raid sirens sounded. The civilian refugees ran toward the station shelter, and the soldiers began to walk the horses carefully back into the boxcars.

We did not feel like following the civilians and spoke to a couple of railway switchmen who were busily switching rails back and forth. They said for us not to worry; even though the Americans were now quite close in northern Italy, there had never been an air raid in Ersekujvar, and there was no reason to fear one now (these were to be famous last words). Regulations demanded that the locomotives be taken out to the open track and strung out along the line about one kilometre apart until the alarm was over, but there was nothing to worry about.

Saving the horses as the bombs rain down.

This was all we needed to know, and I pushed the levers on the old pinball machine. "Let's go down into the cornfield to keep away from the hysterical crowds and play poker as usual." So we sat down about a hundred yards away from the embankment and started a game. A bottle of local red wine accompanied us, and as the time passed, we took swigs from the bottle. We watched as the locomotives were driven out to the open track. There they stood, strung out for about ten kilometres, puffing away in the glorious day as they kept their steam up. The railway line stretched away straight as an arrow for as far as one could see. Time passed. We really did not believe that an air raid would come.

A faint buzz sounded from the west, and a single-engine small plane appeared in the sky. We did not pay any attention until this little plane flying above the railway tracks reached the farthest locomotive. There it executed a neat circle and issued heavy smoke from its belly, which formed a perfect ring in the air over the locomotive. It kept repeating this manoeuvre over each and every locomotive. By now, the little plane had our full attention. When it got to the railway yard and station, we could see it clearly. It was a scout plane, and the last smoke ring, blown as casually as a cigar smoker in his club chair, encompassed the whole yard and station. There was no wind up, so the rings floated immobile where the plane had formed them.

An officer draws his gun to force the grooms to stay with the horses.

By now, we had stopped the card game and were watching the sky for developments. The little scout plane disappeared, and there was total silence. After a little while, a deep murmur could be heard, at first faintly, but then with ever-increasing strength. Looking down the railway lines about thirty kilometres away, up high in the sky, we could see many dots glittering. They approached rapidly over the railway line. They were American superfortresses, flying thirty thousand feet up in perfect formation as if they were promenading at a spa. When they reached the first smoke ring, ten kilometres away, they casually dropped a few bombs from the sky. A few seconds later, up went one locomotive, then the next, and the next; all went up in front of our eyes just like the targets in a carnival shooting gallery. Now the planes were almost over us. It happened so fast that there was no time to get nervous. When they reached the big smoke ring floating over the station, the 24 superfortresses released their remaining bombs, which came down with unearthly banshee noises. We could see the clusters of bombs falling through the sky, swinging from side to side. Then there was a sudden tremendous roar as they all exploded almost simultaneously. This was called carpet bombing. All the bombers had had to do was drop their load into the smoke circle. The water tower went first, then the ammunition train. We could see the boxcars flying up in the air like toys, with human figures flying with them. The earth was shaking under us. There must have been a thousand bombs. Then it was quiet. By this time, the formation had disappeared to the east. A great human cry started from the station as one voice. There were smoke, flames, and exploding ammunition everywhere. Some of our friends started to scramble up the embankment, but I held Johnnie back, "Let's go up the country road towards the little forest." The road was dusty, and it was not easy to walk on the gravel; behind us, a gigantic cloud of dust and smoke was rising into the blue sky. Quite a few other people also headed in that direction, and immediately ahead of us was a girl with a German shepherd dog, also going towards the forest. We were following her, and just as we reached the little forest, we all realised that a new wave of bombers was approaching. The murmur was still barely audible, but I knew that at 300-odd kilometres an hour, it wouldn't take long before they were overhead.

The people from the dusty road quickly disappeared into the forest, believing they were lucky to be that much farther from the railway station. The girl and the dog also veered off from the road and sat down in the roadside ditch. The noise above was ever-increasing; the whole sky now reverberated with the sound. It was time to take shelter. Johnnie said, "Let's go and sit down with the girl." But something held me back. "Let's watch from here, they are not going to bomb a forest." So we remained standing about ten metres away from the girl and her dog, and shading our eyes, we watched the bomber formation. They must have figured that all people running away from the railway station would have reached the forest, and they unloaded their bombs above us. We could see them and hear them as they swung on their path down from heaven. Suddenly their bombs began to explode, the explosion getting closer every second. Finally our nerves gave way, and we threw ourselves down where we were standing, protecting our heads with our arms. There came one more gigantic explosion. I could feel the earth moving under me. Then an unearthly quiet. Only clumps of earth were now raining down on us.

Slowly, carefully, I stood up. There were uprooted trees all around us; others had had their branches blown away; here and there I could see human flesh hanging from the broken branches. Next to me, about a foot away from where I stood, was the edge of the crater left by the last exploding bomb. The crater must have measured about 50 feet in diameter, and in its centre, about ten feet down, a red-hot part of the casing of the exploded bomb still glowed, at almost the exact spot where we would have been had we followed the girl. There were no traces of her or her dog.

We dusted off our clothes and started moving farther up the road. I was limping slightly because a major clump of earth had fallen on my back, but at the time I felt no pain. Half an hour later, we arrived at the village which we had seen from the railway yard. This was far enough away to be safe. In fact, most of the local farmers had been sitting on the veranda of a small inn with their half-litres of wine and mineral water, watching the bombardment and the rising smoke quite coolly. We got ourselves some wine and sat down, trying to blend into the environment. We were not exactly at liberty to wander around away from our unit. Night came, and in the dark we could see the distant fires still burning. We left the veranda, and through the autumn fields, we cautiously began circling in the direction of the railway station. About one kilometre away from it, we reached a vast cornfield where in the dark, groups of soldiers and civilians could be seen silhouetted against the fire. They were moving about, but keeping a safe distance from the station, and we kept our distance even from them. From a few people who wandered in our direction, we found out the extent of the damage at the main station. Many people had gone into the air-raid shelter, both civilians and soldiers. This had received a direct hit, and it seemed that 800 people had perished there. Now the field gendarmes were rounding up people in the fields to help dig out the shelter. We kept away from the crowds, not wanting to be caught and enlisted for this work. A crazed soldier from the artillery regiment appeared; we learned that as soon as the bombs started falling, many of the grooms and soldiers had wanted to run for shelter, abandoning the horses. The duty officer, an artillery captain, ordered them to stay with their horses and had stood there with his service revolver pointing at them to reinforce the order. He blew up with most of the horses, soldiers, and grooms as the bombs scored direct hits on the train. The crazed soldier thought that he was the only survivor.

It was time to say goodbye to the Hungarian Army and for a new strategy. Johnnie agreed. The air raid had made up our minds. Where our unit was heading, there was much more of that.

Home with the SS to Budapest

Up to this point, the balls in the pinball machine had spun in my favour, but the future now looked uncertain, to say the least. The original theory, in fact the general wisdom, when we answered the call in the spring to join the Christian white-band labour unit was that it was safer in than out, that is, safer to be a member of a Hungarian Army labour battalion than to escape and hide with false papers which were not much help if one got caught.

I believed, of course, that I had made a false move, a foolish move, when I left the seeming safety of the Rasko Company to accompany Ligeti to exile in Transylvania. This move had almost been fatal. But now there was no doubt in my mind that I had to escape; the risk would be far greater if I stayed in the transport.

(I was not to know until after the war that the decision to go with Ligeti had saved my life. I had missed being transported to Bor in Yugoslavia, where the company met a terrible fate. To the last man, the company was machine-gunned down by an SS unit).

After Nagyvárad, back in Jaszberény, and then at Matraderecske and on the trip to Ersekujvar, there had been any number of opportunities to escape and disappear with false papers. However, by this time, I had come by a lot of experience, and until the bombing it had seemed the safest policy to stay with the unit. Escaping meant going underground, a much greater risk. For a young man at that time, to be at large in Budapest, even with the best false papers, was inadvisable. To be caught by military field gendarmes meant summary execution. It had not been difficult to decide that it was better to spend the summer in Matraderecske with our good commander. Now the risks had to be weighed.

In the aftermath of the bombing, I realised that a human flood was pouring westward into Germany, and that the safety of the company was questionable, to say the least. Even with goodwill, could the Hungarian Army protect us once we crossed the German border? Even though the temper of the Hungarian government had turned more liberal during the summer, it was obvious that a Wagnerian Gotterdammerung was approaching, and Johnnie and I began to believe that it was the lesser risk to go back home by whatever means we could and hide away in Budapest until the cataclysm had passed over our heads. We were not as afraid of the Russians as we were of the Germans, who now approached their final agony.

So during the night, while we dodged field gendarmes in the dark and watched flickering fires from a distance— we heard occasional explosions as the fires reached more ammunition caches—Johnnie and I decided that, rather than continuing to travel west with our company, we would head back to Budapest without papers and take gamblers' chances. It was a risky decision, and my hands were not too steady as I played that pinball.

We started to move towards the Danube, south, away from Ersekujvar and the remnants of military units now being reorganised to work in the ruins of the railway station. Our escape did not last long. As the day dawned, we saw our tattered company, our good Commander and staff, rapidly marching away from the bombing, also in the direction of the Danube! Though our decision to escape was now firm, we quickly rejoined the company. We found out that only two people were missing and that our Commander also thought it better to try to postpone the trip to Germany. He ordered our group to march to a small village on the left bank of the Danube, ostensibly for a few days' rest and reorganisation. We reached the village early in the afternoon and settled down in some available barns, while the Commander set himself up in the company office in a house on the main street. He immediately phoned the district command and got permission for R and R in the village for the next week.

*We are caught in an American bombing raid over the
Vienna-Budapest highway. September 1944.*

There were no refugees in this area, and the village was quiet—we had walked to it through country lanes—but opposite, on the other side of the Danube, ran the Budapest-Vienna highway, which was clogged with military and refugee traffic. Almost directly across, on the main highway, was the small town of Almasfuzito. I knew this place well because in the 1930s my father and some partners had owned a linen factory there.

By now, Johnnie and I had no inclination to spend even one more week with the company, so next morning we went to the company office and, while Johnnie and another member of our white-armbanded unit, a former regular army sergeant, diverted the attention of the company clerk, I removed three marching-order forms from the desk and carefully stamped them with the company seal.

It took little effort to persuade our Commander to let the three of us, accompanied by our sergeant major, cross the Danube on a provisioning mission. I was well acquainted with Almasfuzito, and our little village had absolutely no supplies.

We walked down to the river and talked a couple of fishermen into rowing us across (the nearest bridge was 50 miles away). On the other side, we climbed the embankment and had just reached the highway and its river of traffic when the air-raid sirens began howling. Instantly all vehicles drove off the road, and people ran for safety. Almasfuzito was an industrial centre; bauxite and oil were shipped from here on the river and by rail, and there were a number of important factories.

We ran off the road ourselves into a clump of bushes and lay down. Across the Vienna highway, there was a freight yard full of oil tank cars. No sooner did we reach the bush than the air raid started. This was different from the one of two days before; it started with low-flying American fighter bombers strafing the road, which were then followed by the usual high-flying superfortresses. The clump of bushes turned out to be a camouflaged Bofors antiaircraft battery which not only was infernally noisy, but also drew the attention of the fighter bombers, which strafed it (and us) with 50-mm machine guns. Somehow we again survived, and as soon as the raid ended, the three of us, accompanied by the sergeant major, ran out onto the highway. This was enough; we were going home. The war was getting serious.

Traffic started slowly on the highway. Heavy black smoke rolled over it from the burning, exploding oil tank cars. We stood on the far side of the road and tried our luck as hitchhikers. A convertible field-grey wanderer car was the first to approach. It was going towards Budapest. Inside were the driver and two SS officers calmly smoking their cigarettes. We waved them down, and they stopped. Johnnie, who had been to the Reichsdeutsche Gymnasium (German National School) in Budapest and spoke beautiful flawless hochdeutsch and who was the smoothest talker anyhow, did the negotiations.

We hitch a ride home with the SS.

We said that we had orders to get to Budapest to resupply our company that had been bombed out. The German officers were very nice, but their car was so full of luggage that they could not take us; however, the younger officer got out and flagged down a German Gestapo truck which was escorting them. The truck was empty, with two SS soldiers up front. The officer told us to climb into the back through the tailgate. Our white-armbanded sergeant companion had second thoughts, so only Johnnie and I got into the truck—with the help of our sergeant major! As we drove away, he stood in the middle of the highway, waving goodbye.

We dropped the tarp and sat down. We had our papers, but we did not know how acceptable they would be to the Hungarian field gendarmes who were manning checkpoints on all the highways. But our trip to Budapest was uneventful; twice the truck was stopped, but being an SS truck, it was waved on without a search.

It was dark when we got to Budapest. Soon we were in the centre of the city. There was the usual traffic, and the city was bright with lights, for at that point, there was still no blackout. When I saw we were on St. Stephen's

Boulevard opposite the Comedy Theatre, I knocked on the wall of the cab. The truck stopped. We jumped off over the tailgate and walked forward to the cab to thank the soldiers for the ride. They did not accept our offer of cigarettes and, wishing us luck, they drove off. I will never know what they thought of the two 20-year-old civilians they had transported.

Just as the truck drove off, a streetcar came to a stop. We climbed aboard. We were home.

Countdown to the Siege

After all I had witnessed during the last week—the bombings, the chaotic flood of refugees, the movement of troops to the front, and the evacuation of entire regiments westward to Germany—life in Budapest seemed completely peaceful. Lights glittered in the shop windows, crowds waited in front of the cinemas, crowded cafés where life appeared to continue normally went flashing by our streetcar windows.

The two deserters got off at the corner by the National Theatre, and I took Johnnie to my aunts' apartment. They were overjoyed to see me and, though it was not without danger, they agreed to hide Johnnie until he had figured out a way to get to Nagymaros and his family.

Ten minutes later, I arrived on foot at my uncle Charles' apartment building on Stahly utca. Mr. Nagy, our crotchety caretaker, gave me the key to the elevator without asking any questions, even though he knew that I had no business being in Budapest. He was a good man, his bark much more ferocious than his bite, and was very helpful in those difficult times.

I went up to the fourth floor and Charles' apartment, where I found that I had arrived home to a complete family reunion. Present were Charles and his wife Ilka, my Uncle Julius and his wife Manyi, Colonel Tusa, an army man who was an ex-beau of Ilka, and to my great surprise, my father. He had arrived that day from Szentes across the

167

Tisza River with my future stepmother, Eta. Apparently early in the morning a Hungarian sapper officer had arrived at Eta's family house. It turned out that he had been ordered to save my father—it was known that an officer was there—from the Russians who were advancing rapidly. He gave my father and Eta ten minutes to pack and drove with them in an army personnel carrier across the Tisza Bridge to the west side, where he stopped the truck, excused himself for a minute, got out, and blew up the bridge with a plunger. He got back into the cab, and as they drove away, they could hear from the direction of Szentes the rumble of the approaching artillery.

Now it was my turn, and I told my story. But when it was discovered that I had deserted to come back to Budapest, the visiting Colonel and my uncles were horrified. The Colonel told me that, should I be caught, I would be summarily executed. Uncle Julius wanted to drive me back to my company. But I had determined not to be budged, and I stubbornly resisted their entreaties. Finally my father spoke: these were not normal times, he said, and I must do as I thought best. It was my life at risk; I was not a boy, now I was a man, and the last six-month period had proved that I knew what I was doing. This, coming from the ultimate military disciplinarian, quieted all comments. My father alone understood the situation. That night, my father and I slept in the spare bedroom, and the next day, my father went with Eta to her apartment and I went underground.

In the next few days, several more deserters from our company turned up in Budapest, including Pali Rona, who found me through my uncle, and within a week we discovered that our erstwhile commander had managed to bring our company back to Budapest to await new orders. Envoys were sent to encourage us to return to the company without penalty, but Pali Rona and I went to stay with his family in an apartment under the protection of the Swedish Embassy. With the permission of General

Wesemeyer, the SS commander of Hungary, the building, which was situated near Andrassy utca in a very elegant area, had been declared Swedish territory. The coat of arms of Sweden was mounted on the wrought-iron entrance gate, and the Swedish flag flew above the building. The SS protection of the building was the insurance needed to make the Swedish gesture work. The premiums were paid by all residents in hard currency. In addition, the Germans were mindful now of future benefits accruing after the war, which they now knew was lost.

For the moment, in the constantly accelerating pinball game, this was a perfectly safe place, out-of-bounds to Hungarian Army patrols, and many friends had taken shelter there, including some very good-looking girls, two of whom were the sisters Hanna and Teti Feldbaum. Hanna's boyfriend, Alexis (Lexi) Strommer, who was not affected by the Nuremberg laws, spent all his free time there. The only drawback was that, under the agreement with SS General Wesemeyer, all young men had to go each day to the SS headquarters to assist in the construction of a deep bunker being built for the coming siege.

The SS headquarters was on the Buda side of the Danube, high up in a very large villa on Gellert Mountain. Every day, we had to go to Buda by streetcar across the graceful Elizabeth suspension bridge. This was named after the Empress Queen Elizabeth, the great friend of the Hungarians, and looked like a smaller version of the Golden Gate bridge. Through the windows of the streetcars that took us across, we could clearly see, exactly at eye level, yellow-painted explosive packages affixed to each vertical support. These had been visibly wired together and to a central plunger by the careful German sappers. We learned that all the bridges, the Chain Bridge, the Margaret Bridge, and all the others, were similarly prepared. It was not a pleasant feeling to rattle across as we did.

At the SS headquarters, we managed to get light work in the gardens and the basement storage areas; deep in the rock of the mountain, Hungarian miners were working night and day preparing the SS command bunker.

From the quiet garden where I worked, I had an uncomfortably close view of the SS. In the villa, the general and his staff were in constant conference, and many guards were on duty around the villa with Schmeisser machine guns and a few German shepherds. The action was at the front, where the guards were constantly presenting arms as staff cars came and went with arriving and departing officers.

In my section of the garden, however, there was little activity, and I had found a shady bench where I was able to sit and enjoy the beautiful fall weather. From here I could look over the Taban valley to the Royal Mountain and the Royal Palace. From my vantage point, I could look into the terraced palace riding school, which was directly opposite but below me, and where every morning, Admiral Horthy, the Regent, regularly exercised his famous white stallion. Even from about a mile away, I could clearly see the erect posture of this 70-year-old man and admire his beautiful seat on his mount.

From the villa, the city below seemed eerily peaceful, and only two events hinted at what was to come. One day as I took my sandwich to the bench, I noticed through the large plate-glass windows what appeared to be a major meeting going on in the upstairs living room of the villa. General Wesemeyer was at the map table surrounded by his staff officers. Suddenly a shot rang out, and the big plate-glass window cracked under the impact of the bullet. Immediately there was an alarm, and I was dragged with Pali and two other friends to a basement wall. There we stood with hands raised, awaiting reprisals. I thought about what a circuitous route had brought us here, where I was sure we would soon be finished off. The guards, who usually were friendly enough, did not look reassuring. Fortunately nobody was hurt, and by looking through the bullet holes in the double-glazed window, the SS could draw a line to the open upstairs window of a nearby villa. Immediately two Kubelwagens rushed to the empty villa, but all they found was an empty room and a brass shell case on the floor. Lucky for us. We were released, and everything went on as before, except that the curtains on the General's windows were drawn. Once again, we had survived.

About a week later, on another beautiful sunny day, I sat in the garden enjoying the picture-postcard view of Budapest and its well-known landmarks: the Royal Palace, the elegant row of hotels facing the Corso on the Pest side, the glittering ribbon of the Danube splitting it all into Buda and Pest, with the famous bridges holding it together. My eyes were following the river. Nearest me was Elizabeth Bridge, and about a mile upriver the oldest, Chain Bridge, built for Count Szecheny by Adam Clark, the Scottish engineer. Farther up still, past the colossal neo-Gothic Parliament, I could see the widest bridge on the Danube, the multi-spanned Margaret Bridge which had our favourite Stamboul Café at its Buda end. My eyes lingered there on the noonday traffic—yellow streetcars, blue busses, cars, trucks, and pedestrians. As I watched, something extraordinary seemed to happen. It seemed that two or three spans of the bridge began very slowly to sink downwards at the midspan. The streetcars stopped moving, and then, ever so slowly, began sliding on the downslopes towards the water. I could see buses, cars, and people trying to scramble up the slopes; then suddenly everything cascaded into the river with the collapsing spans. Only then did the sound of the explosion and the pressure wave hit me. I stood there frozen. Even from my distance, I could see streetcars and vehicles disappearing into the water. By accident, the Germans had blown up the bridge. (The other bridges would have their turn one cold night in January). Little white propeller-driven boats rushed to the scene, gathering like a flock of geese below the bridge, snatching people from the water.

The text in the image reads: "October 1944, the Danube flows on! germans accidentally? blow up part of Margaret bridge. I watch from Gellert Mountain SS HQ. Rescue operations start. Admiral Horthy rides in Palace Rink"

The Germans blow up the Margaret Bridge over the Danube.

After this event—although I am sure not directly connected to it—the SS command decided to leave Budapest and suspended the building of the bunker. Our job now was to load all the contents of the basement into a continuous stream of trucks. Ever curious, I opened the corner of one of the cases; inside were 12 cans of whole goose liver, two pounds per can, packed by Globus, the Hungarian cannery. By this time, the SS soldiers were willing to barter, so for some dollars and a gold coin, the soldiers sold me three cases. They also agreed to make a detour on their way to the Vienna highway and deliver the goose liver to Eta's house on Molnar utca, where it formed part of our diet during the siege. But I am getting ahead of my story.

About a week later, on October 25 to be exact, as were listening to the radio, we heard the sudden announcement that Admiral Horthy would address the nation. He came on the air with his voice sombre but firm and spoke in his peculiarly stilted Hungarian. He announced the end of the war for

Hungary and ordered the Hungarian Army to surrender on the spot to the Russians. The Rumanians had done the same thing in August, but they were closer to the Russian advance. Sombre music followed, along with further announcements of the surrender order, interspersed with more funeral music. We clung to the radio, awaiting further news. After a while, the sombre music imperceptibly got less sombre; in a short while, it became rousing martial music. We did not like this new mood, and our fears were justified. After an hour or so, a Hungarian Army general came on, and in the name of the new government, ordered the army to fight on. He announced that Horthy had resigned and that the new regent was Szalasy, the leader or Fuhrer of the Arrowcross, the most extreme right-wing Hungarian Nazi party.

I went down to the Boulevard to see what was happening. German Tiger tanks were advancing in the middle of the road, their turrets open and their cannons traversing in a menacing manner from side to side. On the tanks, infantrymen were sitting, holding their Schmeisser guns and with hand grenades in their belts. The Arrowcross bands were not far behind, with their submachine guns and shiny Bilgeri boots. I had no doubt that balls were now rolling in another pinball game, and not wanting to test the now-questionable safety of the Swedish apartment building, I immediately hiked to Molnar utca and joined my father at Eta's apartment.

The next day, we found out that as soon as Hitler heard of Horthy's attempted surrender, he ordered his giant henchman, Otto Skorzeny, and his thugs to fly to Budapest. It was Skorzeny who had abducted Mussolini from the Allies and his mountaintop captivity and flown him to the Wolfshanze in July, just hours after the ill-fated bomb attempt on Hitler's life by Count Stauffenberg.

Skorzeny wasted no time. First, on arriving, he drove with some of his men in commandeered tanks to the Archducal Palace, where Horthy's son Miklos had an office. When Miklos Horthy resisted arrest, Skorzeny shot him in the stomach. He was rolled in a large Persian rug and removed in an armoured vehicle.

Then, sitting upright in the turret of the lead tank, Skorzeny headed across the Chain Bridge to the Royal Palace. The Palace was defended by a regiment of Horthy's personal bodyguard. Skorzeny stopped his tank in front of the first concrete pillbox in the centre of the palace drive. He ordered the cannon lowered towards the pillbox. His other tanks chose similar targets, whereupon the bodyguard surrendered without a shot. Horthy was taken to Germany, where he spent the rest of the war under guard in a guest villa.

The Hungarian officer corps, pampered though it had been by Horthy for the past 25 years, did not remain loyal to its supreme commander, but defied his orders, taking an oath to Szalasy, now the Hungarian "Fuhrer," and went on fighting. As Horthy's career ended, it may be that he recognised the irony: he, after all, became Regent in 1919 by forfeiting his oath and betraying his ruler: Charles, the last Austrian Emperor and King of Hungary.

My Uncle Julius was the oldest brother of my mother. A reserve officer in a Hungarian horse artillery regiment, he was extremely good-looking, with wavy silver-grey hair, tall and spare. Until he met his future wife Manyi, a fashion model and a member of the Budapest movie colony, he was the black sheep of the family, contributing heavily to the dissipation of my grandparents' fortune. But Manyi correctly assessed his potential for success and gradually weaned him off car-racing and the lifestyle that went with it, guiding him into a very senior position at the "Raba" truck, light armoured vehicle, and tank manufacturing company in Gyor. Here his native ability and experience with motor engines in his racing and flying days helped him carve out a unique position. Right to the end of December, he split his time between working in the head office on Andrassy Street next to the Budapest Opera and in the factory in Gyor to the west, halfway to Vienna.

Uncle Julius arrived back in Budapest from Gyor late on the evening of December 23, and his driver dropped him off in Sandor utca, at his town apartment. Early in the morning on Christmas Eve, December 24, the German Gestapo came for him with a black Mercedes car, arrested him, and took him up to the Gestapo headquarters in the Majestic Hotel in the Buda Hills on the far side of the Danube.

Manyi phoned in the morning hours of December 24, desperately reporting Julius' arrest. Immediately we held a council of war. The Gestapo was not known for its gentleness, and there was no way to tell whether Julius would be able to resist the pressure to talk about the whereabouts of family members.

Guszti and I had to disappear from Eta's house; it was decided to move us out of there immediately. After some hesitation, Ottus, Eta's brother, a staunch Nazi and chief engineer of the Budapest Gasworks, agreed to allow us to go to his apartment for a few days. To protect themselves, he and his wife Elsa were to move in with some relatives. Guszti went to friends of his, and around noon, my father, Eta, and I set out to negotiate the trip to Ottus's place. This was not easy, because he lived quite a long way away, towards the city park at the end of Andrassy utca. Because streetcars were regularly raided by the Arrowcross, we decided to walk, taking a roundabout way, avoiding main streets and their crossings. Eta and my father had come with me to give the journey the aura of a respectable family Christmas Eve outing. So there we were—Eta with her blond hair and Wagnerian proportions, my father with military bearing, and I leaning on a cane, limping on account of my healing "wounds," and each of us carrying a few Christmassy-looking parcels. We walked along Custom House Boulevard to Calvin Square. At the Calvinist Church where I had been christened twenty years earlier, we took the left fork to Ulloi utca, where most of the university medical clinics were located, now jam-packed with wounded soldiers. As we walked along beside the stone-based high wrought-iron fence of the surgical clinic, the gate suddenly opened, and a stern-looking army nurse in uniform came out; above her white armband emblazoned with the Red Cross was a second band with the ominous Arrowcross insignia. So suddenly did she appear and begin marching in our direction that I almost dropped my cane. With her heavy brogues clip-clopping on the concrete sidewalk, she came up to us and cast a suspicious glance at me. I mixed up the rhythm of my limp as we passed her. A few steps beyond, there was sudden silence as she stopped short. I cast a surreptitious glance in her direction, and there she stood, following our retreating figures with suspicious eyes. We went on, my limp improving in my desperation. Finally I could hear her steps again going away from us. We passed the gates of the clinic and, reaching the corner, took a sharp left turn. As we turned, I glanced back, and again she was standing watching us with her suspicious glance. We took a zigzag course across several small streets and happily lost her.

Without further incidents, we reached Hernad utca behind the eastern railway station and were only about six or eight blocks from Ottus' building when a horse-drawn flattop wagon overtook us, the driver urging on the bony hag. Arrowcross thugs were standing on the rattling flattop, their machine guns pointing at a group of unfortunate people huddling against the driver's seat. They did not spare us a glance, so busy were they watching their terrified prisoners.

The flattop rattled out of sight, and we finally reached Ottus' house, where my father and I took the stairs to the third floor, carefully avoiding the janitor. Eta returned home, an uneventful journey by streetcar. My father and I spent a long slow Christmas Eve with no guests, no gifts, no carols; only the forbidden BBC news kept us company. At last, after midnight, we fell asleep.

In the morning, Eta arrived back with good news. Uncle Julius had been miraculously saved. As he waited with other miserable arrested men, an Arrowcross soldier marching across the room called out, "What are you doing here, Mr. Julius?" Julius looked up and saw the son of the caretaker of his villa on Rozsadomb standing there. Without further words, he took Julius's arm, walked him out of the infamous Majestic Hotel, and took him home. He also reported that the approaching Russian Army had formed two gigantic prongs, and instead of attacking frontally, had crossed the Danube north and south of Budapest. During the night, they had succeeded in completely surrounding the city and were attacking from all sides. A German SS army of 200,000 motorised troops and a Hungarian Arrowcross army of about the same strength were caught inside this Russian ring of iron. The siege of Budapest had begun in earnest.

Around noon, we returned to Eta's house, and just as we arrived, Ottus phoned from his office at the Obuda Gasworks. He said that as he was looking out the window, Russian tanks were pulling up outside. We later found out that he managed to get out through the back of the building and walked home across the Danube bridges. By now, the sounds of artillery were booming from the east and north and west.

The curtain was rising on the last act.

[IV] The Russians are Here

In my early teens, one of the greatest pleasures came when I woke up with a sore throat and a slight temperature. Madame, our housekeeper, a former head nurse, would announce that school was out of the question. This meant that I could spend my day with my various mechanical toys, but my real pleasure was always to take out our large illustrated Breugel book and, while sitting at the window with its views of the snow-covered roofs and parks of Budapest, immerse myself in the study of Piet the Droll and the elder Breugel's wondrous paintings. I particularly loved *The Peasant Wedding* and *Peasant Dance* and *The Massacre of the Innocents in Bethlehem*. I could spend hours studying the details in the revelling or fleeing crowds—the little things hidden in these magnificent paintings of humanity in abandoned action. One picture could tell so many stories: the tired hunters with their dogs, descending to the right to the village in the snowy dusk; the skaters on the pond; the old woman, walking in the half-foreground to the left across the little stone bridge, dragging her twigs to the home fire to keep her warm in the coming night. But behind the church, far away, a chimney is on fire; the family on the roof is trying to stop it, while a neighbour is rushing with a ladder across the snowy field. All of humanity, moving, active, engaged in a myriad of trivial activities, added up to a most exciting world, worthy of a week in bed with a very bad cold.

On the morning after the night the Russians arrived, I was fully awake at the first light of dawn. The noises of the siege were gone: no mortar fire, no hammering of machine guns,

179

no explosions. Instead there was a humming noise of voices and muted sounds. I threw the heavy blanket aside from the window and, for the first time since the siege began, dared to lean out fully; the scene was Breugel alive.

Among the fallen debris in the dirty snow, people were swarming through Molnar utca up towards Matyas Pinkes and down all the way to Custom House Square. As I looked down, I could see in the middle distance a group of horsemen with black fur caps set like tricorns, altogether well uniformed, with the obligatory "balalaika" submachine guns. The horses nervously pranced around the multitude in the snow. I took them for Cossacks. People came out from the entire neighbourhood dressed in all kinds of raggedy coats, some held together at the waist with old ropes. Women were similarly dressed, but their heads were covered with black scarves. It took me a while to figure out that many of our usually well-dressed neighbours had decided to camouflage themselves for the Russians. The camouflage chosen was their idea of proletarian garb, with the result that they had the air of ghosts from a badly staged Russian classic. The little hunchbacked tailor right under my window was engaged in a lively trade with a group of Asiatic-looking soldiers, the carcass of a German personnel carrier serving as a counter and his flaming red-haired daughter acting as bait as well as assistant. Across the road, beyond the almost totally carved-up frozen body of the German horse in the snow, I could just barely make out the shape of some German soldiers also frozen in grotesque forms where they had fallen in agony. Nobody seemed to pay attention. Beyond, some shabby figures were digging in a desultory manner in the ruins of the old patrician building that had collapsed in front of my eyes during the siege. A few diggers were tugging at something that emerged, dirt- and snow-covered, from the ruins. It was a human leg in boots. They kept dragging, and a pants-clad knee emerged. They almost fell back when it gave way and slid out of the rubble. The rest of its owner remained behind. Two old women were loading salvageables from a collapsed larder.

Acquaintances kept talking excitedly to each other among the Russian soldiers, who did not pay much attention. Young women were not visible, having heard of Russian atrocities from Arrowcross propaganda.

In front of the neighbouring building, a young Hungarian Army lieutenant, who used to commute from his apartment to the front, was standing to the right, now in proletarian garb, having a tug of war with a couple of Asiatic soldiers over his motorcycle that he had hidden in the ruins. The Russians had found it and determined that he was the owner. He gave up, having more important things to hide, and showed them how to kick-start it. Two of the soldiers climbed aboard and took off through the rubble, the motorcycle wobbling crazily. Just before Pinter utca, they ran into the ruins of a fallen archway, and with a terrific crash, the motorcycle threw them off and turned sideways. The motor was still in running gear, the rear wheel turning as the gas poured from its tank and caught fire. The Russians walked off, laughing. They were happy that they were still alive after the siege and now this "crazy machine."

Part of the tank trap at Custom House Square had been removed, and through the opening came three farm wagons with squeaking wheels pulled by the poorest-looking old nags. When they pulled up with their drivers, big-boned, droopy-moustached Hungarian farmers in short sheepskin coats, I saw that they were loaded with plucked, frozen turkeys, their white bellies shining. It took a siege to keep the Hungarian farmers from delivering their Christmas turkeys to the market, and now, finding it ruined, they drove into the street for a "quick sale." The "proletariat" gathered around them, and in no time at all, the turkeys disappeared. Because they did not take cash, everybody paid with what they had: rings, jewellery, clothes, the last of their Schnapps. Some old men, assisted by children, were dragging laden sleds which were skidding every which way on icy patches. Nobody helped. Two men were working on the remnants of an upturned command car, removing all they could for salvage. Soldiers dragged remnants of a four-poster bed, loaded with looted clothes and a bronze chandelier. Instead of twigs, an old lady carried away bits of wood from the ruins for her fire.

Meanwhile, some rumours filtered through from people who came from other parts of the city. All fighting was over on the Pest side of the Danube. The tremendous explosions the previous night had been the four remaining beautiful bridges of Budapest, all blown up simultaneously by the retreating Germans at midnight. There were no German or Hungarian fighting soldiers left on the Pest side. They abandoned all equipment and, changing into civilian clothes, melted into the populace. In the Buda fortress, the German were still holed up around the ruined Royal Palace, and they kept up a bit of artillery fire from there, aimed at the "enemy" in Pest (that included us), but they were now surrounded by Russian forces. They were trying to hold out until German relief could reach them from the west. Indeed, there were rumours circulated by the still-hopeful Arrowcross sympathisers that a huge SS Panzer force was coming from the direction of Lake Balaton.

January 19, 1945. The first Russian roundup.

Up towards Matyas Pinkes, a Russian military truck pulled up, a three-and-a-half ton lend-lease truck of Ford manufacture, laden with flour bags which the driver and two soldiers started to trade. They were too far away for me to make out their faces, but I could see the Red Star twinkle on the front of their fur-lined caps. Many people now surrounded the truck, which was parked opposite the former Arrowcross district headquarters. Watching them, I could see rather than hear a commotion, and a man, raising his hands to protect himself, was dragged protesting out of the group. He was beaten viciously by the crowd and then dragged out of my sight. He must have been an Arrowcross man whom somebody recognised.

The crowd kept ebbing and flowing. People dragged bits of furniture, hauled boxes and bundles, all seeming purposeful among the ruins. After six weeks of siege, of hiding in cellars, of having bombs and artillery rain on them, of having the SS and the Arrowcross hunt them, people were happy to be out in the dull snow-covered street under the grey clouds. They were happy to be alive—their future uncertain, but for the moment safe.

Altogether, but for the lack of colour in their clothing (except for the Cossacks' uniforms), they were hustling and bustling like the characters in a Breugel painting. I felt that for me, the war was over. I had been permitted to live, and (foolishly) I thought of the Russians as our liberators, that the rumours of atrocities and political dangers were just rumours. And the Russians seemed pretty harmless. My father thought so also, and we decided to venture out and walk through the back streets to Uncle Julius' apartment to get some news of the family. We emerged on the street, dressed normally—no camouflage for us—my father with his scarf and a winter coat, a recent English charcoal-grey creation of Knizek bacsi, and myself similarly attired, but hatless.

Julius lived in Sandor utca, not very far from the National Museum, in a nice patrician area about half an hour's walk from Molnar utca. We took off in the general direction through some narrow old-town streets, crossing Vig utca to Szerb utca, which got its name from the beautiful old Serbian Orthodox church whose ancient cemetery backed onto it. Everywhere there were ruins from the siege, hulks of burned-out vehicles and trucks scattered where they died, often belly-up. There was absolutely no traffic; the streets were piled high with rubble. Footpaths meandered through the mess and snow. The sidewalks had become impenetrable with all the fallen masonry.

January 20, 1945. The Hotel Astoria, its portals empty and ruined, and before them, the frozen body of a Hungarian captain.

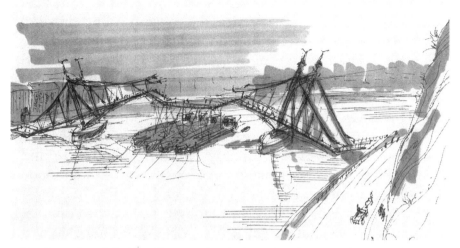

The Franz Joseph Bridge, blown up by the departing Germans, January 18, 1945,

We trudged along beside the scarred yellow-painted stuccoed wall of the cemetery, arriving at the badly damaged but padlocked tall wrought-iron gate of the Serbian cemetery. In front of it, somebody had dropped an army stretcher and abandoned it. The body lying on it was that of an army officer who must have died in agony on that spot. The stretcher and the body were almost completely covered with frozen human ordure; luckily a light sprinkling of snow was beginning to cover everything. Unburied dead soldiers and civilians were lying everywhere, and the footpath wound its way around them. We were getting used to the scene and tried not to look. Through Karoly Square, we finally got to Museum Boulevard, a major thoroughfare. This we crossed carefully in a hurry and entered Sandor utca at the corner where the Museum Coffeehouse stood. This was a traditional meeting place of the intelligentsia, now totally in ruins. Only the scarred masonry arches stood where behind plate glass, the marble-topped tables had given comfort to so many academicians and scientists. On the opposite corner was the beautiful National Museum garden surrounding the Museum building. Here the wrought-iron fence was completely demolished, and in the garden we could see burnt-out tanks and abandoned infantry trenches. We proceeded faster, past the Tattersaal on the corner of Eszterhazy utca, the covered riding rink and club of the aristocracy. Its huge domed roof had collapsed into its walls, and all was burnt out. After passing the abandoned Budapest radio station, we arrived at Julius' apartment. He and Manyi received us with open arms, and we caught up with the news.

All my maternal aunts and uncles had survived the siege and at the moment were at my Uncle Charles' large and undamaged apartment two short blocks away. Manyi made us strong aromatic espresso coffees and gave us the most precious gift anyone could have thought of. It turned out that although the water and electricity services were long gone and the gasworks had also stopped manufacturing gas, the mains were still full, and because they had a gas-geyser-operated bathroom, they could offer us a bath. First my father and then I submerged in their huge old-fashioned tub and soaked away all the accumulated dirt of six weeks.

Then it was time to go home. It was late afternoon, and it began to get darker. We followed the same route by which we had come, past the radio station and the Tattersaal and along the Museum park. On the corner of Museum Boulevard, next to the bombed-out museum café, we walked smack into a crowd of men standing around two Russian soldiers with the usual balalaikas. They looked friendly enough, but they were looking at everybody's identity cards. People in front of us were busy getting out their papers and lining up. I grabbed my father, who was ready as any good citizen to line up, but my instinct was to back away, and I pulled him into Sandor utca. "Why did you do that?" he said. "We have proper papers and nothing to hide." "I don't know why," I answered, "but since Nagyvárad I like to avoid all armed people asking for documents." My father grudgingly followed me, and we crossed Museum Boulevard no more than fifty yards from the corner where the Russian solders stood with the people. Oddly enough, they were letting no one go, and I could see that as in a fisherman's net, more and more people were gathering there.

It was completely dark when we reached Szerb utca, and as we wound our way back to Molnar utca through the rubble, suddenly out of the darkness a solitary Russian soldier stepped in front of us. He was of short stature and had a pockmarked slant-eyed Asian face, and his eyes lit up with a warm friendly smile. He stepped in front of us and greeted my father with a definitely pre-revolutionary form of address: "Goszpdin! Goszpdin! Sir!" "You see," said my father, "he knows what we are." The Russian said next in a commanding way, "Dawaj Chaszi Dawaj Dawaj" (give me your watch, quick quick, as we later found out), and because we did not move fast enough, he pushed his machine gun aside and took off my father's wristwatch, then mine, pushed up the sleeve of his down-filled field jacket, and strapped both watches onto his left wrist. His arm as far as I could see was covered with watches. He wished us Godspeed in a friendly manner and disappeared into the dark. Without further incident, we reached our building in Molnar utca and found the heavy oak door not only bolted and barred, but also barricaded from the inside.

The street was empty and dark. With all my strength, I banged on the door until Eta, who was anxiously waiting for us upstairs, heard the noise and got the caretaker, a peg-legged old man, to remove the barricade and unbolt the door for us.

Gratefully I helped from the inside to shoot the bolt and rebuild the barricade. No sooner did we get upstairs than Eta told us that the whole street had heard rumours of Russian atrocities; consequently all buildings were shut as tightly as possible. Sure enough, ten minutes later, five or six Russian soldiers tried noisily to break into one of the buildings across the road. All the windows filled up with people yelling and screaming, "Patruj, Patruj" (Patrol! Patrol!) until finally the soldiers were unnerved by the racket and moved off to try elsewhere. The looting and raping had started everywhere, as we found out the next day.

My decision to avoid the Russian patrol on the corner of Museum Boulevard turned out to have been sound. By the second day, we knew that the Russians had set up control points at all major intersections and that any man running into their net, regardless of his documents, was seized. Those rounded up were escorted in groups of forty into a nearby courtyard so that a large crowd did not cause passers-by to get the wind up. When they had about 500 men collected, they marched them in columns five abreast, heavily guarded on both sides at every fifth row, to a large collecting camp in Kistarcsa to the east of the city. It was eminently suited for the purpose because it had been erected by the Germans in 1944. From this place, all captured men from 16 to 70 or so were shipped by trainloads to an even larger camp in Rumania called Focsany. From there, the road led straight to a P.O.W. gulag in Siberia, and only a small number of them were ever released alive, and then only many years later. The chances of escape from the Russians were slim once they captured somebody, and the further away from the point of capture, the slimmer the chances got. The supposed justification for this procedure, as presented to the so-called "Allied Control Commission," set up according to the Yalta Agreement and in Budapest at that time staffed sparsely by American, British, and French representatives, was that all the 200,000 SS and an equal number of Hungarian troops surrounded in Pest had disappeared, which indicated that they had all melted into the civilian population; therefore, any man of military age found in civilian clothes was considered a soldier and a P.O.W. Of course, the Russians given this task could not read the Roman alphabet of the Hungarian documents and, quite deliberately erring in what constitutes "military age," took just about anyone they could catch.

By noon of the second day, I nevertheless overcame the effect of the bad news and, giving in to my need to find out what was going on, decided to set out to investigate. Knowing about the Russian control system, I decided to venture forth carefully. I sneaked around the back streets and carefully peeked around corners. Sure enough, near the National Museum, the Russians were on the corner, surrounded by a group of civilians. I ducked back and made a wide swing to Kecskemeti utca and arrived at the corner of Kossuth Lajos utca at the old church across from which, on the corner, my Uncle Feri used to hold his noon-hour audiences. Everything was in ruins; in the middle of the square stood the burnt-out bunker from which the Germans proposed to defend the approaches to Elizabeth Bridge and the fortress of Buda. The Franciscan church seemed to have survived, but my childhood row of shops—Habig, Berath and Toth the barber, and Knizek bacsi's building were all destroyed; what remained was completely looted out. Kossuth Lajos utca had many pedestrians plodding through the debris on the wide sidewalks. I noticed quite a lot of traffic in the middle of the road, too, mostly grim-looking people pulling and pushing handcarts of various shapes laden with God knows what kind of bundles. Heading towards Stanley utca where my aunts and uncles lived, I passed the Hotel Astoria, its portals gaping empty and ruined. In front of its once-elegant main entrance, I saw on the ground, half-buried in debris and snow, what looked like a human shape. Although together with the other pedestrians I now passed many frozen bodies without really looking, this time I was drawn to examine. It was the corpse of a Hungarian Army captain, his face staring into the sky. His right hand remained rigidly clamped to his other hand; it seemed that he had been in the act of pulling off the glove of the left hand. He had obviously tried to look at his wristwatch. On his wrist lifted towards his face, I could still see the marks of a metal strap. The watch was gone. I moved on, wondering if he registered the moment of his death before one of the liberators tore off the watch.

On I moved along Rakoczi utca, past the ruins of the Hotel Pannonia, where not so many years before, my Uncle Kari had had his wedding reception. Finally I reached Stanley utca and

Kari's apartment. The reunion with the family was joyous. All were there and in good condition except my Uncle Francis, the youngest, who was a doctor and had been marched off with one of the labour battalions towards Austria in November. Nobody had heard of him since.

I did not stay too long. I wanted to explore more, and after crossing at lesser intersections and being careful about Russian control points, I entered the area that since the previous summer had become the Budapest ghetto. After the deportations in the east, Admiral Horthy, who really did not have his heart in it, had managed to put a more liberal government in power in July, thus staving off the deportation here. But only the old people and children were left; the men had all been rounded up and marched in a death march westwards after the Arrowcross took over in October. Here the crowds were more dense because the old people were unable to move very far. They all looked emaciated. The food situation in the ghetto at the end was disastrous.

Suddenly an old lady detached herself from a group and rushed towards me. "George! George!" she cried as she embraced me, tears on her wrinkled emaciated face. It was my father's secretary, Gabi. She was 35 years old. She told me of the fear and desperation in the ghetto, where after October the Arrowcross raided day and night, and of all the atrocities. She told me that as one got deeper inside the ghetto, the scenes became grislier and grislier. She wanted me to go to Klauzal Square to see the worst. I kissed her goodbye and promised to come back to see her the next day. I did, and I looked for her for days, but could never find her among the 200,000 dying old people. Nobody knew of her, and I never saw her again.

Klauzal Square was where the so-called "hospital" was located. It was a convenient place; the dead bodies of thousands of people were piled up like logs in huge mounds. All were obscenely naked (all clothes had been removed), their bodily fluids frozen as they leaked out from every orifice. Fortunately the winter had covered them all with a merciful sprinkling of snow. I could not watch the scene long with its the dead and the ghostly shadows of the half-dead. I kept marching, and in ten minutes I came out of the inferno onto Paulay Ede utca, just outside the ghetto, only a short march from Andrassy utca.

This was a main thoroughfare which everybody tried to avoid because of the Russians, but the traffic here was quite active. These people were not ghetto survivors, and they moved around in the usual rubble quite purposefully, carrying bundles or dragging little handcarts. I was breathing again and started heading towards Octagon (formerly Mussolini) Square, where I heard that a huge open-air barter market had begun to develop. I was happy to have the war and all of its infamy behind me, and I found myself walking along with a middle-aged man with a little handcart, heading for Octagon Square with all kinds of household goods on his cart for trading. He, too, seemed confident that the worst was over and hoped to get some food for his family.

Paulay Ede utca ran parallel to Andrassy utca, the big radial boulevard pointing straight at the Buda Palace, where the Germans were still holding out. Suddenly I could hear the whistling of a few artillery shots from Buda. One exploded overhead, and shrapnel came raining down on the street, then silence. I resumed my talk with my companion, but he was no longer there. He was lying face down in the rubble, blood pouring out of his head. He joined the thousands of corpses all over the city.

The war was not really over yet. Still I was determined to survive, once I had made it this far, but as a precaution decided to avoid streets into which a cannon could shoot directly from Buda and began to zigzag towards Octagon Square, crossing dangerous streets fast.

Octagon Square was another Breugel scene. Four sides of the octagon were major arteries, separated by huge buildings which delineated the other four sides. I approached the square carefully, but it appeared that many hundreds of people were undisturbed in their activities. I could see crowds around some Russian trucks loaded with flour bags and other basic foodstuffs, for which people were busily trading old watches, odd bits of jewellery, and bottles of wine. Other groups seemed to be standing and gazing at the square's four giant candelabra-type cast-iron lampposts. These had been festooned with the bodies of four figures. The men had been lynched by a mob, perhaps days ago. They were hanging by their broken necks; before they were hung, they had been severely beaten. Broken canes had been thrown under each lamppost. One man had had an eye gouged out; it was hanging down his face, frozen.

While some of the crowd stood morbidly looking at the spectacle—probably Arrowcross thugs who had been recognised and lynched on the spot—business was going on undisturbed. It was time to go home, but having seen the brisk trading, I decided to come back next day with some bottles of liquor and French cognac that Eta had stashed away.

Next morning, armed with a shopping list and a knapsack filled with eight bottles of invaluable liquor, I set out. On my way, I observed many Russian control points where people were being held up and arrested. At the same time, I observed that the Russians were only interested in what to them seemed idle passers-by and paid no attention to people going about in the middle of the road dragging their handcarts. I figured that the comrades did not interfere with people on serious business and decided to get hold of a handcart as soon as possible. I found out later how right I was; an army officer, I heard, walked all the way back from Austria along the Vienna-Budapest railway tracks, having got hold of a railwayman's long-handled hammer used to test the rails for weakness. Every time he saw Russians, he started banging away at the rails. The Russians would not interfere with a man so busy with a useful task. All men in Budapest at this point were only thinking of getting around safely without being captured.

At the square, I approached one of the trading Russian groups and began to observe the bartering. While walking around, I ran into Pista Kakonyi, a tough, talented graphic artist who was with me at the artists' colony in Nagybánya and who had been my graphics instructor at the Hungarian Academy of Fine Arts. We exchanged stories of the last year and began to discuss the present problem: the Russian action against all men they could catch. Pista said that he was working on a solution. He asked me to come with him to the Academy, which was only a few blocks away on Andrassy Street and had survived the siege unharmed. We walked there and along the deserted corridor to the graphics department, where all kinds of printing machines stood silent in the semi-darkness. Pista took me to his office where, taped to a drawing board, was a strange document written in the Cyrillic alphabet, adorned by a large circular stamp and a signature. He explained that it was a document issued to a friend of his by the Russian commandature, stating that the bearer was employed by them in some capacity and ordering everybody to give every assistance to that person. It was a *laissez-passer*, a "propuska" in Russian, and Pista decided to copy it with my help, complete with the stamp and signature; he proposed to make a woodcut negative and to print only a few copies, adding our names and thus providing us with security. Pista was a master woodcutter, and my role was to hold a magnifying glass and a carbide lamp while he worked. He had a beautiful piece of hardwood clamped down, and slowly a near-perfect copy was cut into it. It was hard work, and it was early afternoon by the time we rollered the ink onto the wood, wiped off the excess, and clamped the whole thing into a printing press. Carefully we made a few test prints. Then making two good copies on paper very similar to the document, he carefully wrote his name on one and mine on another, and after they dried, we folded them up exactly like the original. The sun was setting when I took my full knapsack and started the trek home. I did not barter anything that day, but I had my document. I don't know up to this day whether it would have been effective, because I never used it for identification.

By the time I arrived back at Molnar utca, the weight of the eight bottles had become very heavy, and the straps were cutting into my shoulders. Eta let me in and was disappointed that I had come back empty-handed. I only wanted to get rid of the knapsack and backed onto the kitchen table, loosened the straps and stepped away to sit down. The knapsack teetered on the table and before I could catch it, it fell on the kitchen floor. There was a tremendous crash, and the smell of Cointreau, Schnapps, and cognac all mixed up filled the kitchen with its wild aroma. Nothing could be saved, and it was a long time before Eta could forgive me for the loss, which in those days seemed enormous.

Visit to the Hill of the Roses

Every day I spent going further and further from Molnar utca, visiting friends and trying to gather information on the future. This was hard to come by because nobody knew what was going to happen. Everybody knew about the Yalta Agreement, according to which, at the end of the war, all occupied countries were to be allowed free democratic elections. But nobody believed that. We all thought that the Russians were here to stay. There were no newspapers, no radio, only rumours. We knew that the war was still on, that the allies were penetrating deeper and deeper into Germany, and that the Russians were on the Austrian-Hungarian border. Meanwhile, I had obtained from our peg-legged caretaker a rickety old four-wheeled handcart with an empty cardboard box tied to it, and indeed with it I had been able to get by the numerous Russian nets.

One day, I was heading towards my old school along a rubble-strewn frozen back street behind the ruined opera house. Suddenly two Cossack riders pulled up in front of me and jumped off their horses, after which one of them pointed a pistol at me and handed over the two sets of reins. In sign language, he explained that I was to hold onto the reins while they went upstairs to visit a barishnya (girl). I stood there with the two impatient horses while they went upstairs, figuring that as soon as they disappeared, I would leave the horses and scoot off with my handcart. This proved to be difficult, because every few minutes one of the Cossacks leaned out a window and threatened me with his pistol while the other attended to the barishnya. I was getting cold, and the horses were restless, prancing about, and I had to turn around with them several times, the reins twisting around me. Finally a man came along, and I gave him the reins for a moment, then hurried away with my cart. When I was just about to turn the corner, I heard the Cossack yelling and shaking his gun at my substitute.

I returned to Molnar utca, temporarily parked my handcart, and then headed off once again without it for my old school. I had got fairly close and was crossing an old square full of debris and blowing snow when suddenly Johnnie Vago emerged from the other direction. I had not seen him since the time we escaped the army together in September, and we were delighted to see each other alive. He immediately invited me to a little flat he was sharing with a Greek friend, Theo Argiriadis Panayotis, who had somehow ended up in Budapest. He had good connections with the Greek Red Cross, perhaps because his father was the governor of the island of Mitilini in the Aegean Sea, and had obtained a barrel full of hazelnuts which Johnnie offered me, telling me to eat as much as I wanted. I was delighted with the new delicacy until the nuts turned out to be rancid and wormy and not very enjoyable.

It was soon time for me to go home, but we agreed to go together next day down to the Danube to try and go across to Buda. Johnnie wanted to find his father who he thought was over there, and I wanted to visit our villa on Rozsadomb. The Germans had surrendered in Buda, so there seemed no reason not to go. The bridges were all gone, but we had heard that a few entrepreneurs were rowing people across the Danube in keeled rowboats.

We arrived at the embankment laden with bartering goods, ready to negotiate our way across. (Hungarian currency, the pengo, at this point was not accepted by anybody). We found a long queue waiting for the five or six former rowing-club boats now plying the icy waters to Buda. Finally our turn came, and with a few others—the boat had only a few inches of planking showing above the grey swirling water—we headed out into midstream. Skilfully dodging the numerous ice floes, the boatmen delivered us safely in fifteen minutes to Buda.

We walked along past the ruins of my favourite prewar café, the "Stamboul," and then Johnnie went in the direction of the Regent House, a modern apartment building at the foot of the Hill where he thought the father might be, and I took to the Hill on Gul Baba Street, anxious to see how our villa had survived the war. It was near the top, a good 20 minutes on foot, and it was a sad sight to see when I arrived. The seven-foot-high cast-iron fencing was all down, and an infantry trench wound its way through the front garden. But the house, badly damaged from being hit by over 40 artillery shells and mortars, was still standing. Big holes were gaping in the slate roof, and most of the stucco had fallen down, showing the naked masonry walls. Downstairs, the caretaker's apartment was relatively undamaged, and Gosztonyi and his wife received me with a great welcome.

Upstairs there was only one livable room where Takacsi, our tenant, was living with his wife, who was the sister of my friend, Pali Fabo. They also welcomed me and suggested that I spend the night there. I settled in at the caretaker's, and we all got together to catch up with events. Gosztonyi produced a few bottles of wine from a hiding place, and I brought them up to date on my last few months. Then I listened to their story.

Apparently the Germans, towards the end of the siege, moved a battery of Bofors antiaircraft guns into our garden, dug running trenches, and in the last few days, lowered the sights of the anti-aircraft guns, pouring their shots straight up the hill almost at point-blank range at the approaching Russian tanks. One night the shooting stopped, the Germans were gone, nobody knew where, and next morning the Russians were everywhere. The sappers came with long poles with foot-long needle-sharp metal spikes at their ends and started to poke them gently into the frozen ground, searching for hidden land mines. They did not find any, but in our backyard their needles struck a solid object which they dug out carefully. It turned out to be my 100-litre wooden barrel of rum which I had dug into the soil last September to save it from the invaders.

Then followed an event that has not been forgotten in the neighbourhood to this day. The Russians began drinking the rum and by early afternoon were highly intoxicated. One of them found in one of the neighbouring villas a Roman Catholic priest who, not wanting to be caught by the Russians, had abandoned his habit and dressed as a civilian. To increase his protection, he also had put on a Red Cross armband. A roving and drunken patrol found him and, thinking that he was a doctor, took him to an empty villa. Other patrols meanwhile rounded up all women in the neighbourhood who had not been able to hide successfully. Ever worried about venereal diseases, the Russians then ordered the "doctor" to examine each woman for diseases at pistol point. The unfortunate priest had no choice. After this event, the Russians raped all the women, forcing the poor priest to watch, and then let them go. Immediately the news had spread that my barrel of rum was to blame for the outrage, and the Takacsis and Gosztonyi and his wife thought it best that for a while I should discreetly keep away from the Hill. A lynch mob had been looking for me ever since.

Takacsi also gave me bad news about his brother-in-law, my friend, Pali Fabo, whom I had not seen or heard of ever since that fateful day in May when on the parade ground we were separated by Colonel Zentay. Apparently, in the fall Pali returned from his battalion and was given refuge in the condominium of another friend and classmate, Harry Eidlitz, who being an Italian citizen, was safe from Nazis of the German and Hungarian kind. During the siege, Pali Fabo was wearing the uniform and had the papers of a Hungarian Army officer; he went out one day and had not been heard of since. I promised to visit his parents.

After a quiet night, I sneaked out of the house and walked past the row of Lombardy poplars that lined the footpath from the street entrance. I saw that the frozen ground around the sixth poplar was not disturbed. Just as well, because in the early spring of 1944, just after the invasion by the Germans, following my father's instructions, I buried there about 12 kilos of gold. As he had instructed, I dug them in close enough to the roots so that, should the Russians come looking for land mines with their pokers, they would be unlikely to find them. And once again he was right. They had not dug that close.

Escaping the Liberators

It was still half-dark when I reached the bottom of the hill in old Buda. Here large three-hundred-year-old houses lined the embankment. I saw no one around and proceeded. Instantly, a huge Russian stepped out from an archway and, without asking for my home-made "propuska," he shoved me into a dark courtyard where hundreds of people captured the day before were milling about. Half an hour later, sitting in the bottom of a huge steel pontoon, we were tugged to Margaret's Island, to the pier of the former Royal Hungarian Athletic club, a very exclusive establishment before the siege. Here a large crowd of prisoners and Russian sappers were busy building a temporary bridge out of huge wooden piles driven into the river bottom and bolted together by the sappers. The bridge was urgently needed so that traffic could once again cross the river. Since the night when Pest fell and the Germans blew up the bridges, Buda and Pest had been cut off from each other.

When the motor boat towing our steel pontoon docked at the MAC pier on the island, the work was already well underway, aided by previously captured forced labour. The Russian sappers were of obviously different racial origin than the mostly Asiatic fighting troops: large-boned, blonde, purposeful. They seemed competent and not unfriendly. Under their instruction, hundreds of captive Hungarians were at work. On a small hill in the centre of the island, the Russians had deposited a huge pile of 40-foot-long round wooden piles, each of which just a short while ago must have been a proudly towering giant fir tree in the Carpathians. Under the sappers' direction, the Hungarian prisoners tied huge manila ropes to the logs, and in groups of ten, they dragged them down to the embankment on the Buda side of the island. It looked like a giant tug of war, everybody huffing and puffing and dragging. Once the logs arrived, the sappers went to work with pile drivers mounted on anchored pontoons, while others drilled and bolted the logs together with large steel bolts.

I helped drag a load of logs, but always looking for a way to keep up my strength, I found an easier job: somebody had to take the ropes immediately back to the log pile on the hill, and I appropriated this task for myself. While the others were tugging, I walked beside them. When they arrived at the embankment, staggering from exhaustion, I unhitched the rope and casually dragged it back to the hilltop. I had a clearly defined job, and with everybody accepting my self-imposed assignment, I spent the day walking downhill and then dragging the rope back.

There were no provisions to feed us; when the work stopped at noon, everybody just collapsed where they were. I had become quite friendly with the Russian sapper who was in charge of the woodpile and the boxes of steel bolts, and so managed to sit down with him at lunch time. Another soldier brought him a huge aluminum bowl of steaming "kasha," a kind of porridge. I watched him eat, shivering. He smiled at me and handed me the bowl half-full. Without hesitation, I quickly filled my stomach with the hot gruel, a good training for Siberia, I thought. After we finished eating, he gave me a further lesson in gulag customs. From a copy of the "Red Army" newspaper, he tore off two ten-inch-wide strips. Folding them in half lengthwise, he then reached into the pocket of his padded field jacket, pulled out a handful of dried leaves, small twigs, and various other dubious matter mixed here and there with black tobacco, and proceeded to pour this into the two folded sections. Arranging the material in long even rows, he than rolled up the newsprint around it and giving each a healthy lengthwise lick, made two gigantic cigarettes, about the size of a Churchill cigar, handing one to me and lighting up both of them. The first puff nearly knocked me out, but I bravely went on and survived. The name of this cigar-cigarette, as I found out from him, was "Mahorka," and every Russian smoked them. There was always a newspaper around, and pockets were always full of flammable items.

As soon as we finished our smoke, it was back to work again until it became dark. At night, we were allowed into a huge gym room and, without food, left to rest. There were no guards outside. The Russians were sure that we were not going to escape by swimming across the nearly frozen river. It was very cold in the hall; the wind blew furiously through the cracks of this unwinterised building. I played with ideas for escape; this initial introduction to gulag living did not appeal. Having no ideas, I then concentrated on finding better quarters; sleeping side by side on the floor spoon-shape had little appeal. I found a small adjoining storeroom, where in the dark I stumbled on some cardboard boxes full of what apparently were neckties. I pulled them all out and, partly lying on them, partly covering myself, managed to create a warm corner and finally fell asleep. I woke up with the false dawn, feeling very chilled. In the light, I saw that I was covered with hundreds of navy blue, gold-striped MAC club ties.

The day started with the banging of the pile drivers and other noises. Again there was no food, and I was determined to spend the day finding a way to escape. The construction site was surrounded on two sides by a high barbed-wire fence, and the other two sides bordered on the riverbanks. The river was flowing fast, carrying large ice floes. Down I walked with the tugging crew and back with the rope every five minutes.

Around noon, as I returned to the log pile, I saw my friendly sapper walking towards the Pest embankment with two men. One more shot on the pinball machine, I thought. I ran after them and, catching up, asked them what they were doing. The two men said that the sapper had ordered them to come with him to row across the Danube to the bridgehead for some crates of bolts. With body language, I explained to the Russian that I was a powerful oarsman; he laughed and sent one of the other fellows back. I rowed us across in a flat-bottomed wooden rowboat, the kind that Danube fishermen used. It was more stable than the keeled sports boat in which Johnnie and I had crossed two days before.

Rowing hard, and after scraping several ice floes, we got across to the bridgehead, which was a fenced-in area in front of what was known as the Palatinus houses, a row of waterfront apartments. Towards the wrecked Margaret Bridge, there was a large wooden drop gate for trucks, guarded by two Russian soldiers. Our sapper guided us to a basement entrance, which was behind a yellow telephone booth, peppered by machine-gun shots, but still standing. Beyond, on St. Stephen's Boulevard, I could see the usual post-siege crowd busily going about, dragging handcarts and sleighs or carrying bundles.

The sapper started down the steps and beckoned us to follow. The other chap went after him, but I waited behind the phone booth. The guards, noticing me standing around, walked over from the gate curiously. In my best Russian, I said "Tovarich sapper dal" and pointed down the steps. The guards trundled down with their submachine guns, and as soon as they disappeared, keeping the phone booth between myself and the basement entrance, I carefully backed towards the gate. One more escape, I hoped. When I was close enough, I turned and ran, ducking under the post. Once on the other side, I slowed down and quickly melted into the crowd. I was free again.

The next day, I found out that Johnnie had not found his father. He had been staying in a building which received a direct hit. It had a German ammunition dump on the second floor, and when this exploded, the ten-storey building collapsed onto the air-raid shelter, burying perhaps 800 people. It was years before the ruins were removed. Coming back to Pest, Johnnie also was captured by the Russians. He, too, managed to escape.

As for the bridge workforce, I later learned that all were shipped to Siberia, like all other captured men.

The First Day's Work in the New Life

Sometime early in February, after the siege, Mr. Gulyas, my father's wine-cellar master, appeared at Eta's flat, and my father decided to pay a visit to our cellars, which he had not seen since October 1944, the time of the Arrowcross takeover. As one of the leading wine exporters of Hungary, his main business before the collapse was the buying up of whole crops from some of the big landowners. The new wine might be processed in the cellars of the estates for direct export or sent to Budapest as soon as the fermentation had stopped and stored in my father's wine cellars, which were located under the freight yard buildings of the Western Railway, just behind the Eiffel-designed Western Railway Terminal of Budapest. These freight yards consisted of extensive, long, single-storey warehouses which all had loading ramps on one side and railway sidings on the other. Most of the goods coming into Budapest from the west or being shipped out arrived here, and the shipping companies were located in these buildings. The huge basements underneath were not suitable for hard goods, and so there, in the 1930's, my father built his "transit lager," a transit wine cellar, of approximately 30,000 HL capacity (3,000,000 litres). The young wines were filtered here, processed, and stored for short periods before being exported to their destination. Before the war, the wines went mainly to Switzerland, which at that time was the centre of the European wine trade, but some were exported to Germany, Czechoslovakia, and Poland as well. As a sideline, he also kept up a lively trade to local pubs and restaurants.

The location was well suited for both large and small shipments, the loading ramps serving the local trade in 7–8 HL (700–800 litre) transport barrels, while the wine for export was shipped by train in enamel- or glass-lined wine-transport tankers which were leased from specialist shipping companies. These tankers could carry up to 100 HL each. On the outside, they looked exactly like oil tanker cars.

In the cellars themselves, the wine was stored in huge oak barrels of 100 HL (10,000 litres) each. These, 12 to 14 feet high, stood in endless rows along both walls of the long cellars facing on a central corridor which served as a working aisle. Each barrel had a filling hole at the top, through which the wine was pumped in. Long catwalks ran from barrel to barrel, permitting daily checks to make sure that the barrels were full (there was always evaporation) and that no air pockets had developed. The wine had to live in a bacteria-free environment. Along the centre aisle, each barrel had a large door in its face, kept in place through the pressure of the liquid, but through which, by means of a tapped opening, quantities could be drawn off for local shipping or, using large pumps, transferred into the tank cars above. These doors also let the coopers get inside to clean and maintain the barrels.

The barrels were originally beer barrels made of three-inch-thick oak sections They had been dismantled in the brewery cellars, carried in section by section, and reassembled. The sections were held together by huge steel rings, and as long as the barrels did not dry out, they were water- and airtight. In my father's wine cellars, they never dried out because the wine kept coming and going all the time. Some were a hundred years old or older, and quite a few had on their faces beautiful carvings of the original owner's coat of arms and other decorative motifs.

Of course, this wine cellar at the Western Railway Yards was not suitable for maturing special wines for years because of the unstable temperature and atmosphere. It was strictly a transit cellar. While my father's export business demanded a constant flow, he like all the great wine merchants followed the tradition of laying in quantities of the best wine for the long term.

There were two reasons for this: first, up to a certain number of years, the wines kept improving year by year, and it was, so to say, money in the bank, bearing good interest.

But there was a second, more important reason: every three or four years in Europe, there was an exceptionally bountiful and outstanding harvest, The market would be unable to absorb the vast crop, the prices would drop, and those with available capital and organisation bought up all they could and put it away for the future. In addition, about every seven years, there was a truly disastrous crop, with the result—in those days of stable currencies—that prices doubled or even tripled on the European wine markets. These were the years when the great wine fortunes were made. In these disaster years, the profits tripled and quadrupled. As a result, a wine merchant measured his wealth according to how many hectolitres of wine sat in his cellars, all paid for, waiting for the right moment. My father had played this game for decades, and when the time came to buy, he scraped together all his resources and bought and bought. For his long-term storage needs, he leased wine cellars in Budafok, like most of his colleagues. It was here that the vast State Wine Enterprise, the largest in Hungary, was located, as well as the Oenological Research Institute, which inspected and certified all export shipments of wine.

Budafok had perhaps one of the world's greatest concentrations of wine cellars, with a total capacity of about one million HL (100,000,000 litres) of wine. Until the middle of the nineteenth century, it was a sleepy little village on a flat peninsula just south of Buda, with a few vineyards nestling under the great limestone escarpment that the Danube carved for itself eons ago. The modern city of Budapest, with its elegant apartment buildings, boulevards, the famous Fishermen's Bastion on the Palace Hill, even the abutments of the Chain Bridge of Count Szechenyi, were all built of limestone quarried in Budafok in the nineteenth century.

But instead of quarrying helter-skelter and leaving ugly scars in the escarpment, the builders had a better idea. They burrowed into the hill, creating the wine cellars. These were stone tunnels about 50–60 feet wide and two stories high, and at first the builders went straight into the mountain for perhaps half a kilometre.

Later they started branching out in "Y" shapes as the demand rose for more and more stone for the growing metropolis. Eventually railway sidings were built along the centre of each cellar, so that the wine could be pumped in and out directly from the barrels into the tank cars. All the great wine merchants had occupied vast sections of the cellars. Not only were they practical for shipping and receiving, but the steady year-round temperature and atmosphere were ideal for long-term storage and maturing of wines and for making sparkling wines in the Champagne manner.

Father established his own holding cellars here, and as a teenager, I loved to visit. The layout was similar to the transit cellars at the Western Freight Yards, but instead of a railway siding outside the sheds, here whole trains of tank cars were shunted right in for loading and unloading. Each great wine cellar had wine-tasting rooms furnished with great care, and in traditional Hungarian style, sometimes with beautifully kept carved antique barrels as decoration. I visited them all and the cellars behind.

There was less hustle and bustle going on in our Budafok cellar than in the transit cellar. Here, any time one visited, tens of thousand of hectolitres of wine were quietly maturing for years, so there was less activity.

The cellar had a straight main branch and from it, in a "Y" shape, two lesser ones. The rail siding did not go beyond the main branch. Here in the summer of 1944, on the longer of the two secondary branches, my father stored 10,000 hectolitres of Takaji Szamorodni wine for the time, for retrieval once the war had ended. As the Russian armies poured over the Carpathian mountains heading into Hungary, he decided to take measures for the survival of his stock. He and his cellar master Gulyas supervised the walling-up of this storage area by the local mason. After the wall was completed, the mason carefully disguised the structure with rocks and boulders in irregular shapes, and my father and Gulyas were satisfied that it looked absolutely natural to the eye.

By February, my father was restless and wanted to visit both facilities, but because the transit cellar had been practically empty before the siege, except for the barrels, he and Gulyas decided to visit Budafok first. Gulyas organised a horse-drawn farm wagon and a driver in Buda, and we set out on the trip across the Danube in a rowboat and met the wagon on the other side. It was past noon when we reached Budafok and the wine cellars.

There was little activity around the champagne factory, but here and there, cellars were being opened up, and a few workmen could be seen. Budafok saw little fighting because the Russian pincer movement of the previous Christmas Eve took everybody by surprise and such defenders as there were withdrew towards Buda, so we drove up quite optimistically to the entrance of our cellar with our wagon.

Electricity was not yet restored, and we entered with carbide lamps held high in our hands, which cast an eerie light around us. The main branch of our cellar was in good shape and so were the rows of barrels, emptied long before the siege, but as we neared the end and approached the walled-in section, we had a rude surprise. The secret wall had been demolished, and as we looked inside by the light of the lamps, an unbelievable sight greeted us.

At the bottom of the cellar, there was a lake of evil-smelling wine stretching as far as our eyes could see. In it swam every kind of flotsam: clothing, parts of barrels, empty oil cans, buckets, anything that could float. The storage barrels had huge holes in them, and we could see dried streaks where the wine had poured out. We waded into the pool and walked down partway in the cold liquid. Everywhere the same scene: demolished and partially demolished barrels, totally empty. Our feet were cold, and we had to get out.

Near the Oenological Institute, we found some staff who had stayed right through the Russian advance, and they told us what happened. A day or two after the Russians occupied Budafok looking for loot, they found the great cellars, but they were empty—the merchants had shipped the wine out to Germany in front of the advancing troops. The Russians then got ugly and threatened the population with reprisals. So the stone mason took them to our cellar and opened up the hidden wall. The Russians swarmed in, but could not open the taps of the huge barrels. They brought in heavy machine guns and started shooting into many of them. As the barrels were holed, the wine poured out in great gushes.

The soldiers caught the wine in their steel helmets, oil cans, anything handy, or simply lay down under the stream and drank. For a day, they remained there, drunk in the pool of wine, unable to move. Then the feared military police, the Russian NKVD, heard about the bacchanale and came and carted off the drunk soldiers, perhaps to the gulag, sealed the cellar, and posted a heavy guard. A few days later a train of tank cars appeared, guarded by machine guns, and the remaining wine, about 7000 HL, was pumped into the tankers. These were marked "Destination Kremlin, Moscow," and the train departed with perhaps the greatest single bounty of the siege.

Now not only was the hidden cellar empty, but all the equipment and many of the barrels were ruined. With that train went my father's fortune, built up with hard work and considerable business acumen. The value of the wine at that time in Switzerland on the market was 20 cents U.S. per litre wholesale, or $200,000 for the million litres of wine stolen or spilled out. My father was 57 years old, and he had just been ruined.

He shrugged and said to Gulyas: "Let's go home now, it is very cold out here, I need to warm up. Tomorrow we will go to the transit cellar, and we'll see what's left there." We had a few blankets with us, and we rode under them shivering as the wagon rolled down the cobbled streets of Budafok. I never heard him mention the loss again.

We expected to find much less of value at the transit cellar, yet when we arrived there next morning, descending through the steep basement steps with our lamps, and walked by the wine-tasting room, we found a pleasant surprise: although the cellar had been looted and some barrels were partially drained, most of them still had some wine in them, as we established by carefully tapping on the barrel faces. We found an ancient hand pump with a long handle, and Gulyas and I started pumping from the less-full barrels into those that were not so drained. After a few hours, we had four full barrels of 100 HL each and enough wine left to fill to the top two 7 HL transport barrels as well.

Now all the barrels that were full had to be stoppered. The ancient system for this was to cut a piece of jute material and, wrapping it around the wooden plug, to hammer it into the top hole of the barrel. We found enough plugs in the storage, but no jute material. I went with my lamp in search of jute, and sure enough, in the wine-tasting room, tossed under a trestle table, I found a strange but brand-new large jute bag. There was something in it, and the bag was sealed. To see better, I dragged it up the steps to the loading ramp. Then I saw the explanation, stencilled on its side with black lettering: "Wehrmacht Leichen Sack" (Wehrmacht Medical Corps body bag). There was something inside, frozen solid, but much smaller than a body! We needed the jute, and I was also curious, so I slit the bag open. Out came a frozen leg, its Wehrmacht boot still on it, amputated somewhere above the knee and below the hip. By then I had seen so many frozen bodies all over the ruined city that I took this discovery quite calmly. I carried the unknown soldier's leg to the rubble heap nearby, and because we needed the jute, I cut the cleanest parts of it into ten-inch squares. In no time, Gulyas had sealed all the barrels in the prescribed manner.

Just as he was finishing, a group of men noisily descended the steps. Lifting our lamp, we saw the figure of the Hungarian freight-yard chief, whom we knew well, surrounded by armed policemen. He had come to see whether looters were at work in the cellar. Father, Gulyas, and I greeted him happily. The Russian command had left him in his post to look after the freight yards, to organise the freight trains, and to protect the many valuable items stored in the sheds. The shippers had not yet returned to their stores, and in fact we were the first who had come to reclaim our facility.

The Russians allowed the police detachment of the freight yard to be armed. These police were the first Hungarian authorities I saw carrying weapons. They told us that they were not permitted to carry the rifles beyond the freight yards, which they patrolled day and night. The only looters were stray groups of Russian soldiers, and they were authorised by the Russian command to use their weapons if necessary and had done so on occasion. Later, when the Russian soldiers realised that the wine cellar was stocked, these policemen defended it, sometimes fighting pitched battles.

My father asked them to keep an eye on the cellar, and Gulyas, ever practical, found two large ten-litre raffia-covered glass "demijohns", a type of wine container, filled them with quite a nice Riesling, and handed these over for encouragement. It always helped to give a good reason to an official to be cooperative, and in these times, when money held no sure value, when barter was the order of the day, two demijohns were a powerful inducement. From this time on, our cellar was as safe as the National Bank.

So my father had some wine stocks, a cellar master, and although the political situation was not clear, he saw that he was back in business. We all trundled up the stairs, Gulyas put a huge padlock on the wooden doors, and shaking hands all around, we went our way after the first day's work in the new life.

Currency Trading and Other Adventures

As the weeks passed, Russian atrocities and taking of prisoners diminished as the front-line troops moved out towards Austria and the more disciplined NKVD-led occupation troops took over. There was still no water or electricity or any kind of transportation. The war news was passed on by word of mouth, though some people had battery-operated radios and could hear Allied news which was quite accurate. The noose was tightening on Germany, but resistance was fierce, and the end was nowhere in sight. They were now drafting 12- to 14-year-old boys, and rumour had it that Hitler was planning to draw back to the Bavarian Alps for the final battle, where, it was said, he could hold out for years.

I reinstated my handcart and continued my trips around town. One day, I was walking along Maria Valerie utca, where in my motorcycle days we used to hang out at the Paradiso bar. All the grand hotels along the Danube had been ruined by low-flying Russian bombers; there had been special orders to demolish these redoubts of the upper classes. Only the Bristol Hotel had not collapsed, although it was heavily damaged. Here with my cousin, Peter Laszlo, who during 1942 and 1943 was apprenticing at the reception desk, I had spent many happy hours in the lobby bar and at afternoon tea dances. I got to know all the staff and was particularly friendly with Peter's bosses, Mr. Kossowitz, the distinguished-looking chief receptionist, and Mr. Miszla, the wicked chief concierge. Now I scrambled into the ruined lobby, past the blown-up reception desk, and thought of the good times we had had in the little office behind, being treated by Miszla and Kossowitz to French cognac and packages of "Darling" cigarettes, the Hungarian copy of Camels (even down to the packaging). There was nobody around for a treat now.

Everything was covered with rubble and mortar dust, and the little steps leading to a basement storage room, where according to my cousin, Kossowitz and Miszla had hoarded vast numbers of cartons of Darling cigarettes, were buried under debris. Looking closely, I decided that it would not be impossible to clear the area enough to get to the storeroom. The next day, I organised an expedition with our peg-legged caretaker. Equipped with a few shovels and a pickaxe, after hours of work, we cleared a passage. The legend of the hoard was real; we found almost 2,000 cartons of Darling cigarettes. These we loaded on our little handcart, covered them with a dirty old tarp, and successfully returned to Molnar utca. Cigarettes were the best currency at this time; anything could be had, if you had them. For 15 percent of the loot, Mr.

Pegleg stored it in our coal cellar, and I felt like a genuine millionaire.

Shortly after this, Johnnie and I heard that an open-air currency market was operating in Nador utca behind the former Bourse. Sure enough, there was a beehive of activity there. Although the Hungarian pengo at this point had dubious value, U.S. dollars and gold, in the form of Napoleon coins (worth about $12) and all kinds of gold chains at $1/gram, were trading fast as if on a commodity exchange. Some traders specialised in dollars, some in gold, and around them were crowds of people wanting to change one thing or another. We ran into a comrade from the labour battalion, an older man, a merchant of some kind in the past, who was trading in U.S. dollars and gold. Small amounts traded every minute, and each trader's stock was carried by a partner who for reasons of security waited across the wide street on the other side, carrying the bank. It was interesting to watch the lively activity. With the curfew still on, the market dissolved every day around dusk so that everybody could get home safely. I had some beautiful white tissue-thin one-pound notes that I bought through a friend in 1943, and I tried to buy some gold from a friend. (Alas, these pound notes were not tradable: the Germans had faked them beautifully using Jewish concentration-camp inmates, trained chemists, and printers; even the Bank of England could not tell the difference between the real and fake notes, and eventually, before the end of the war, they withdrew them all from circulation).

Nevertheless, after Johnnie met a former French officer whose family were famous Strasbourg pâté manufacturers and who was buying goose liver by the ton from the Hungarian farmers (and who through some quirk of fate ended up in the siege of Budapest, perhaps as a German prisoner), an interesting business proposition came our way: hidden in his clothes, Pierre had a neatly folded crisp $1000 bill. Not knowing his way around in the chaos of post-siege Budapest, he entrusted us with the job of making change for him. A 1000-dollar bill at that point was as useless as Mark Twain's famous 1,000,000-pound note. The dollar was the favoured currency in Budapest, but in denominations of $1, $5, and $10. A $100 bill was already unheard-of, and a $1000 bill was at once very valuable and useless.

So we undertook to make change for him on the black market. We arrived early behind the Bourse one morning. I had the bill hidden on me and stood with the other bankers on the far side of Nador utca while Johnnie mixed with and talked to the dealers. Our old comrade at first thought we were crazy, but finally we approached a group of bearded Hassidim, who were known to be the most powerful traders. They went around to various other traders, formed a consortium, and agreed to change the bill. First, however, they wanted to see it and to take it to an associate who was an expert in these matters. We were loath to let it out of our sight, but in the end a solution was found: we handed the bill over, and they left two of their partners with us as hostages. They took off with the bill, and an anxious hour was spent waiting. But the Hassidim were meticulously honest, and at the end of the hour, they returned with the money and an offer: for a $200 fee, they would change the awkward bill. We agreed, and two young Hassidim appeared with a huge cardboard box labelled "Red Cross Aid." This contained an amazing series of bundles of $1 and $5 bills, tattered and worn. Surrounded for security by all members of the consortium, we counted out the $800, then repackaged the lot, taking $50 as our commission. We hastily disappeared from the trading sidewalk and repaired to the apartment, where the French captain was anxiously awaiting us. Up to that moment, this transaction was the biggest on the young currency market of Budapest.

Because there was nothing better to do—no cafés, no espressos, no school—we took our $50 and spent part of our days with it as our capital on the currency market, buying and selling as sub-agents on behalf of our ex-comrade. Although there were no ticker tapes, the market was a central point where all the news was also traded, with many old friends turning up regularly.

Lexi (Alexis) Strommer, whom I had known at university, an exceptionally good-looking man, appeared one day. His story of the Arrowcross times was interesting. One day he was going to a house protected by the Swedish Wallenberg group to visit his Jewish girlfriend, Hanna Feldbaum, and as he approached the group of apartment buildings bearing the Swedish flag, he noticed a large Arrowcross unit entering the first block, obviously on a major raid. He arrived just in time to sneak Hanna, her sister Teti, and their parents out through the back stairs. He managed to take them to his apartment on Korond (the Rotonde), where they all survived the siege and where they were still living. Lexi was also trading in currency in a small way, but he had a large group to support and was more devoted to the practice than Johnnie and I. Later Lexi become a rather famous figure and lived an unusual life to which I will return later.

Amid all the carnage, a classmate of mine from the Fasor Gymnasium, Tomi Dick, had a story to tell with a happy ending. He had been rescued by his daredevil best friend, Tomi Schmolka, who had been living in disguise with the help of his stepfather, Paul Javor, one of Hungary's finest dramatic actors.

Tomi Dick, disguised in the uniform of a Hungarian Army private, had been living in a modern apartment in a group of buildings surrounding Saint Stephen's Park. This was a predominately Jewish area built in the 1930s and nicknamed the Budapest "Tel Aviv." The Jewish residents had all been moved into the ghetto before shipment to the death camps, and the apartments had quickly filed up with refugee families from the eastern provinces fleeing the Russian invasion. This made the district an excellent place for melting into the crowds; Tomi Schmolka got hold of an apartment there and hid his girlfriend and her family there, and also Tomi Dick. Many other apartments were also occupied by those who wished to hide. The Arrowcross figured this out and made a major raid, advancing building by building during the night and collecting about 50 people in their net.

Tomi Dick was one of them. In the pitch-dark park, the group huddled miserably under the eyes of their guards, waiting for the end of the raid, Tomi was determined to escape. He realised that the group would march across the darkened park supervised by only a few armed guards and whispered to others that at the signal of his cough, they should run in all directions. Some might get caught, but the majority would get away. Soon they were marched off, and at an appropriate moment, Tomi gave the signal and ran for his life. But the others stayed with the guards. Two of these easily caught Tomi, beat him up, and pushed him back into the column.

The march continued across a bridge to Buda and upriver on the Danube embankment to a killing ground just about level with the Lukacs Spa Bath. There they lined their prisoners up on the edge of the embankment over the ice-cold river which rushed by below, carrying ice floes in its current. One by one, the guards shot the prisoners in the neck and pushed them forward as their knees buckled. Tomi could hear the shots getting closer and instinctively turned his head. At that moment, a bullet hit him, but because his head was turned, it entered through his jaw, travelled through his tongue, and exited just below his right eye. He fell unconscious into the Danube. A mile and a half downriver, he recovered consciousness in the ice-cold water and painfully swam among the ice floes to the embankment. He managed to crawl up the stone steps and fainted again.

He was found by an army patrol from the infamous military police barracks on Margit Boulevard in Buda. Because he was in army uniform, they took him into custody and dragged him away only half-conscious. Luckily the Hospital of the Good Samaritans was on their route, and because he was bleeding profusely, they took him there to be bandaged. The doctor on duty, quoting the Geneva Convention which prohibited him from releasing a dying soldier, told the patrol to come back the next day. As soon as they left, the doctor asked Tomi if he knew someone who could come for him with fake military orders before the military patrol returned.

Tomi gave him Schmolka's phone number, and next morning, Schmolka miraculously arrived in a sergeant's uniform with a submachine gun, an ambulance, and acceptable fake papers. The hospital released Tomi Dick on a stretcher, and he was put in the ambulance, which drove away at high speed.

This was not the end of the story. The ambulance, in this, the second week of the siege, drove from hospital to hospital. All of them were so overfilled with wounded soldiers that none would accept Tomi. On and on they drove, until finally at the Octagon Square, the famous crossing at Andrassy utca and the main circular boulevard, their ambulance crashed into a huge Horch car flying the pennants of the Commander of the defending Hungarian forces. The ambulance was wrecked, but the Horch just shook its fenders. The General's military driver got out and helped Schmolka remove the shaken Tomi from the wreck. Then the driver offered to take him in the General's car in search of hospital accommodation. When they arrived at a private hospital, the Fasor Sanatorium on Queen Wilhelmina Boulevard next door to our old school, Tomi was presented as the General's favourite soldier, wounded in the battle for Budapest. Naturally a bed was immediately prepared for him. Here he spent the end of the war recuperating in the best possible circumstances, all things considered, safely awaiting the arrival of the Russians.

My own life was not without interest. One day, standing on the far side of Nador utca, I met an extremely attractive dark-haired woman who had just come out of one of the elegant apartment buildings. There we started to chat, and she told me that she lived upstairs with her daughter; her name was Mrs. B. She invited me for a drink, which I accepted. Her rather dignified apartment had survived unharmed and was well stocked with wines and liqueurs of all kinds. These were times when people needed companionship, and it was natural to form new friendships. We drank a few glasses of wine, and she told me her story, or some of it.

Her husband was a gendarme Colonel, quite a famous one, aptly named "The Terrorist of Ujvidek." In 1941, the German

215

and Hungarian armies marched into the Bacska, a former Hungarian province, which after the First World War was taken away from Hungary in the Trianon Treaty and attached to the newly formed Yugoslavia.

After the German-Hungarian armies arrived, the gendarmes followed, and under Colonel B's command, an early "ethnic cleansing" began. The Danube was frozen, and the gendarmes cut a hole in the ice. The cleansing affected mostly the unfortunate Hungarian Jewish population. Lined up on the riverbanks, helplessly queuing under the guns of the gendarmes, all received a shot in the neck, and one after the other disappeared under the ice. We all had heard details of this story: a huge pool of blood on the ice, gendarmes surrounding the queue, while the Colonel with his officers watched from the banks of the river. When this story began to circulate in 1941, there was shock in Budapest, but the Colonel did not get even a reprimand. Right after the siege, the Yugoslav army caught him and took him to the Ujvidek military prison, where he was now awaiting trial for his war crimes. Mrs. B. told me that she was abused by her husband all their married life; she and her 18-year-old daughter hated him, according to her story, with good reason.

As the sad tale unfolded, time was passing, and I suddenly noticed that it was getting dark outside and made moves to go. In view of the curfew, Mrs. B. felt I should stay with them, and it seemed like a good idea. By now, my father had agreed that if I was caught by the curfew, I should stay wherever it was convenient, and because I could not call, I encouraged him to feel assured that I would turn up sooner or later. After more storytelling and quite a few more glasses of wine consumed by candlelight, my hostess produced an acceptable dinner. It was quite late by the time she made up a bed for me on the sofa in the pleasant Biedermeyer living room. Huge down-filled pillows and a warm duvet welcomed me. She and her daughter shared a large double bed in the only bedroom. Slipping under the warm duvet was a luxurious comfort in the unheated apartment. I was wondering what would happen next when the bedroom door opened and my hostess quietly slipped in next to me, her lithe body burrowing into the warmth. She held me desperately, and I will never forget the night this lonesome passionate woman gave me. Next morning, back in Molnar utca, I told my father to be prepared for further absences. Day after day, I appeared at the currency market, waiting for the afternoon when I could go to Mrs. B and a warm welcome. By now, Mrs. B's daughter had also accepted me, and the evenings passed pleasantly, drinking, talking, and playing cards. Mrs. B did not talk much about the Colonel, although she seemed to receive regular news of the course of the trial, a military tribunal, where all the horrors at Ujvidek were recounted. The day of judgment drew near.

One night we had a particularly good champagne and lots of wine with the simple meal. Afterwards she told me that her husband had been sentenced to death by hanging and would be executed in Yugoslavia at dawn the next day. She did not talk about it again, but when the time came to go to bed, she did not make up the sofa, but led me into the bedroom together with her daughter. In between these two beautiful women, there I lay, drinking from a bottle of fine French champagne. Not another word was passed between us, the candles burnt down, and this most unusual night passed. Drink and passion were sedatives for them as we made love together. All my thoughts were of the fearful year that had just passed, and I wondered what fate had in mind with this encounter. In memory, I could see Nagyvárad, Baby Ritter and her family, beautiful Éva Hochteil, and so many friends whose fate I did not know.

After that night, the friendship faded; we all felt a little embarrassed. But I believe that in her way, she, too, had revenge that night.

Journey to Szeged and Life in Fur Storage

Although my father was determined to start up his business again, most of Budapest was still only slowly recovering from the siege. There was no electricity, no streetcars, no public transportation, no fuel for heating and cooking, hardly any food, schools and universities were closed; the future was uncertain. The streets were covered with mountains of ruins, snow, and burnt-out vehicles. The population was dazed, still wandering around in the rubble, searching for relatives, food, and fuel. Everywhere people were dragging little carts or carrying bundles on their backs.

The Russians had eased up on capturing the men of the city; it seemed that they had filled their quota. The new danger on the streets was press gangs of unarmed police taking anybody they could catch to start the cleaning up. First those shanghaied removed the thousands of frozen bodies, loading them like logs onto large carts which were then pulled away by three or four men or women to mass burial sites. Luckily it was very cold, which prevented the outbreak of epidemics. Other forced labour began to remove the most dangerous ruins, working sometimes three or four stories high on top of dangerously swaying structures. This was not only risky, but very unpleasant work in the cold winter, with the wind blowing through the tall structures. The reward after a hard day's work was a cup of hot soup of undetermined content from a soup kitchen.

I was very careful to avoid being rounded up as I made my daily aimless travels with my handcart. The street markets were the only source of food or other items. Money was of no value; all purchases were based on barter, though by now most families were running out of barter items. The cafés, restaurants, and hotels were either in ruins or stood as empty shells. There was no place to go, except to friends and relatives, who sat shivering in their homes, wrapped in blankets. As soon as dusk came, everybody hurried to get off the streets because the curfew was still on.

To the west, the war was still raging; news was mostly passed on verbally; there were no newspapers and of course no radio, because there was no power. Rumour had it that to the east there were a few cities where the army had retreated without fighting, and according to some well-informed sources, in these areas life was returning to normal. Desperate people, mostly women, for it was not safe for men to travel, began to walk east in the hope of buying food. Women dressed in shabby winter coats with black babushkas on their heads, disguised as poor peasants, fanned out to the east from Budapest with empty bundles on their backs. They hoped to return with the bundles filled with food from the farms on the great plains, where there was an abundance of food to barter. Soon this became known as the march of the "bundle women," or Bundlers.

I was restless and had begun to think about going east myself when one day I met Pista Horvath, who had been slated to be the director of the Molière play that we had planned to produce and for which I had designed the stage sets, just before the German occupation, less than a year earlier. John Kolozs, my good friend, had introduced him to the group. They had been classmates at the Szeged Gymnasium. Pista had survived the war on his own in Budapest after his family had been deported from Szeged the previous summer. He wanted to go east to Szeged, where he had friends and hoped to settle down. This city had escaped the ravages of war intact and was supposed to be almost back to normal. It was one of the largest cities outside of Budapest, with a famous university where at the medical school Professor Albert Szentgyörgyi synthesised Vitamin "C" out of the paprika plant and received the Nobel Prize in recognition of his discovery. It was also my father's home town, and I had a few friends there, too, so we decided to go together the next day.

At the freight yards where my father's wine cellar was located, I heard from the policemen that every night empty freight trains went east to pick up ammunition and other goods for the Russian Army, which by now was fighting hundreds of miles to the west of Budapest on the Austrian border. They told me also that groups of bundling women left daily on the trains towards the east in search of food. So I arranged with the chief of the freight yards that we should go on one of these trains.   Late at night, he led us to the train that was scheduled to leave next, and together with hundreds of women, we climbed up onto the roofs of the boxcars and sat there shivering, waiting for the train to start.

A few hours later, huffing and puffing, it pulled out of the yard, but it did not go very far. After traveling the huge circle that curved around the city, it turned in an easterly direction, but then came to a halt on the open track. After a while, the day dawned, and we could see a working-class suburb in the distance. The train showed no sign of moving again. I stood up on the roof, and I could see shivering masses of women huddled together on the roofs of all the boxcars. Having had some recent experience with freight trains, I decided to climb down, and with the help of Pista, managed to open the big sliding door of our boxcar. It was empty. We called the women down, and in a few minutes, all the women on the other cars had climbed down, too, and found every boxcar empty. About 20 to a car, the Bundlers disappeared inside the empty train.

We sat down on the dirty wooden floor, the women surrounded by their bundles and baskets. All of them were city folk, but they had dressed for this trip for safety's sake in black peasant garb, with heavy black babushkas on their heads. No sooner did we settle down than the train began to move. We felt quite proud that we had managed to get inside.

After about ten minutes, with furious whistling, the train came to a halt again. I poked my head out and saw a group of Russian soldiers, machine pistols at the ready, around the locomotive, which was about 20 cars ahead of us. Two soldiers were climbing up into the first car and came down after a few minutes. They worked their way towards us, car by car. We were the only men on the train, and we were trapped; there was no way to get off. Luckily the women were anxious to save us from the Russians, each donating a piece of her black clothing. By the time the soldiers reached our car, we were sitting amidst the group, dressed as women, with babushkas on our heads.

One of the soldiers, a big beefy blonde young man, climbed up to our level with his "balalaika" machine pistol and looked us over carefully. To his disappointment, the women with us were past middle age. He looked from one to the other until his eyes bore into me. Even the big black babushka could not hide my young rosy cheeks, and I could sense his interest in me. My blood froze as I became aware of this, and pulling my rags even closer around me, I cast my eyes to the floor, hoping with all my power to survive this latest threat. All the women were holding their breath with me. After a very long moment, the soldier shook his head, turned, and jumped off the wagon. I started breathing again when I heard his boots crunching on the gravel ballast. But suddenly his retreating steps stopped. I could hear him turn around and come back. Pulling my babushka further down, I resolutely fixed my gaze downward.

Later, the others told me, he had poked his head back in through the door and, looking wistfully in my direction, stood motionless, as if unable to make up his mind. Then he was gone again. We did not speak until the checking of the train was finished. After a long while, the locomotive started up, and with the usual jarring and clanging, the wagons began to roll. Only then did we relax. Had he followed through with his Russian instinct for rape, I for sure would have ended up with a round of bullets from his machine pistol when he discovered what was hiding under my babushka.

But the odyssey of this trip was not over yet. Most of our companions were going to the town of Kecskemet, halfway to Szeged, about 100 kilometres from Budapest, in the rich heartland of the great Hungarian plain, where they expected to load up with food for their families.

Normally this trip should not have taken more than two hours by train, but ours lasted about 16 hours, with endless stops on the open track and at various small towns. It was past midnight when we finally arrived at the darkened, bombed-out station of Kecskemet. We knew that from here we would have to find some other transportation because the tracks to Szeged had been demolished in the war.

Pista and I planned to wait for the morning in the station, but once we were standing on the platform, it became evident that this was not possible. All was in ruins. Our companions and many of the other travelers scampered off and in no time disappeared in the darkness. The town lay some distance away; there were no lights, and the curfew was on. We had to find some place to wait for the morning, and reluctantly, we put our empty knapsacks on our backs and began to walk in the snowy darkness towards the direction where we thought the centre of the city lay. It was bitter cold, and the wind was blowing unhindered across the plains from the faraway mountains. The snow absorbed the noise of our steps as we trudged along a road with a few darkened houses here and there.

Suddenly, out of nowhere, we saw the lights of a vehicle approaching from a side lane. It came level with us, and its wheels crunched to a stop. It was a Russian jeep with military markings. Two huge figures jumped off, dressed in bulky overcoats. They were Russian female sergeants, their enormous bosoms bulging out from their uniforms. As we stood frozen with fear, one of them shone a flashlight on us and pulled out her sidearm pointing in our direction. They must have liked us, as they started laughing and yelling, "Dawaj! Dawaj!" and seconds later powerful hands started unbuttoning our pants, tearing at the material. It was too much, after the train ride and all the excitement there, to be attacked by two hungry armed Amazons. My only conscious thought while Pista and I were standing with our pants around our knees and their hands all over us was that they would surely kill us if we didn't perform. But it was evident that even with all the rude coaxing, we would disappoint them. What saved us was the appearance, far down the main road, of another pair of headlights from another approaching vehicle, bouncing along among the snowdrifts. In a second, our attackers jumped back into their jeep, backed around, and disappeared in a spray of fine powdered snow. We had just enough time to pull up our pants and hide behind the snowdrifts. The lights came closer and passed on in the direction taken by the jeep. As they went by, we saw clearly the stern faces of Russian military police under their fur hats, their machine pistols glistening in the light reflected by the snow. We were saved.

Hazard of the time

When the red taillights faded in the gloom, we ran to the nearest darkened house and started knocking furiously on the door. We were lucky. Inside, the farmhouse was already filled to the gills with bundlers from Budapest. The farmer understood our problem and let us in for a small payment. Ten minutes later, Pista and I were lying on the warm floor of the farm kitchen, with our knapsacks under our heads amid a bunch of people snoring away in the night. There was nothing else to do but to join them.

Early next morning, the farmer got us all onto his farm wagon (for a price), and his two strong horses began the long trip east on the snowy highway. Shortly after we left town, it became evident why the trains could not proceed to Szeged; a deep trench with tank traps stretched in both directions across the road. The endless flat plain was dotted with the wrecks of all kinds of armed vehicles, blown-up cannons, and burnt-out German tanks, all partly covered by snowdrifts. The train rails were bent into grotesque spaghetti-like configurations. A few ruined homesteads were also visible. Obviously a major battle had been fought here not very long ago. The concrete road stretched away straight as an arrow; there was no sign of life in this lonely plain.

The wagon moved slowly but steadily towards the next town, from where, beyond the battlefield, a small train still shuttled back and forth to and from Szeged. All the while, we were traveling southeast, and the snow began to disappear in patches; finally we arrived at the railway station, where a small regular passenger train was beginning to fill up with the bundling women and other travelers.

We got aboard. The train started, and hours later, early in the afternoon, I saw a mirage in the distance: church spires, large buildings huddled around them. But the mirage turned out not to be a mirage, but the city of Szeged, untouched by the war, hustling and bustling. Even streetcars could be seen from the train. Here was a miracle. For many months, I had seen only ruins and bedraggled straggling crowds patrolled by Russian soldiers in their jeeps. Suddenly here in front of us was a scene from before the war; even the railway station was untouched.

Pista and I got off with our knapsacks, and he began to lead me away from the station through the neat, clean streets, past the main square, to the house of an old classmate of his, George Rosman, who was also an acquaintance of mine from the long-gone days of summer holidays on Lake Balaton. George's father was a well-known furrier in Szeged who specialised in sheepskin coats. I had never been at his house in Szeged, and I was quite surprised at the large patrician residence where we now arrived.

Even more surprising were the fur storage and offices, located in the back in a separate loft building. Here we found George, who looked well-fed and well-dressed compared to us. Like me, George had been in a labour battalion and at the end of the war had found himself near Szeged when the Russians arrived. He joined the Russians as a partisan. George received us in the most warm and welcoming manner and led us into the huge fur storage, where he said we could stay as long as we wanted. The animal furs were stored ready to be made into fur linings and coats, one on top of another, filling most of the vast room to an even height of four feet or so. Around this huge island of furs, along the walls, were the suitcases and briefcases of many people, all of whom came from Budapest and knew George. He had welcomed them all and told us that they were out now all over town, but would be back at night and would sleep up in the furs. He said there were more than 50 male and female guests. We were invited to share the same accommodation.

I was anxious to walk around town, and after depositing my belongings in a corner, I left Pista and George and went for a walk. What a surprise it was to see life going on again as it had before the war, the population moving about on its business in a normal way, streetcars coming and going, disgorging their passengers and picking up new ones. All the little pubs and restaurants were open for business, and even the famous confectionery and café on Klauzal Square was open. Inside, the atmosphere was just like that in a pre-war café in Budapest: marble tables and bentwood chairs, all occupied by people chatting, smoking, and reading newspapers in bamboo frames, as was the custom in the central European cafés. Well-fed rosy-cheeked waitresses in black shiny uniforms with little white aprons were carrying cakes with espressos and glasses of complementary soda water and of course heaping plates full of rich whipped cream from behind the counter to the grey marble tables. I had to pinch myself to make sure that I was not dreaming. Soon, however, my eyes got used to the semi-gloom in the smoke-filled baroque interior. I realised that I was not dreaming; half the tables were occupied by friends and acquaintances from Budapest. They, too, recognised me, and I was asked to join many different tables with people who were all survivors of the siege, all with stories to tell and wanting to get the latest news of Budapest. It was truly miraculous. Quite a few were also boarders at George Rosman's fur hotel, with girlfriends and wives all sleeping atop the mountain of fur, all passing the day in town, just enjoying the holiday atmosphere.

Around dinnertime, a large group decided to go to the Hotel Tisza for a meal, and I joined them. There were no taxis, but just around the corner at the cab stand were ancient fiakkers and what in Hungary were called konflis (a one-horse coach), with grizzled drivers sitting on the box, waiting for custom. We all climbed aboard and in a convoy of three proceeded to the hotel. I found out that here the pengo, the Hungarian currency, was acceptable for small services; only major purchases, hotel bills and the like, had to be paid with U.S. dollars or gold, of which everybody was carrying a sufficient amount from Budapest.

The main dining room at the hotel was as I remembered it from before the war. Even the same old head waiter was there, carrying around his waist the traditional leather money pouches fastened to an ancient money belt. The menu card was not too elaborate, but the food tasted good after Budapest, and the local wine and soda water in siphon bottles helped to wash it down. The place filled up mostly with Budapest visitors, but there were a few high-ranking Russian officers, an unheard-of thing in Budapest. I was just getting used to the atmosphere when we paid our bills and marched out towards George's Fur Hotel. Those in the know told me that at 9:30 the lights went out in the warehouse, by order of the host. We made it back just in time. Pista Horvath was already up in the furs and was holding a place for me next to him. Many others, including quite a few couples, were also already stretched out. It was warm in the warehouse, but just in case, all seemed to have covered themselves with a soft blanket of furs. The lights went out as predicted, and we were ready for a good night's sleep after our strenuous trip. But sleep did not come for a very long time to Pista and me, the two weary travelers.

Everybody at George Rosman's inn was young, and all could have died a hundred different ways in the last year, but each had survived somehow, and now they were ready to resume living with extra vengeance. They were like maple trees after a long cold winter when the sun shines on them in the first warmth of spring, with the heat reflecting from the snow: the sap starts running fast with the joy of life. And in this fur storage, too, the sap was running. At first we could hear only a little stirring in the dark as the couples began to turn to each other. The mountain of fur muted the noises, but soon we had no doubt; new life was being created as nature took its course in this wonderful spring that against all odds these people had lived to see. It was quite late when finally everybody seemed to fall into exhausted sleep. Only Pista and I felt lonely, sleeplessly tossing among the warm smooth furs.

Bringing Home the Bacon

The days in Szeged went by fast. Pista began to negotiate for the reopening of the local theatre. He was determined to become a producer. I volunteered to design the sets for the first performance. We had had enough of the fur storage, so Pista moved in with some friends, and I moved into the Tisza Hotel.

I also visited the university and, although everything was still closed down, I heard that in April they planned to start lecturing again. After a day or two spent considering the future, I registered for the first year of medical school, because that was the most interesting faculty. Never before had I thought of becoming anything but an artist, but here we were, with the new world starting uncertainly, and being a doctor sounded like a good idea. This arranged, I went on day by day with the routine of Szeged life: confectionery, cafés, restaurants, and long walks. The weather kept improving.

As March came to its end, more travelers came from Budapest with the news that although food was still scarce, life had begun again there; even a few espresso bars had started up, and there was talk about the university opening again. My dollars were running out, and so I began to think of going back home for a visit to see how things were. An old classmate of mine from the Lutheran High School, John Dick, whose younger brother Tomi had the frightening adventure of being shot on the Danube banks by the Arrowcross and somehow surviving, had also turned up from Budapest some weeks earlier and wanted to return again. And so one morning, after saying temporary good-byes to Pista Horvath, the Rosmans, and other friends (I still fully intended to come back in a few weeks' time), with knapsacks and bundles bulging with Szeged salami and other goods unheard-of in recent months in Budapest, we climbed back into the little shuttle train and started the return trip. By noon, we were back at the station where the rail line ended.

Hundreds of bundlers from the train were still getting organised on the platform, but we were already outside, where on the little square, farm wagons were waiting to hire out for the highway trip to Kecskemet and the main rail line. After quick negotiations with a farmer, our little group was first on a big wagon, our bundles and knapsacks on the floor boards. Six similarly laden people joined us, and the heavily loaded wagon pulled away.

The farmer soon got us out onto the concrete highway, and the return journey commenced. But the steel-shod wheels ground against the concrete, and the wagon laboured, protesting under the load, the horses and the farmer not too happy either. The landscape was just as bleak as a month ago, and although the snow was only visible in a few patches, the wind was still howling from the north. Our backs turned to the wind, we tried to keep warm. Conversation was impossible because of the wind and the groaning of the wagon as it lurched forward. Then about an hour into the journey, one of the axles broke under the load, and the wheels buckled as the wagon settled against the concrete with a grinding noise. There was nothing to do for all of us but to gather up our knapsacks and bundles and start up the road, walking.

As the other six people started towards Kecskemet, I had a sudden idea—I was still playing the old pinball game. "Let's go back towards Szeged." So as the six people began hiking up the road, we began to move in the opposite direction. We did not walk longer than ten minutes when from the direction of Szeged, a camouflaged military truck appeared, bearing down on us. I flagged it down. In the cab were two soldiers dressed in uniforms like the Russians. They turned out to be Tito's soldiers coming from the Yugoslav border, which was only ten kilometres from Szeged. They were heading to the Yugoslav Embassy in Budapest on some mission. Offering them ten dollars, I negotiated a ride. We climbed up into the open back of the truck, which was filled up to the sideboards with some load covered with an old tarpaulin. We hunkered down behind the cab for wind protection, and the trip to Budapest resumed. The truck gathered speed, and soon we passed the farmer, who stood scratching his head by his broken wagon. The six bundlers were by now quite a long way ahead, but we caught up with them, too, and as they were standing off to the side, trying to flag down our truck, we waved proudly, as with their faces turned up, they receded and disappeared from our sight.

It was bitterly cold up there on the truck, which was now hurtling down the road at a speed of at least 50 miles an hour. John Dick and I were lying on top of the canvas, exposing ourselves as little as possible to the biting wind. After a while, my curiosity compelled me to lift up the corner of the tarp to find out what the uncomfortable hard cargo was under it: we were sitting on about a ton of hard, frozen slabs of bacon. Obviously the soldiers came from the rich farm area just south of the Hungarian border (which before the end of the 1914–18 war, when it was sliced off and given to newly created Yugoslavia, had been the granary of Hungary). Wheels turned in my head, and I knocked on the window of the cab. The soldiers stopped the truck, and I climbed down for a conference. In broken German, they explained to me that, taking advantage of their mission to Budapest, they had loaded up the truck illegally with all the bacon they could get and were planning to sell it on the black market in the hungry city. It took me only a few minutes to convince them of the difficulty of unloading all this bacon there at once, and they were quite happy to sell it to me on the spot for a promised $100, agreeing to deliver their cargo to Molnar utca. Two hours later, I guided them there, to Eta's apartment. At the last minute, the soldiers had an afterthought: they raised the price to $150. In those days in Budapest, it was still a bargain, and I agreed. Luckily Eta was at home, and while she dug out the money from a secret hiding place, I waited with the soldiers and the idling truck. The money came, and the exchange took place. The two soldiers carried all the bacon into our part of the cellar, while the old caretaker was excitedly hopping around on his peg leg, pointing the way down the steps. Afterwards the soldiers carefully counted the money, a collection of tattered one-, five-, and ten-dollar notes, and drove away in a spume of blue smoke, the engine roar reverberating in the narrow street.

Only then did I enter the vaulted portals of our building, dragging my bulging knapsack with me. I had brought home the bacon! My triumphal entrance was observed by many of the residents lining the arcaded corridors upstairs; I had left Budapest to find some food in the country, and I returned with loot of legendary proportions. I felt like the conquering hero, a Roman proconsul returning from Africa, marching through a triumphal arch at the Forum, his slaves behind him, staggering with the booty.

Blue Horizons

January 18, 1945, was the day I survived World War II, but the elation over that much-awaited liberation had been short-lived. We had thought of the Russians as true allies of the West, and during the war, we were quite aware that the social fabric in Hungary would have to change. A degree of idealism even enabled us to overlook the horrors of early Communism, the murderous Moscow show trials of the 1930s. We believed that Stalin, "Uncle Joe" to the Americans, was going to be grateful to the Allies for all their help and, once reconciled with his people through the Great Patriotic War, would change over to enlightened socialism, giving all Russians a good life after their great sacrifices. The soldiers, the fighters against Nazism, would be good people, we thought, and no harm would come to us from them.

This theory did not survive two days of Russian occupation. We had to make a quick 180-degree turn in our thinking. The Russians, we realised to our dismay, were a new enemy, dragging tens of thousands of people to their gulags and raping and pillaging all over the country. The Asiatic soldiers were utterly primitive; most had never seen a water closet, never owned a watch, and had hardly any education. The exceptions were the NKVD, the uniformed secret police, who came with their lists and, just as they did with Raoul Wallenberg, caused many prominent Hungarians to disappear.

We decided then that we had to dig in, without much hope of restoring our national life, and prepare to live under Russian Communist rule. In Szeged, we saw that a semblance of the old life did exist, but we could not really believe in the mirage.

Now at the end of March 1945, when I returned to Budapest, miraculously in four short weeks everything had changed. Spring had come, and like daffodils from under the snow, cafés and espresso bars had sprung up from under the ruins. With the sunshine, the population seemed to have shed their skins from the siege, digging out lighter clothing. The Russians seemed less visible, there was more food available on the black market, the worst of the mountains of ruins had retreated from the streets, and, like my father, other businessmen and factories were beginning to try to operate again. Suddenly people became optimistic; Communism and the Russians appeared less threatening. There was another 180-degree revolution in our thoughts. Perhaps law and order would return. Newspapers began to appear, and with them the news of the new Hungarian provisional government, approved by the liberators and with a temporary seat in Debrecen.

The new government consisted of respectable middle-class opposition groups and small landowners' groups mixed with socialists and representatives of the Communists who had returned from Moscow. One of its first acts was to bring in agrarian reform. Until this moment, the majority of farmland in the country had been owned by the great landowners, the gentry, and the aristocracy; 400 holdings represented almost all the large farms in Hungary and employed about three million peasants. By decree, these large estates were now divided among the peasants, 30 to 50 acres to each. (Future compensation to the former landholders was promised, but up to the day of writing, has failed to materialise.)

Land reform had been the hope of the Hungarian peasantry for generations, and this Communist-inspired gift was greeted with enthusiasm by all except the land magnates, and at the time, nobody worried about them. It was a shrewd move, a reassurance to the farmers that the policies that led to the deaths of millions of peasants in Russia in the 1920s would not be repeated; rather, the new government recognised small private holdings. No wonder that these nearly five million formerly disenfranchised, poverty-stricken farmers lined up solidly behind the new small landowners' party.

This happened almost immediately after my return from Szeged and confirmed my belief that Hungary would be given free democratic elections. Nobody doubted that an election would go against the socialists and Communists and that the occupying Russians would return home.

At the end of March, the Palatine Joseph Technical University reopened its doors, and, forgetting about returning to Szeged and becoming a doctor, I registered in the faculty of architecture, a discipline nearer my old dream of becoming an artist. The vast halls and lecture rooms were full of shattered glass and other wreckage, and there was no heating. Under the guidance of the professors, the students began the term by removing the debris. More than a thousand engineering and architectural students had come back to continue their education where the war had interrupted it, and to these were added the influx of new students. About 200 students registered in the first year of architecture, among them myself. For weeks, we enthusiastically worked away with shovels and pickaxes until, early in April, about the time the Russians chased the last German and Hungarian armies out of the country, formal lectures began.

The professors were all of the old guard, serious dignified people, and they taught us exactly as they had in past years, as if none of the cataclysmic events of the past months had happened. The windows had not yet been glazed, and teachers and students alike turned out in tattered overcoats for the lectures that now went on in a regular manner. It was nice to be a student again. At this time, the politicising of the university had not yet started, so no time was wasted with that. The students were a mixed lot, from all social classes, and with quite a few girls, too. Most of us were determined to do well, and I discovered that my years studying art and the two years at the School of Economic Sciences had not been wasted. Design in the first year was pretty elementary, but I enjoyed every minute, and I made many good friends.

Rebuilding Prosperity

Meanwhile, my father, with more energy that I could ever have mustered, proceeded not only with the reorganisation of his own business, but also with the revitalisation of Hungary's wine export trade. Wine was always an important hard-currency earner for Hungary. Now, with the war nearing its end, wine would become the only major export item that the country could produce, promising hard currency earnings of several million dollars. This was desperately needed by the country for the rebuilding of the economy, something that even the Communists in the provisional government understood and were therefore willing to support all efforts to promote the wine export trade.

My father convened the surviving wine exporters, restarted the Wine Exporters' Association, and was promptly elected president. My uncle Salusinszky, the father of my cousins, Pista and Marika, and one of the leading pre-war corporate lawyers, had died suddenly, and his magnificent office and conference rooms were standing idle next to the family residence on Bathory utca. By luck, the building had escaped all the ravages of war, and because their mother needed extra income, the Wine Exporters' Association moved in and set up its office.

The first task of the wine exporters was quite obvious: regardless of whose army was occupying the land or even whose property it was, big landowner or small farmer, year after year, each spring, the vines came to life, and the new leaves and fruit began to grow. From that moment until the grapes were ripe and ready for harvest in the fall, the crop was threatened by a multiplicity of disasters. The leaves could freeze in the cold early spring; there could be too many rainy days in the summer; clouds obscuring the sun could slow the ripening process. But the biggest danger of all came with the beneficial hot days of summer, when myriads of insects and creepie crawlies found the grape vines, particularly the ripening grapes, the most delicious of snacks. Their attacks could ruin the most promising crop.

The traditional defence of the farmers in these less environmentally conscious days was the careful spraying of all individual grape plants with a copper solution, which had a devastating effect on the fauna. The exporters realised that to have wine to export, they must find a way to supply each individual farmer with copper solution. This presented almost insurmountable problems. Copper was one of the rarest wartime materials, and our little war-torn country had none. Thousands of tons of copper crystals were needed. Where to get them and how to pay for them were the big questions.

Meanwhile, the provisional government moved to Budapest in April, the various ministries started to function, and the moderate civil servants who had not escaped to Germany in front of the Russian armies crawled out from the cellars, brushed off their good suits, and were back at their desks. In pre-war years, a delegation consisting of the heads of the Wine Section of the External Trade Office, accompanied by the leading exporters, would go to Switzerland to negotiate the annual export agreement. Similar delegations would go to Germany and Poland. It was obvious that this year there would be only one market, Switzerland, and that the best of the crop would have to be sold on that market. The provisional government was enthusiastic at the prospect, and thanks to the advice of the External Trade Office, it realised that the complex task of bringing in the year's crop could be handled only by the wine exporters. Only the wine exporters had the contacts with the farmers and the connections in the wine-importing countries necessary for commercial negotiations. Planning was well advanced, even before the war finally came to a halt, as the Allied and Russian troops met on the Elbe and the Russians hoisted their flag on top of the Brandenburg Gate.

Of course I was faithfully attending lectures at the university, but I followed my father's activities in the afternoon and evening. By now, my father had a driver, Szücs, who had been our truck driver before 1944, and who now was also acting caretaker for the family of a former classmate of mine which had a villa almost opposite the Lutheran Gymnasium on Queen Wilhelmina Allee. He kept our car in the garage of the villa and reported to Molnar utca early every morning. My only way to get hold of the car was to volunteer to drive my father to his meetings, wait in the car outside—unattended cars were immediately stolen to disappear without a trace—

and when my father was through for the day, take him home and then take off with the car myself for a few hours. Late at night, I would pick up Szücs at his favourite pub, after which he would drive me home and then take the car to his villa's garage. As a result of this program, I was always up to date on the Wine Exporters' activities.

To resolve the copper problem, my father got in touch with the owner of the largest chemical and fertilizer company and negotiated a loan from the government of several hundred thousand dollars, repayable in Hungarian currency. With the funds available, the chemical company purchased the necessary copper in Switzerland. This was shipped to the plant via already-liberated Austria, turned into copper crystals, and packaged ready for shipping to the farmers, who would mix up the preparation for spraying.

By now, inflation had begun to speed up, and the government loans were based, not on the currency, but on an inflationary factor connected to the future wholesale price of wine. The farmers had no money to pay for the copper solution, but eventually my father figured out a formula according to which, after the harvest, the farmers would pay for each 1 kg (plus or minus 1 litre) of copper crystals with ten litres of wine of a set quality. In practical terms, this meant that each farmer would give in payment about one-third of his crop. He was then free to sell the balance to the exporters at the going rate. The exporters had to pay for the copper and its manufacture into crystals, and they ran a very high risk should the crops fail. In any event, this did not happen, for the God of the Hungarians gave the farmers that year the biggest bumper crop in recent memory.

Meanwhile, the Hotel Bristol, the only one of the hotels on the elegant Danube promenade to survive the systematic Russian bombing more or less intact, had been patched up sufficiently so that with my old friends Mr. Miszla and Mr. Kossowitz at the front desk and my cousin Peter as a bellhop, it reopened its doors. I began to divide my time between university, my father's transportation, and the hotel. Often

Peter and I would sit in the little back office, drinking for the first time in our lives a strange dark liquid that an American guest had donated to the reception desk. It had the odd name (to us) of "Coca Cola"! Having been brought up on wine and Turkish and espresso coffee, we were not impressed and soon returned to coffee drinking. Until this day, I have not succeeded in getting used to it.

Kossovitz and Miszla kept reminiscing about the good and bad old days, and they never failed to complain about the mystery of the disappearance after the siege of their huge stash of "Darling" cigarettes. I listened, but never ventured any opinion on the disappearance, merely noting that like Camel cigarettes, which the Darlings were imitating, I had heard they were harmful to health. The upstairs bar, a small intimate affair, had also reopened with the same pre-war North African bartender and legendary coffee maker, Ali, with his red fez, in charge. On certain days, a well-known piano player, Agiacs, used to play at the bar piano. By now inflation was rampant, so I opened an account with Mr. Kossovitz by depositing $20 in his safe. Every time I charged at the bar, he deducted an amount equivalent to the value that day of payment in Hungarian pengos, the currency in which Ali conducted transactions.

Having organised the production of the all-important copper crystals, the wine exporters sent out their troops all across the country. Contracts were made with the wine growers, and then the exporters' trucks began to ship the necessary materials. This way, the exporters pre-purchased one-tenth of the best of the upcoming vintage.

My father now had to turn his attention to the all-important task of organising the team that would negotiate the sale of the best of the crop in Switzerland. Although my father was already a leading exporter before the war, the government-to-government negotiations were always led by Mr. Graf of the megafirm of the time, Graf and Lessner. Graf had been my father's predecessor in the president's chair, but as a devoted Nazi, he had departed Hungary before the Russian onslaught.

Happily his partner, Mr. Lessner, a Jew, had survived the German occupation, and so my father approached him for advice and know-how. Just about the time Hitler committed suicide and the Third Reich finally collapsed, Father arranged to see Mr. Lessner at his villa on St. Gellert's mountain.

This was an event that I did not want to miss, and having brought Szücs along for the drive, I was able to accompany my father while Szücs watched the car. Lessner was approaching the biblical threescore and ten years, and in addition, we had heard that he had a very severe heart condition. Nevertheless, because he had known and liked my father for many years, he had agreed to the meeting. The door of the villa was opened by his housekeeper, who led us upstairs to the master bedroom. Mr. Lessner received us in his large double bed, propped up on huge pillows. He was a very distinguished elderly gentleman with gracious manners, and he seemed very ill. He turned his pale drawn face towards my father, greeted him affectionately, and indicated two armchairs for us to sit in. My father's chair was drawn quite close to the old man. I still remember the furnishings of the room, which were antique Viennese Biedermeyer pieces, the two armchairs upholstered in a corded hunting-green material. Mr. Lessner knew that my father was the new president of the wine exporters, and before talking business, he enquired about my father and myself and about a few wine-exporting colleagues. He heard that my father had rehabilitated Feri Wiedman, his partner in the twenties (who was also my godfather) and had accepted him as a member of the association. Smiling feebly, he remarked that the scoundrel deserved worse treatment, but admitted that his main sin was opportunism; he had done no harm to anybody and could not be held responsible for the fact that his nephew was the personal pilot of the recently departed Adolf Hitler.

Meanwhile, coffee and little cakes were served and a glass of mineral water brought for the patriarch, who already seemed exhausted. He revived for a two-hour conversation, which was perhaps more of a lecture or a monologue. My father stayed silent, listening to every word, occasionally asking a question, but mostly just absorbing the flow of information. I did not understand all the details of the conversation, but I knew that Mr. Lessner was passing on the baton to the new generation. My father had many friends in the wine business in Switzerland; many had been his customers for more than twenty years, but he knew little about the actual annual marketing negotiations which he would now lead. Mr. Lessner did not short-change him; he told all about the methods and tactics of official negotiations, elaborating on what my father might expect from the Swiss government representatives. As far as the Hungarian government team was concerned, Mr. Lessner recommended that he rely without hesitation on the knowledge of Dr. Kurtzi, head of the wine section in the foreign trade office, an honourable man and a wise and shrewd negotiator.

At this point, Mr. Lessner leaned back in his pillows, reached over for a pill, gulped it down with the remainder of his mineral water, and because he was now clearly totally exhausted, we quickly took our leave. As we headed to the door, he opened his eyes and said, "I know, John, that you will be successful, and I wish you good luck in your enterprise." Then he asked to be kept informed and added, "Don't hesitate to call if I can do anything further." I was sure that I saw tears in my father's eyes as we descended the stairs, which was very unusual for this tough retired soldier.

We got into the little BMW sedan, not without difficulty because it was a two-door model, Szücs engaged the clutch, and we descended St. Gellert's Mountain on the almost-empty streets. "We will keep calling on the old man regularly," my father decided. This was not possible, because two weeks later we heard that his heart, undoubtedly weakened further by the recent trials of hiding from the Arrowcross, refused to work any longer. The end, we heard, was peaceful.

Preparations for the trip to Switzerland went on. My father spoke to Dr. Kurtzi, so highly recommended by Mr. Lessner, but this, too, was not an easy task because Kurtzi lay at home, ill with cancer of the lung, which according to the doctors had been brought on by smoking two packs of Darling cigarettes a day. Nevertheless, he, too, rose to the occasion like an old cavalry horse when the bugle calls for a charge.

So, fortified by good advice, my father was now ready for the Swiss negotiations. The war was still not yet over when plans were made for travel to Switzerland. This was easier said than done because there were no trains from Budapest to Vienna, although from Vienna we heard that the famous Arlberg Express was regularly commuting overnight to Zurich, travelling through the Alps and arriving in the city in time for breakfast. With the blessings of the provisional government, the delegation finally managed to depart from Budapest on a Russian troop transport truck driven by a Russian Army driver. The delegation consisted of my father, my godfather, Feri Wiedman, and Rudi Habel, head of the third-largest wine-export firm, together with representatives of the Central Bank, the Ministry of External Trade, and the Hungarian Wine Export Agency. Knowing that, unlike in Budapest, there was no food in Russian-occupied Vienna, the delegation arranged to travel with a large suitcase of meat and other essentials. Their favourite hotel, the Meissel and Schaden, just off Kartnerstrasse, had been bombed to the ground, but luckily the Hotel Kranz across the road (now called the Ambassador) was largely intact, and it was here that the delegation climbed off the truck and checked in. In Vienna at that time, even with ration coupons, little food was available. Looking at the people on the street, it was evident that hunger was the biggest problem. Immediately upon arrival, a few members of the group visited the kitchen and handed over their imported Hungarian veal schnitzels and other edibles not seen on the tables of Vienna for many months.

The next day, the group drove to the railway station and boarded the formerly glamorous Arlberg Express, the Austrian cousin of the Orient Express. It was dirty and shabby on the outside, but inside it retained some traces of the old glamour. All went to their allocated sleeping compartments, and then after dark they walked along the narrow jarring corridors to the dining car. To their surprise, the car was full, all tables already taken. The delegation had to line up to await the second service. "Who are all these well-dressed Austrian ladies and gentlemen, and where are they going?" my father enquired. The head waiter explained, "This is an international train, and there are plentiful good foods and drinks, all served without coupons. All the passengers you see are Viennese, coming with us to the border—they are not allowed to go beyond—for the purpose of eating a good dinner, breakfast, and lunch, and the same on the return trip." Sure enough, at the border in Buchs, after having crossed the Russian, American, and French occupation zones in Austria, our fellow passengers presented their identity cards to the succession of military authorities and disembarked, disappearing down the long platform. When the express pulled into St. Gallen in Switzerland after crossing the border, only the delegation remained on board.

Two weeks later, the delegation returned to Budapest with a multi-million Swiss franc agreement. They came back on another Russian transport truck, and my father arrived at Molnar utca, not without presents for Eta and myself from the undiminished plenty of the stores on the Zurich Bahnhofstrasse. Not the least memorable of these was a huge bunch of ripe bananas, a delicacy not seen in Hungary since 1938, and I could not resist the temptation to walk down the noon promenade on the newly functioning Vig utca, chatting with friends and all the time casually peeling and eating bananas. There were enough for all my friends, and after all we had been through, the danger of slipping on a banana peel did not worry us.

From that time on, life in Budapest accelerated. In June, the electrical power was restored, which made studying and working much easier. With electricity came the streetcars, radio, and cinemas, and the famous spas and steam baths reopened as well. A professor of engineering, using various diameters of cast-iron gas pipe, the only possible construction material remaining, designed an ingenious temporary bridge which crossed the Danube near the Parliament buildings. Apart from the Russian army's temporary wooden pile bridge, on the construction of which in January I had briefly assisted myself, this was the first new bridge connecting Buda with Pest. All day long, a line of trucks and horse-drawn carriages, as well as a few motorcars, lined up at both bridgeheads, waiting for hours to cross the narrow bridge. All the other beautiful Budapest bridges were now rusting structures dangling into the swiftly flowing Danube. Only the arched Franz Joseph Bridge near the technical university had been temporarily repaired. Here a gap of 100 meters where the centre had been blown away was filled by a wooden truss structure mounted on ten Danube barges. This was connected to the remainder of the original steel bridge on both sides by hinged wooden ramps which enabled the structure mounted on the barges to ride with the river as it rose and dropped in response to rains or floods. The traffic, mostly pedestrians, horse-drawn wagons, and the occasional truck, first had to climb up onto the original bridgehead, then drop down on the ramp to the wooden structure, then up again on another ramp, until finally on the remainder of the truncated old bridge it could descend onto the opposite embankment. It was an interesting trip which I and my classmates had to negotiate twice a day on our trips to and from the university.

But never mind; the two halves of the city were again connected, for commerce and for pleasure, and with the weather improving, masses of city dwellers took to the Buda Hills, on foot or by streetcar, and a few, like us, by motorcar.

My studies had progressed in the most rewarding way, and we were nearing the end of the first semester. My father's firm was hard at work organising the distribution of the copper-spraying solution, and Eta and my father took to crossing the river on Sundays with me at the wheel to picnic in the garden of our villa on the Hill of the Roses. While there, they inspected the progress of the reconstruction of our house, which had taken about 40 artillery shots in the siege. In a quiet city hall ceremony one day, they got married, and we planned to move back into the villa when the repairs were complete, as we expected they would be by fall.

I had plenty of time to drive around while they picnicked, and I acquired a girl friend or two, nothing very serious, mind you. The semester ended, and to make up for the lost year at the end of the war, the University decided to have only a three-week break before the second semester, which would last through the rest of the summer up to mid-September. Immediately we would then go into the first semester of the second year and be back to normal.

That spring, the biggest problem facing our war-torn country was the inflation of the Hungarian pengo. At the end of the war and immediately afterwards, no one would accept the pengo, and all commercial transactions, even the buying of basic foodstuffs, were done on a barter basis. But by February, as business started up again, the pengo was back in use. Wages and salaries were paid according to a scale set by the government. But immediately inflation began to spiral, first by 50% per annum, a month later by 500% per annum, because the government was printing valueless currency. At this point, the government could not reset the wage scale fast enough.

What saved the workers was that employers began to pay in goods as well as money. This for us was not too difficult, because we already had a strong personal currency in the wine. Every week, employees received substantial amounts of wine, which they and their families then used for bartering. In addition, my father dispatched trucks laden with wine to the countryside; this was then traded to the farmers in exchange for eggs, flour, bacon, meat, milk, and other products. Each Friday morning, these were distributed to the staff, who were then given the rest of the day off to spend their wages, which were of course paid in cash. Everyone rushed to the markets to get rid of their money, buying whatever was on sale. No one wanted to be caught with money, because by now inflation was rising exponentially on an ever-steeper curve.

For instance, one pound of tomatoes would cost 1000 pengos on the market one day; by the next, it cost 5000. A week later, the same tomatoes would go for a million. The farm wives set out small blackboards on top of their stalls on which they marked the prices hourly with chalk. To keep up with inflation, the government kept printing bills in larger and larger denominations. In the end, the farm wives lost control of the dazzling figures and simply nailed the corresponding notes onto the board: 1 pound of tomatoes = one purple note (one million pengos) plus one blue note (500 thousand pengos) plus two green notes (100 thousand pengos each). The wages could not quite keep up; it was the weekly allocation of goods that enabled families to survive.

Everyone was not as lucky as a wine exporter, of course, so to obtain the necessary foodstuffs, firms which sold or manufactured non-barterable goods usually had to send out their trucks to trade with the farmers in U.S. dollars or gold. Everybody traded, and everything was traded. Soon the middlemen arrived, the black marketeers who put themselves between the bartering parties. These made large profits in dollars, gold, and goods, but they were a necessary element now in the conduct of commerce, because in these postwar days, the traditional infrastructure no longer operated. Although the black marketeers profited, few were dishonest, at least not in a scandalous way. Moneychangers were also part of the food chain. These opened little storefront banks around the former bourse. Strange to say, they created a stable market in dollars and gold, and because the government had no resources other than their printing presses, a laissez-faire attitude developed.

Back to the Brickworks

Early in the summer of 1945, lectures came to a halt. Most people passed their end-of-semester exams easily, and then came three short weeks of holiday before the second semester started. Pali Rona, who immediately after the war had married his girlfriend Joli, and I decided to take a few days to visit

Matraderecske where we had spent the previous memorable summer at Bell's brickworks. We had made friends in the village, and we wanted to know how they came through the war.

My father agreed to let me take our little BMW for this trip. Trains and buses were still not operating. To take a hundred-mile trip with a car was a major undertaking. There were no gas stations or repair shops in the country. With the help of our driver Szücs, we lashed four jerry cans of gas to the rear bumper and in addition to the two spare tires, we carried about half a dozen inner tubes of various German "ersatz" Suva rubber materials. The tires were the real problem because all of them were retreads and in the warm weather had the habit of regularly stripping their treads. Even if they held, one could expect several punctures on a trip, because the only transportation that the farmers had on the country roads was horse-drawn wagons, and the roads were littered with the nails that dropped out of the horseshoes.

Our preparations got underway just about the same time that Roosevelt, Churchill, Charles de Gaulle, and Stalin were getting ready for the first postwar conference at Potsdam. This was of no interest to us; we were not aware of the significant decisions that were to be made there which would affect our future and the future of our country.

On a beautiful summer morning, I picked up Pali and his wife, and soon we had left the ravaged city and were merrily rolling with the trusty BMW on the dusty road towards the Matra mountains. After Gyongyos, the road started to climb, and about every twenty minutes, the radiator boiled over, and we had to stop on the roadside to wait for the water to cool. This was not because of lack of oxygen, as can happen in the Alps, but mainly because the radiator was leaky. In those days, the cure for this problem was to throw a bit of linseed into the water. This temporarily plugged the holes, but the pressure of the overheated water reopened them. This was routine. We pulled up under the shade of a mulberry tree, spread our blanket, ate a few sandwiches, and drank a little wine. As soon as the water cooled, I removed a handful of linseeds, and we were on our way again. To replace the radiator was an impossible task at the time.

After a few stops for this, and to change punctured tries, late Saturday afternoon we rolled into the main street of Matraderecske, the peaceful and unchanged village that we had come to visit. A car equipped for a fair was an unusual sight for the inhabitants of this remote place, and soon we were surrounded by many villagers. "Brer" Nagy and Imre Kovacs, "the Milk," the two foremen, appeared and, recognising us, greeted us in the warmest way, together with the other villagers. Imre Kovacs invited us to stay in his farmhouse, a beautiful old whitewashed house with its two shuttered front windows facing the street. A long covered brick-paved porch led to the barnyard. Its carved wood balustrades were topped with flower boxes in which red geraniums were already blooming.

The front room, called the "clean room" in farmers' houses, was a museum piece. It opened from the huge farm kitchen and got its name because it was never used. Or hardly ever, because this is where Imre Kovacs and his wife led us. It was symmetrically furnished: one narrow bed on each side of the two front windows, and a smaller one abutting the one at the left. Each bed had about six feather mattresses, the top one about four feet from the floor, covered by bedcovers embroidered in colourful traditional Hungarian patterns. One large and one small pillow sat on top of each bed and had similarly embroidered pillowcases. We had never slept in such beds. In the middle of the room stood a large wooden table with carved legs, surrounded by six chairs. The table was covered by an ornamental table cloth, over which hung a copper and green-glass oil lamp. On the wooden floors were hooked rugs made of strips of coloured cloth.

He bade us put down our small bags and led us back into the kitchen, where we sat down beside the whitewashed corner country oven with its traditional rounded bulky shape on an oak bench that ran the full length of the kitchen. This was the traditional sleeping bunk in farm homes, the preserve of granny.

By this time, "Brer" Nagy and many other old friends and their wives had come along, and we all sat around the rough-hewn kitchen table. A demijohn of wine and glasses appeared, and the conversation started. They all wanted to know what had happened to us after the little train took us away last year. A lot had happened, and we kept talking for a long while. Some food appeared also, and we ate together.

We were curious about their story, too, and knew enough not to be deceived by the unchanged appearance of the village. Slowly they began to talk, and from the events they related, we learned that trouble had reached paradise, too. Around November, late in the fall, the Hungarian Army retreated through this area, with the Russians only hours away. A lot of village soldiers came with the army and deserted when they got so close to home. Their families hid them in barns, attics, root cellars, and the like and went on with business as usual. Just ahead of the Russian Army—people could hear the booming of the artillery and machine-gun fire—an army truck drove in with a few harried field gendarmes who wanted to make a quick job of rousting out the deserters. They went to a likely farm and began to search.

They seemed to know their business and in no time at all dragged out a frightened soldier from a little tool shed behind the manure pile. With his mother crying and begging, they tied his hands behind him and took him to the village square. By then, all the villagers were there in front of the church. The sergeant of the field gendarmes had the truck back up to a large tree at the side of the church. A rope was hastily thrown over a strong branch. The gendarmes surrounded the truck with their machine pistols facing the crowd. Two of them climbed on the platform of the truck and hoisted the boy up between them. The crowd surged forward, but the guns were cocked. In just a few minutes, the rope was put around the young soldier's neck, the motor started up, and while the terrified farmers watched, the sergeant ordered the driver to move forward. When the body stopped jerking and they were sure that the soldier was dead, one by one the field gendarmes climbed up, still facing the crowd, and the truck drove away, raising the dust as it went. The gendarmes knew what they were doing; by the time they drove off, about 20 other village boys had come out of hiding, and working their way through the backs of the gardens and fields, ran to rejoin their units. The gendarmes drove off to another village. Most of the boys survived the war and worked their way back from the prisoner-of-war camps. These were the days when many victims of the war—soldiers, deportees—from whom until now nothing had been heard, began to reappear, giving great joy and raising hopes of more lost people turning up.

It was quite late when the last of the wine was finished and the last visitor left. We climbed up into the marvellously soft tall beds, Pali and I in the ones on each side of the windows, and Joli in the bed at Pali's feet.

We woke early with gigantic hangovers, but a breakfast of double-smoked bacon and a couple of shot glasses of Schnapps woke us up. "Brer" Nagy invited almost the whole village to join us for the Sunday meal after the noon Mass, but first we went on a nostalgic walk, starting at the little railway station, which was deserted, the weeds growing between the unused tracks. Near the freight shed on the ramp stood abandoned all the pallets of tens of thousands of bricks that we had manufactured. These never managed to follow their owner, Mr. Bell, to the west.

The track from here led to the Bell Manor, which stood empty, locked up, but obviously cared for. Next door was the observatory tower, its door hanging open on its hinges. Joli wanted to climb up the narrow winding stone steps, but Pali, still hung over, lay down in the tall neglected grass. So I climbed up with her to the top to see the view from where we had never been allowed to come before. It was worth the climb: the rolling hills with the fields below and the distant vista of higher mountains beyond, dark green with their pine forests, were magnificent from six stories up. The telescope was long gone. We descended and wound our way towards the brickworks. The drying sheds where Pali Hirsch had kept his pemmican depots were empty; only some birds flew through their open sides. The factory, too, was deserted. Now here we were at our former barracks. I found my bunk and my initials carved into the rafter just at the spot where I used to feed my domesticated mouse. The wooden box where Samuel Feder, our "batman", kept our utensils was still there, its hinges rusting. Had I known about Andrew Wyeth then, I would have thought that the scene was familiar. The only difference was that in his pictures, the houses stand empty, the people gone, it seems forever; on the other hand, we were alive, we survived, we came back. It was all a powerful reminder of what had happened, of what could have happened. But we were alive, alive and well after all the pinball games. As I wandered around, I was thinking of the many friends lost in the wild games. Of George Ligeti, who but for his desire for one more ice cream, would have been here with us through the summer of 1944, would not have disappeared into the German machine.

The clay pit, too, was just as we remembered it in the hillside, the narrow-gauge rails of the pit train now rusting, together with a few siding switches and some of the clay gondolas tipped over after the last day's work. We did not climb up into the hills; instead, we walked down the meadow to the spot where we used to have our picnic lunches on visiting Sundays under the willow trees on the banks of the little creek. Beyond that, I could see a few houses of the gypsy quarter and the place where on the night of the wedding we danced to the gypsy music with the beautiful gypsy girls.

In the distance, we heard the noon bell ringing in the church spire. It was time to return to the village. By the time we came out of the meadow to the road and reached "Brer" Nagy's homestead, everybody was gathered in their Sunday best, the married women with their dark babushkas, the unmarried ones bareheaded. Tables were set with huge plates laden with breaded spring chickens. The farmers kept their habit of preparing the chickens, the drumsticks with the scrawny claws left on.

A barrel of beer was on tap, and demijohns of wine on top of all the tables. Everybody that we knew was here; even some of the gypsies were around, the same band that had played on the wedding day were tuning their violins. We spoke, drank, spoke to more and more people, and a wonderful tipsy feeling came over me. We were all alive, filled with life. The party went on long, long after the sun set. It was a wonderful reunion with the wonderful honest Hungarian farmers, friends in those difficult times and now.

Next morning, we said our farewells to the village and, promising to return, climbed aboard the old BMW. I quickly put the car in gear to force myself to leave. On the way back, we drove to Parad, the target of many of our forced marches. The beautiful main square was empty, no tourists, no spa visitors. We drove past the village of Recsk, the site of an ancient gold mine. We did not know then that in later years this mine and its surrounding area would become a most infamous punitive camp where thousands of Hungary's intellectuals slaved under the harshest conditions. The car held up and took us back to Budapest, and by dark I was back in Molnar utca.

My 22nd birthday came two days later. We celebrated this at lunch in Eta's flat in Molnar utca. That day, I received two wonderful birthday presents. Just as Eta was bringing in my chocolate birthday cake with its 22 candles, there was a knock at the door. I rushed to open it, and there in the arcaded corridor, in an impeccable pearl-grey flannel suit, stood my beloved Uncle Francis, the doctor, who had been taken away the year before on the death march to Austria. We had not had any news of him since. He looked a little thinner, but suntanned and healthy. I embraced him, and he came in and sat down with us and shared the cake. He had been liberated at the Mannhausen camp near Luz by the American Army. He had worked there as a doctor under the SS command, helping as many as he could until the camp was liberated. Then he collapsed with spotted typhus. The American doctors nursed him back to health and, growing impatient waiting for transport, he walked from Luz to Budapest. He arrived that morning, and after a little celebration with family, he dressed in his fine flannel suit and came for my birthday. My joy was more than I could express.

A few days later, my friends and comrades from Nagyvárad organised a party at the house of Doni (Donnenberg), the son of a baker, who was already beginning to take over his father's bakery. Everybody was there, Pali Rona, my cousin Peter, and a few other friends. Doni lived in a modern apartment on the sixth floor, with a huge balcony overlooking the Danube and St. Gellert's mountain. The sliding doors were open, but the view was obstructed by a billowing curtain. We talked about friends: Erwin Leichter, who at the end had been taken on the march to Austria and so far had not been heard from; and Ligeti, who for the love of ice cream got separated from us in Nagyvárad and ended up going to Auschwitz. The curtain parted, and there stood my dear friend George Ligeti, hale and safe. Ligeti was always a great clown.

Days on Late Balaton

The three weeks of summer holiday were unreeling fast. To make the best of it, a classmate of mine and I decided to spend the next ten days at the one remaining resort on the Hungarian "sea", as Lake Balaton is called. Indeed, it is the largest body of water in central Europe, about 70 miles in length, with beautiful volcanic hills on the north-westerly shores, covered with vineyards like those beside Lac Leman in Switzerland. The centre of this wine-growing district is the famous Badacsony mountain, near which we had a small vineyard ourselves, while the south-easterly shore is completely flat, with beautiful sandy beaches along which over the years some quite pleasant resorts developed. Most of the better-known had not yet recovered from the ravages of war, but we heard that Balatonlelle, a lesser but pleasant spa, was open, and this was where the holiday-seekers on this first summer of peace were heading.

We arrived in my friend's father's car and checked into the only lakefront hotel operating. The guests were a mix of people from all levels of life, because this was the only hotel available: married women, lots of children, a few teenaged girls. The husbands stayed in town and came for the weekends. We quickly settled into the routine: beach life in the daytime and good meals. It was an all-inclusive plan, and we heard in Budapest that payment had to be in gold, so we arrived with a pocketful of gold chains. These we deposited with the cashier on arrival. The rooms were minimal, with a washbasin in each and shower rooms and toilets for common use at the end of the corridor.

One day, as we were swimming around the small pier jutting into the lake, we observed a tall, lean, good-looking man of about forty in bathing trunks walk down the pier in animated conversation with a beautiful slim woman also dressed for swimming. The couple was followed closely by a middle-aged man in a dark three-piece suit with shirt and tie who looked like a cleric, but for the lack of a dog collar, carrying a briefcase—a decidedly unusual combination. At the end of the pier, a dory was tied up. Into this the three climbed, the "cleric" took the oars, the tall slim gentleman cast off, and he and his lady sat down on the stern seat. It was a beautiful warm sunny day, not a ripple on the surface of the lake as the "cleric" slowly pulled away; they proceeded to a point about 200 yards away, well beyond the bathing children and the swimmers. We watched curiously. There the cleric let go of the oars and immersed himself into some documents from his briefcase, while the couple descended into the velvet waters of the lake and swam around the boat. They were obviously enjoying themselves, diving and splashing in the water; we could hear their laughter clearly. Then they climbed up and started a serious sunbathing session. We could have sworn that the woman, who somehow seemed familiar, untied her shoulder straps and rolled down the top of her swimsuit. This in those days was in itself an unusual act, but even more unusual was that the cleric, without a glance at her, kept studying his papers.

When the sun began to descend across the lake towards the vineyard mountain at Badacsony, the crowd on the beach began to gather their towels and bags and get ready to walk back to the hotel. The strange threesome returned in their boat, leaving the pier in the same order in which they came, and walked some way in the sand to a small beachfront bungalow which we had not noticed until then. This bungalow was part of the hotel property and had a wide covered porch. They climbed up and disappeared inside.

The next day, while we were soaking in the sun on the beach, the door to the small bungalow opened, and, dressed as they were the day before, the trio reappeared, walked to the boat again, and cast off. That night after dinner, when darkness came, we walked along the beach past the little house. The three of them were sitting on the porch, having dinner in the light of a lamp suspended from the wooden rafter. We were puzzled. The three had obviously politely separated themselves from the noisy crowd and, though enjoying the water, the sun, and the beach, paid no attention to anybody.

That evening, I asked around, and finally the mystery was solved. The tall man was Prince Paul Eszterhazy, his companion, Melinda Ottrubay, the prima ballerina of the Budapest opera, a truly magnificent ballet dancer, and the clerical gentleman was Prince Eszterhazy's secretary. The Prince was the wealthiest magnate in Hungary, with vast land holdings in Transdanubia and Austria, the senior Catholic temporal leader in the upper house (the House of Lords) of Parliament. At this time, Hungary was still legally a kingdom, although the last monarch, King Charles, had long ago died in exile in the Canary Islands, leaving behind his beautiful Empress Zita, a very large family, and his eldest son, Otto, as official claimant to the throne. King Charles had been delivered to the Allies after the First World War by Admiral Horthy, the leader of the White army, which stepped into the political void following the collapse of the short-lived

Communist revolution of Bela Kun. A former aide-de-camp to the Emperor King Francis Joseph, the predecessor of King Charles, Horthy in 1920 forgot his oath to his Emperor, and after shipping Charles on a gunboat down the river, had himself appointed Regent of the Kingdom of Hungary. The "interregnum" lasted until the forced abdication of Horthy by the Germans in the fall of 1944.

The Catholic magnates of Hungary were mostly monarchists, and even now under Russian occupation, not given to the view that the thousand-year Kingdom of Saint Stephen would not survive the current difficulties, Eszterhazy, an intelligent faithful monarchist, must nevertheless have seen the future as uncertain. Much of his holdings had been (or would be) confiscated in the land reforms, but he was still (and would remain) the richest, most powerful representative of the old regime.

We wondered what were his plans and his future. Little did we know that only three years later, during the trial of Cardinal Mindszenty, he would be accused of plotting with the Roman Catholic Church to bring back Otto of Hapsburg as the King of Hungary and of financing the plot with illegal hard currency. Both the Prince and the Cardinal would be sentenced to decades in prison, and he would be liberated only during the 1956 revolution. Melinda Ottrubay would be arrested, too, and the spiteful Communist regime would send the foremost dancer of the Opera to work in the rice fields.

But all this was in the future. After the hard times of war and siege, the holiday was pleasant for all on the beach, and no doubt for the solitary trio as well. We knew that soon there were to be elections to replace the provisional government, and if we thought about it at all, we thought that the people would have their say and that then the Russians would go home.

When the holiday came to an end, the cashier took out my gold chain from the safe, and having calculated the bill in terms of gold (let's say 40 grams, or about $40), she took a large pair of scissors and snipped off roughly that much in weight. Then weighing again, she found she was short three grams and snipped off some more links. Having satisfied the hotel in this way, we returned to Budapest and the university. As we were driving along past some vineyards, from the road we could see the ripening grapes flash by; they all had a slight bluish tinge from constant spraying with copper solution.

Back to Better Times?

The second semester started in August. There was optimism now, and hope, as the people of Budapest settled in to rebuild their country, and many deportees who had survived were turning up, to the joy of relatives and friends.

One Saturday morning, there was a knock on the door of Eta's flat in Molnar utca. There was my friend, John Kolozs, holding my forgotten umbrella in his hand. "Well," he said, "the war is over, so I brought it back as you asked." My note slipped under his door in March 1944 survived the siege and the bombings. And he survived, too, through the death camps of Auschwitz and Belsen. He finally ended up somewhere in Silesia, where the Russian army "liberated" him. After he recovered, he made his way, mostly on foot, sometimes by freight train, back to Budapest. The end of summer passed, and in mid-September, as the first full regular year started, John also registered at the school of architecture. He started the year enthusiastically, one year behind me and Johnnie Vago. We all worked hard at our studies, sure of our future careers, seeing before us all the ruins that had to be rebuilt. Pali Rona, who had escaped with me from Nagyvárad, and his kid brother Tomi were constant companions.

I was still going out with Marika Salusinszky occasionally, but our friendship was going through severe trials. Marika had a firm unshakable idealistic belief in Communism. Right after the war, at her instigation—but against my better judgment—I visited a district party headquarters to register. I was unceremoniously thrown out. Marika, ever the party liner, told me, "Well, yes, when we needed your help you were not there; now that our side won, naturally they don't want you. You are only interested out of opportunism." This was the beginning of the end of our relationship. Sure, I was a little bit opportunistic, but now I saw that life was coming back to normal, there were other directions for an opportunist. Early in the fall, the first democratic free elections were called, under the watchful eyes of the Russian occupiers. Marika threw herself into electioneering, but I was not interested. I spent my spare time in the city's few new espresso bars and in the second-floor dancing bar of the "My Darling" night club. Here the orchestra played the latest American popular hits, with lyrics translated into Hungarian. These were expressive of everybody's great desire to go out into the wide free world where everything was smiles, girls, beautiful cars, and money! One of the most popular songs went something like this:

"Come, love, and we'll go immediately;
Our apartment waits in Paris,
A garlanded car will drive us to Nice,"

and the refrain,

" 'Cause in Cairo it rains a lot in July.
The people rush around with their umbrellas.
The lords are approaching us, and greet you, saying,
'A more beautiful couple we have never seen.' "

Of course, with these desires, left-wing politics had no appeal.

The Russians allowed only three main parties to run in the election. The small Communist Party was of course their representative. The Socialist (Labour) party, long established, was acceptable to the occupiers; past experience suggested that they could cope with them. And to maintain their commitment to free elections, they then threw in the Small Landholders' Party, the third participant in the Debrecen post-war provisional government. In September, the provisional government tried to slow the frightening inflation that had gripped the country with a pre-election gift, by introduced a kind of scrip money which was to exist separately from the main inflated old pengo and which could be used only for certain transactions. The ultimate hope was that this would become the sole currency. It was named the "tax pengo." The results were disastrous. Instead of stabilising inflation, the two currencies now started to inflate at separate rates, the pengo in free fall and the tax pengo accelerating steadily at about 50% per month.

Fierce propagandising started on the Communist-Socialist side. Marika, as a good party worker, enthusiastically collaborated, while the only right-wing party, led by the Roman Catholic Church, became the grab bag for all anti-socialist groups. Suddenly many people discovered their allegiance to it for political reasons, and a wild debate ensued before the voting. But my group was thinking of Paris, Nice, and Cairo. We worked hard because education was taking us there.

Smoke and Mirrors

In spite of all the manoeuvring on the part of the Communists, including quite a bit of cheating, the results of the election were not quite what they expected. Almost 58% voted for the Small Landholders' party, which in democratic terms meant a clear majority. But at Russian insistence, a coalition government was formed, with the cabinet posts evenly distributed between the Small Landholders and the Communist-Socialist minority.

The real leaders of the Communist Party, and later of the whole country, were the tightly knit, Moscow-controlled, so-called Muscovites: Matyas Rakosi, the party secretary, Erno Gero, and Zoltan Vas. They were the remnants of the short-lived 1919 Bela Kun Communist revolution, and two of them had spent from 1920 to 1938 in the Horthy era's prisons. When in 1938 Hitler made his famous pact with Stalin, Hungary also made a gesture of friendship to Stalin: they released Rakosi and Vas and allowed them to depart for Moscow. The Russians were not entirely sure what to make of this gesture, but felt obliged to reciprocate, so they returned the regimental flags of the 1848 Hungarian revolutionary army, captured at the battle of Segesvar, when at the invitation of the defeated Austrians, the Russians came across the Carpathians and crushed the

Hungarians with their steamroller. The ceremonial return of the flags caused a tremendous celebration in Hungary. I saw the ceremony myself.

In Moscow, the unholy trio did not waste time and worked to effect the rise of Communism in Hungary. In 1944, they came back with the Russian armies and participated in the forming of the provisional government in Debrecen. They became bloodthirsty rulers until the 1956 armed revolution swept them away.

Laszlo Rájk (who in 1946 replaced the first Communist police minister, Imre Nagy). was also a Moscow-trained Communist who participated on the republican side in the 1936 Spanish War, did all the bidding of his Moscow masters, and was responsible for the bloody first phase of police action. However, unlike Rakosi, Gero, and Vas who were international Communists, Rájk combined Communism with fierce nationalism. He wanted to see a nationalist Communist state and to emulate Tito, the Yugoslav leader, who had cut his dependence on Moscow. This was not forgiven either by Stalin or by the unholy trio, and in 1950, Rájk was arrested and later died gruesomely at the hands of the AVO, his own creation. The revolution has always devoured its own.

Zoltan Tildy of the Small Landholders' Party became premier of the first government. The Russian head of the Allied Control Commission did not interfere. A vote had been held, the will of the people recorded, and the Allied members of the Control Commission were apparently happy enough, although the British and French would have been happier with stronger Socialist representation. In all the rejoicing, nobody paid much attention to the Communists' only non-negotiable condition. They wanted the interior ministry (the police) in their hands and appointed Imre Nagy, an old-time Communist, as minister.

Business as Usual

The harvest was as good as expected, the wine tanker cars began to roll towards Switzerland, and the exporters began to earn their Swiss francs. There was one hitch, of course: the money (as per the Swiss-Hungarian trade agreement) was transferred to the Hungarian National Bank, but paid out in Hungarian pengos only. The bank would receive the transfer of, say, 200,000 Swiss francs (payment for about 250,000 litres of wine). They would instantly change this according to the day's going rate for the pengo, which meant that literally zillions of pengos had to be collected when the Bank called my father's office to come to get the money in cash. This required lightning action. Because the pengo was in free fall, by the next day its value would have dropped to maybe 100,000 Swiss francs, half the original sum.

Because I had established contact with the currency market right after the siege, this logistical nightmare was mine. Physically the amount of money was daunting. We took the company truck, Szacs driving and myself and a few strong workers along. On the truck, we carried about two dozen empty suitcases. We drove directly into the underground vaults, where the bank clerks had ready on a huge counter a mountain of newly printed money in blue, purple, and green bank notes, all correctly banded in batches.

We unloaded the suitcases and, as fast as we could, stuffed them full of money. There was no question of counting; there was no time. I signed the receipt, and we drove off at high speed. I had a prearranged group of small storefront banks which I dealt with regularly, and we stopped at each, dropped one or two full suitcases, and drove on. For their part, they immediately started buying up U.S. dollars on the black market through their contacts. Next day, I made the rounds again and picked up the dollars. If we were lucky, in one afternoon they exchanged the whole lot, and we did not lose more on the whole exchange than the equivalent of about 10,000 francs. The times were so crazy that nobody really worried about that. The next day, the agents of the wine exporters spread out over the country's wine-growing regions and started to buy more wine with the hard currency. It was not unusual to end up with 500,000 litres of wine for the original amount of 200,000 francs. As Father explained, in hyperflation, it did not matter how much money you had; the only thing that mattered was how much your inventory increased. This could easily double in two months; meanwhile, the price of wine in Swiss francs remained stable.

It was not only the wine exporters who were having a windfall, but other exporters of agricultural items were also doing well, the goose-down exporters particularly. The Russians and the local Communists knew that big profits were being made, but their policy (not stated) was to allow the businessmen to build up the economy with their skills, will, and know-how, not to speak of their connections. But the Communist plan was to take it all away later, when the talents of the Hungarian entrepreneurs would no longer be needed. The Communists knew that with Communist methods, regeneration would not occur. On the other hand, they figured that they could run the heavy industries themselves, so these got nationalised immediately. The banks escaped for the moment; banking expertise was also needed.

To get their maximum effort, the able businessmen and industrialists had to be lulled into a false sense of security, and the Communists at this stage were very accommodating, even helpful. But secretly, long-range plans were underway for socialisation of every aspect of the entire country, its economy and life. Like the termites in a tropical house, the Communists were working secretly, invisibly, patiently, waiting for the big hurricane that would bring down the edifice. Outwardly the house showed little evidence of this patient chewing away. But there were indications; the careful observer could have noticed the munching sounds. But nobody wanted to believe the danger.

One of the more visible signs was the reorganisation of the police. The headquarters of the Nazi Arrowcross party, 60 Andrassy Boulevard, a huge and prestigious-looking palace, had stood empty since the war. Into this building moved a new branch of the police, identified by the acronym AVO. This was really a branch of the feared Russian NKVD (later the KGB), but we all thought, based on its official title—State Protection

Agency—that its main purpose was to root out from hiding war criminals—the Arrowcross thugs. Why else would the confectioner Lukacs, an elegant survivor of the war, reopen on the corner beside this building? Surely this would not have happened had there been anything sinister going on. We were later to find out that 60 Andrassy was the Budapest equivalent of the Lubyanka, the KGB headquarters in Moscow.

So the time passed; more and more restaurants, theatres, and movies opened up, and the fall of 1945 began to turn into winter. The university was still not properly heated, but the courses were getting more interesting, and we were young and so did not mind the cold. I no longer saw Marika Salusinszky or her brother, although the wine exporters' association was still headquartered in their father's beautiful offices.

A Fruit of Peace

At the beginning of July, at the end of the semester, my father acquired a new car: an eight-cylinder, twin-carburetor sports convertible. It had a white convertible top, white leather upholstery, white steering wheel, and knobs on the dashboard. It had been built for a German air-force general in 1941, and it was by far the most beautiful, most powerful car I ever had up to this day. Even my father, a puritan at heart, appeared for the moment to be as proud of this vehicle as he had been as a young man of his shiny Irish hunters.

For an inaugural ride on a beautiful sunny afternoon, we went for tea to the villa of a bank president who lived not far from our house in a valley below the Hill of the Roses which had been named in the days of the Turkish occupation, the Pasaret, or "fields of the Pasha." (Our house, now nearly rebuilt, was on Turosvesz, roughly translated, "the street of the Turkish threat," and we had moved in only a few days before). For our outing, Szücs the driver polished the car's navy blue body and black fenders with exceptional care, and it waited for us with its top down, glistening in the sunshine. For this occasion, my father and Eta had dressed to kill, and I had done pretty much the same. I let them into the back seat and then took the white wheel and put my hand on the starter. There was a low growl, and engaging the gear, I steered slowly down the hill. It handled beautifully, and in a short while we drove with panache, I thought, through the iron gates into the banker's garden. We swept round a circular driveway to the main entrance, where I stopped in front of the steps leading to the front servant door.

Before I could touch the bell, the door was opened by a uniformed servant who ushered us into the salon, where the banker and his wife received us. The banker was a dignified gentleman in an impeccable English banker's suit; his wife was a matching partner. As we sat down, I wondered how such an elegant house could have survived the siege so intact. While tea was served, the banker explained that after the Russian armies had crossed the Danube both above and below Budapest on Christmas Eve of 1944 and encircled Buda, this part of the Pasaret had fallen with hardly a shot fired. Talk of the luck of the bankers! Conversation went on for a long while, but I could hardly wait to get back into the car and to continue with the drive. When the time came to leave, my father mentioned that our new car was outside, and the couple accompanied us outside and watched from the top of the stairs as Father and Eta got in the back and I took the wheel. The car started with its deep throaty growl, our hosts raised their arms in farewell, and I shifted from first and slowly engaged the clutch. Nothing happened. I gave it more gas, and with a shudder the engine stopped. Several false starts later, the car had not budged an inch. As it later turned out, I had forgotten to release the emergency brake when leaving home, and the ersatz brake lining had melted from the friction of the drive.

The embarrassment was stupendous; our hosts stood frozen until I eventually had to admit that I couldn't move the car. They graciously invited Eta and my furious father back into the house, and I headed up the Pasaret to find a tow truck. This, in the first summer after the war, was not an easy task, but finally I found an old truck whose driver could be persuaded to tow the car away. My father and Eta chose to walk rather than suffer the indignity of a tow. This drive was not soon forgiven.

[V] The Communist Agenda

My Father Loses his Business

By now, we were comfortably ensconced in our villa on the Hill of the Roses. Everybody was beginning to polish and decorate their houses and apartments, if only by repainting the old walls. But the termites were at work behind all the fresh new paint, although for the moment they were invisible. In February 1946, Parliament proclaimed Hungary a republic, ending the 1000-year-old Kingdom of St. Stephen. The premier, Zoltan Tildy, became the first president and moved into a very large villa that during the Nazi era was the German Ambassador's residence, only a stone's throw from ours. Being a republic didn't worry us too much; after all, half the most interesting countries of the world, the United States, France, and all the Latin American countries, were republics.

Already there were skirmishes between the Communist-Socialist left and the right wing of the Small Landholders' Party, but because these occurred under the parliamentary umbrella, they did not seem to affect the functioning of the coalition government. In fact, on the first of August, the government very effectively in one well-prepared move introduced a new currency, the forint, and stopped inflation, profiteering, and black marketers. Among many measures, they stockpiled essential goods so that they were available at fixed prices in the new currency. Dealing in gold or dollars was now illegal. Workers were no longer paid in goods, but in money. Prices seemed to have gone up somewhat, but the money was solid, and optimism prevailed.

Zoltan Vas, the Minister of Trade, a Muscovite Communist, was more than helpful in furthering the success of the wine industry, a chief source of hard currency; he bent over backwards. So it was no surprise that when he asked for large donations for rebuilding the Chain Bridge from the wine exporters, my father reciprocated by pledging from the association a donation of two million new forints (about $100,000), at that time a staggering sum. It would be some months before the game plan of the Communists became apparent.

Christmas 1946 passed peacefully, and in the new year of 1947, the peace treaty with the Allies was signed. But now the Communist agenda began to be visible. The first target was the Small Landholders' Party, their coalition partners, which they now sought to undermine. Its Secretary General was accused of conspiracy to overthrow the Republic, and although Parliament refused to lift his parliamentary immunity, the Soviet Control Commission arrested him and many so-called co-conspirators. A show trial followed, and the leaders were condemned to death.

This was a defining moment. From now on, I had no doubt that the Communists were planning a takeover. This knowledge was profoundly depressing, and not even the arrival of a brand new big apple-green Dodge with "fluid drive", the most advanced system of that time, could raise my spirits. My father had become fed up with the constant "defekts" in the two cars he had bought from Bruck Brothers, where years before he had purchased my Rudge. Of course no one was allowed to import such hard-currency automobiles, and the purchase had taken special intervention on the part of Comrade Vas, still, but not for much longer, helpful as ever. I began to tell my father that we should leave Hungary; he did not buy the suggestion. His attention was focused on the next wine harvest in which he had made much capital despite the nationalisation of the three major banks by the Parliament.

The Communists completed their takeover of the Parliament through fancy manoeuvres surrounding the elections of August 31, 1947. The Minister of the Interior, Laszlo Rájk, (who had replaced Imre Nagy, said to be "soft" on the right) pushed a new election law through the emasculated Parliament. Essentially they wanted the takeover disguised as a legally correct expression of the people's will. Rájk is said to have personally supervised the voter lists, with the result that vast numbers who could not be counted on to vote for the Marxists simply disappeared from the lists. Another new measure permitted the telegraphing of votes; registration cards were issued for casting votes away from home. It is known that thousands of "tourists" cast Marxist votes repeatedly while being trucked all over the country. The Communists encouraged the formation of new parties; anyone could start a new party if he gathered sufficient signatures on a petition. Six new anti-Communist parties emerged, which effectively split the vote. Because of the many irregularities, the most important opposition party demanded that the election be declared invalid. The secret police, with their vast resources, set about examining the signatures on the petitions of the various candidates. They found thousands of "forged" signatures, and on this basis seats were declared void. The wholesale arrest of politicians with voided seats began. Many disappeared into the huge fortress of the AVO on Andrassy utca; among them was a young doctor, Bela Haray, a specialist in sports medicine, who was later to play a vital role in my future.

Now the Communists had the upper hand, and Parliament was no more than their mouthpiece. And the Soviet Army was there to enforce their will. Hungary and the Allies had signed a peace treaty, but Austria was still occupied by the four powers. The Soviets maintained a huge military presence there, and using the pretext that it must maintain a connection between the occupying troops and its territory, Russia declared that the army would remain in Hungary.

The atmosphere in Hungary in the fall of 1947 became surreal. The relaxed lifestyle continued, business was booming, and espresso bars, restaurants, and theatres flourished. But there was now open propagandising in the factories and in the newspapers and more open confrontation with the Catholic Church, the only remaining resistance. At the university, lectures went on as before, but the atmosphere changed; Communist cells sprang up, and daily Marxist seminars were held after the lectures. People began to disappear: some into the cells of the AVO, some simply left the country while it was still legally possible to make trips to the West. It was a mark of the times that our apple-green Dodge was painted gunmetal green so as not to attract attention. A new generation of pinball games was about to begin.

But it was only in March 1948 that one morning two men in dark suits walked past the receptionist and into my father's office. They explained that they were from the Finance Ministry and declared that his business was now theirs and that he was free to leave immediately.

My father stood up and picked up his briefcase. "Just a minute," said the senior of the two men. "We want to take a look in that." In those days, business was often conducted on a cash basis; cheques were rather rare. My father snapped his briefcase open, but only a few papers were there. He picked up his hat and coat and walked out.

The officers followed him down the steps of the building, and Sandor the driver opened the car door for him. "Just a minute," said the Finance Ministry man, "the car remains here." For the moment, my father had the last word. "The car is my personal property," he said. Sandor shut the door and drove off.

My father's business was the first private commercial company to be nationalised. By the end of the month, all businesses with over 100 employees had been seized.

Tu Felix Austria ...

My father remained quite secure in spite of the nationalisation of his export company. He had money in various banks and in the large old safe we had kept in a corner of the garage since 1944, and his iron reserve, the twelve kilos of gold which I had dug into the garden in 1944, was still in place. He also had the vineyard, which in a good year could produce as much as 200 HL (20,000 litres) of the finest Badacsony wine, worth at the time about $5,000 in U.S. dollars, at the time a very adequate extra income. As a result, he was very cool about his future. He did not believe that the Communists would put us out of our house or confiscate the vineyard; therefore he looked upon the seizure of his business as a sort of forced retirement—after all, he was 60 years old. In addition, he still received each month his army pension, which, as he put it, should look after his cigars. So there was no visible change in our lifestyle: the garden on the Hill of the Roses was well tended, and Sandor the driver kept the cars spotlessly shiny. My father turned his vast energy to being a very good wine grower, and his visits to the vineyard became very frequent. He admitted, however, that the future for young men did not look rosy and accepted the fact that I would leave the country once I finished the last semester, passed my exams, and received my diploma.

I agreed that I had to go. At this point, it was still relatively easy to leave the country, and many people felt that they should go now while the going was good. At first imperceptibly, then with increasing frequency, my friends began to disappear from the scene.

I myself did not want to wait for graduation. After all, some of my best friends, Johnnie Vago and Peter Abeles among them, were already on the other side of the border, but my father was firm. The current wisdom in Budapest at that time was that one should leave "under forty or over forty", under 40 years of age or with over $40,000. In his pragmatic manner, my father said to me, "You can go now because you are under forty, but then you are on your own, and there is no comeback, or you can go after graduation with $40,000."

This was in essence a promise to send me into the world once I had my diploma with a well-filled purse, and I decided to wait. But in the ever-increasing tension that accompanied the Communists' carefully plotted day-by-day encroachment into all areas of the country's life, our interest in studying was steadily declining. All the more so as by now the school had become a hotbed of Communist politics, and concentration was impossible. So I decided that the next best thing to leaving the country would be to take a short trip outside. I still had a valid passport, and with the help of a good friend, Peter Selmeci, who worked as a police captain at the passport office, I obtained an exit visa for Austria.

At the end of the month, with $200 of traveling money given by my father (not enough for escaping, but enough for a good holiday), I got on the Budapest-Vienna express train. The train was almost completely empty. Only government officials and a few business travellers still had passports, and they travelled first class; my second-class carriage was empty. Shortly after the train started and the conductor came by to check the tickets, I repaired to the washroom and, using a sticking plaster, hid my $200 behind a toilet on a water pipe that was nearly invisible. To take money out of the country was illegal, and to be found in possession of the now-outlawed U.S. dollars would have meant prison.

Having completed this manoeuvre, I sat back in my seat and concentrated on the familiar landscape sliding by. Just beyond the mountains, a few miles away, was the Danube bend and my beloved Nagymaros, and as we went speeding westward, the train swaying and rattling, we passed Almasfuzito, where in 1944 Johnnie and I had said farewell to the Hungarian Army after the devastating air raid. Just as then, the oil tanker trains were in the yards, but they were not burning; it was only the smoke of our locomotive that spread over them now. We were running close to the Danube, and from time to time the river flashed between the trees. The train sped through Gyor, the only major town before the border, and then began to slow down. Mosonmagyarovar went by with its grim red-brick railway station, and then the train stopped at Hegyeshalom, the border town. There were no would-be passengers on the station platform, only half a dozen grim-faced border-guards with submachine guns. The station doors swung open, and a group of guards and a few customs officials came out with a senior officer. The soldiers crossed over the railway track between us and the platform and lined up alongside the train with their arms at the ready. The customs officers climbed aboard and disappeared into the train. The senior officer in an AVO uniform stood on the platform, his eyes traversing the train from one end to the other. Later I found out that this was the infamous Major X who in his long career would be responsible for catching and torturing thousands of unfortunate escapees. He had no cock feathers on his cap, but to me he looked just like the gendarmes in Nagyvárad in 1944.

I had a valid passport with a valid visa and nothing to fear—even my little stash was safely hidden in the toilet— yet the whole scenario made me profoundly uneasy. For a long time, nothing seemed to be happening. I crossed the carriage to the opposite side and looked out. The train was surrounded by armed border guards here as well. You could leave this place only by train (if your papers were in order) or be escorted out under guard if they were not. Not a happy feeling.

The carriage doors burst open. "Passports," shouted the customs officer. I handed mine over; he looked at my picture, looked at my face a couple of times, then handed it to his assistant, who put it in a wooden box hanging on his chest. The officers left my carriage without another word. When they had gone through the train, they climbed down and marched back into the station; the AVO major now left the platform and followed. The soldiers with the guns remained. The platform was deserted; the only sounds came from the locomotive, which periodically exhausted great plumes of steam. The big white station clock showed 3 P.M.; its large black arm crept forward slowly. Justifiably or not, I was afraid.

Finally the officials came out of the station, crossed over the tracks again, climbed back on board, and began moving down the train. By the time they got to me, I had a few beads of perspiration on my brow. The senior customs man took my passport from the box and handed it over to me after again carefully checking the picture against my visage. Perhaps he thought that in the meantime, by some sleight of hand, I had turned into an escaping enemy of the State. Satisfied, they moved on. Only then did I look at my open passport. A neat exit visa had been stamped into it.

Now they all left the train and walked back to their office. The AVO officer continued to stand on the platform, watching the train through narrowed eyes. Finally the locomotive appeared to clear its throat of accumulated phlegm and, with the usual clanging and puffing, slowly rolled out of Hegyeshalom. The soldiers shouldered their weapons and walked away from the train as we rolled by. The show was over.

I did not know exactly where we crossed the actual border; the weeds between the tracks looked the same on both sides, but in just a few minutes, we stopped again at the little Austrian border station of Nickelsdorf. The station building was painted "Schönbrunner" yellow, just as the Emperor's summer palace used to be. Two customs men came to the train in dark uniforms with green piping. Their trip through the carriages was very short. My carriage door opened, "Gruss Gott," said the two officials, and without much ceremony they stamped my passport. "Haben Sie eine angenehme Reise." They smiled and left.

Shortly the train started up. We were through the border, we were in Austria. At the Sudbahnhof (Southern Railway Station), Johnnie was waiting for me. It was a happy reunion. I could hardly wait to hear of his adventures.

At this time in Vienna, taxis were rare and expensive, but there was a stand for horse-drawn carriages (fiakkers), and we climbed up into the first one. The old Viennese coachman encouraged a horse that had seen better times, and we started down the Mariathilferstrasse, a broad avenue of four-storey apartment buildings and shops, towards the Ring and Kartnerstrasse in the central district, where I was going to stay at the Hotel Kranz, a venerable hotel that had somehow survived the war.

At first glance, the city seemed less damaged by the war than Budapest, but the people on the streets looked seedy and weary. Halfway down the hill on the right-hand side was a huge ten-storey, windowless, square structure with a wide concrete ledge running around the top, about one floor down from the roof. From all four corners of this ledge projected circular shapes like Mickey Mouse ears. Johnnie explained that this grim-looking structure was built during the war with ten-foot-thick solid concrete walls to give safe shelter from bombing or artillery fire. It could house 10,000 people during a raid. Bofors 88 antiaircraft batteries had been mounted on the Mickey Mouse ears, from where they could cover almost all segments of the sky above. They were not very efficient against the high-flying B14 Superfortress squadrons of the Americans, but they made a reassuring racket during a raid. There were several more such structures along the Ringstrasse, and because they defied all postwar efforts to destroy them, they had now been put to use as shelters for the thousands of homeless people. (Some of these structures are still there on the Ringstrasse today; they are hidden now by all sorts of government buildings, but you have only to walk around the back to see them.)

As we got closer to the town centre, the number of ruins increased; the famous Opera House on the Ring stood roofless, with gaping windows, a burnt-out hulk. We turned down Kartnerstrasse just past the Opera and in a few minutes arrived at the hotel.

Austria was still an occupied country divided among the four victorious Allies, each with its own sector. The Russians occupied the eastern and northern parts of the country up to the Hungarian and Czechoslovakian borders; their sector extended as far west as the river Enns near Linz, the former home of Adolf Hitler, and to the south up to the Semmering, where it joined the British Zone of occupation. From Linz, the American Zone of occupation reached as far as Salzburg and the Bavarian border; to the west, between the British Zone and the American Zone, were the French, wedged into the Tyrol around Innsbruck.

The city itself was also divided into four zones, while the city centre (where the Allied Control Commission had its headquarters) was jointly occupied by all four powers, with the actual policing and administration of this area rotating monthly. The military police headquarters was located in the Auersberg Palace, a beautiful late Baroque building. People loved to live in this old inner district, but those who had anything to fear from the Russians had to move out when it was the Russians' turn for policing. This made living rather complicated for some people, like Johnnie, who lived in Burggasse #56, just around the corner from the house where Sigmund Freud had his offices with his famous couch before the "Anschluss", the joining of Austria with Nazi Germany in 1938. The Austrians, those accomplished turncoats, after the war referred to the "Anschluss" as a forceful occupation by the Nazis. Forgotten (temporarily) was the day in 1938 when Adolf Hitler drove down Universitätstrasse at the head of his goose-stepping troops, standing proudly in his big open Horch motorcar, extending a stiff Nazi salute to half the population of Vienna, which stood on both sides of the broad avenue, crying with joy and cheering the homecoming of their national hero. Now, according to what one heard, every second Austrian had been an anti-German partisan (during the war) fighting the conquerors—not very correct historically. The Allied Control Commission was chaired by Marshall Voroshilov, a forbidding-looking Russian soldier. As Johnnie told me in our conversations later, he had had the opportunity to meet him several times.

I checked into a fairly faded small room and immediately went down to the large hall and bar area with Johnnie. The furniture was still elegant, with rose-colored crushed velvet and gilding, but it showed the wear of two world wars and everything in between. But the chandelier was still grand-looking, even though only half the light bulbs were lit. The cocktail hour was ending, with all kinds of very prosperous-looking foreign businessmen taking their last drink with somewhat frumpy-looking Austrian lady friends. The Kranz (now called the Ambassador) was the only "first-class" accommodation in Vienna at that time. The Imperial Hotel was occupied by the Allies, and the Hotel Bristol just around the corner from Kartnerstrasse had been converted into an American officers' club and hotel. The beautiful, elegant Meissel und Schaden Hotel, where my father used to stay before the war, just across from the Kranz, was a burned-out ruin.

The Russians lived, of course, in the Russian Zone, most of them across the Danube Canal in a working-class area (known even before the war as the "Red" district). Beyond this, also in the Russian Zone in the middle of a large park, was the Prater and its giant Ferris wheel, visible for miles. Here, just at that time, the climactic scene of the famous movie, "The Third Man", was being filmed by Carol Reed, with Orson Welles and James Cotten in the lead roles. The movie's sentimental haunting theme song became known all over the world. Its Austrian composer, Anton Karas, played his zither in one of the many suburban "Heurige" (wine gardens) and was discovered there by the movie makers.

Anybody who had any business in Vienna at that time, American, British, and French, all checked into the Kranz. Among them were important people, as well as half the con men in the world. As the crowd in the bar began to thin, we walked over through the Kartnerstrasse to a typical Viennese eating place, a huge basement beer hall called Gabler Brau (brewery). The streets were dark by now, and at least Kartnerstrasse began to glitter. You could not see the ruins for all the garish neon lights advertising the multitude of little bars that had sprung up since the war. In fact, Kartnerstrasse looked like an aging gypsy whore, aging just like the multitude of garishly painted prostitutes who plied their charms in and around Wahlfischgasse as soon as it got dark. My father, who stopped regularly in Vienna from 1945 on, always staying at the Kranz, swore that he could recognise many of the cruising ladies from before 1938. They had certainly survived many conquerors, and just like the street, they were showing the signs of wear.

Anybody who saw "The Third Man" can imagine what life was like then in Vienna. Together with genuine businessmen, the city was filled with purveyors of every kind of smuggled or illegal goods. Penicillin, not available then in central Europe, was traded here as on a commodity exchange, except that this was highly illegal. Around this trade is woven the story of Harry Lime. If like me, you were in Vienna in those days, you were in the middle of it. It was fascinating, exciting, and frightening at the same time. Military jeeps with four uniformed MP's, one from each of the occupying armies, cruised up and down along the crowded sidewalks, but they were not looking for civilians. I knew that Johnnie had many interesting stories, and I could hardly wait to hear them.

Food was still rationed even in the hotels and good restaurants, but foreign visitors were given ration cards in the hotels. Compared to that in Budapest and in Hungary generally, the food was truly awful, lots of cabbage with little pieces of meat and very thin sauce. But the beer was good, and the evening got underway with several bottles of it.

The Third Man's Vienna

When Johnnie arrived in Vienna, he was practically penniless. Nevertheless, he wanted to live in the 1st District, and he found himself a room in Burggasse, behind the Parliament buildings. In fact, it wasn't a room really, but a maid's chamber in an old Viennese burgher's apartment. The sole access was through the rather tatty bathroom, in which, at any time of the day or night, the house laundry was hung to dry. (This laundry will come up in the story significantly, several times). Johnnie did not want to give up his studies and enrolled in the School of Architecture at the "Technische Hochschule" (Technical University). But times in Vienna in 1946 were tough, and Johnnie had great difficulty making ends meet. However, he was an inventive and clever chap and soon began to look for some income. In Vienna, as in Budapest at that time (1946), currency trading was one source of easy income, so in his spare time he joined the trade. This had many dangers—you could be mugged—and it was also illegal. Being a careful man, Johnnie fell back on the old system that had been in force at the Budapest currency market behind the Bourse building: the trader never had any money on him, he just made the deals, while his "bag man" waiting across the street did the actual transfers of cash. Johnnie would casually walk down Kartnerstrasse, where the market was, and his man, with various currencies in various pockets, would walk a safe distance behind him. Johnnie's assistant was the same Theo (Theofratus Argiriadis Panayotis), the Greek boy in whose apartment Johnnie had lived for the first week after the siege in Budapest, and where he and I had gorged ourselves on somewhat rancid hazelnuts donated by the Greek Red Cross.

So Johnnie would meet somebody who needed $50. He would agree on the price, then walk back to Theo, tell him the deal out of the corner of his mouth, and walk on. Theo would walk over towards the customer and consummate the transaction. And so it went, but it was not very good business. The competition was fierce, and by now Johnnie, who always liked night life, needed a stronger cash flow. But soon he had another idea. He knew that the Hotel Kranz was where all the foreign executives and businessmen stayed, and so, dressed in his best suit, he began to visit the grand lobby in the midmorning or afternoon for a coffee and to read the newspapers. He was an easy-going charming young man, and almost daily he struck up conversations with a guest or two. Most could not speak German, and he began to help them with the authorities with whom they had to deal, arranging with the Control Commission for permits and so forth, and when the day's business was over, he would guide them around the restaurants and night clubs, where by now he had become quite well known. The girls of the demi-monde doted on him, and everybody did their best to accommodate the important visitors that Johnnie brought with him. This was better business and more fun. To increase the status of his services, he had an elegant business card printed, which bore the name: Johannes Vago A.G. General Director, Hauptburo Burggasse 56 Tel: ---- -. Roughly translated: J. Vago Ltd., Managing Director, Head Office....etc. Business began to grow. He arranged import/ export licenses, whatever was needed.

All went well until one afternoon he met a serious Dutch businessman who seemed eager for Johnnie's services. The man appeared impressed with Johnnie's firm and was delighted to meet such a presentable young businessman. They arranged to meet in the hotel lobby the following morning at 10 A.M. Johnnie was also pleased with his new contact, and that night he celebrated with his friends at his favourite bar just off Kartnerstrasse.

Next morning at exactly 10 A.M., the businessman waited in the lobby for Johnnie's arrival. After half an hour, he tried to phone the number on Johnnie's card. There was no answer. After some more waiting, he went out, jumped into a taxi, and gave the address of Johnnie's head office to the driver. In five minutes, they arrived at a respectable-looking old building, and the serious prospect hurried upstairs, where the landlady ushered him to Johnnie's room through the bathroom. He opened the door of the "head office" and found Johnnie asleep after a long night's drinking. After this, Johnnie became more careful; he made appointments only for early afternoon.

Time passed, and Johnnie regularly visited the Kranz, though not so regularly his classes at the University. One day, as he was sipping his coffee in the lobby, he noticed an extremely well-dressed, affluent-looking Oriental gentleman. It did not take Johnnie long to start a conversation, and it turned out that the man was Colonel Charlie Chang of Chiang Kai-Shek's Nationalist Army from China, sent to Vienna, or so he said, by the Chinese representative at the Allied

Control Commission—after all, Chiang Kai-Shek was an ally in the war. He showed Johnnie his letter of accreditation, an impressive document printed on beautiful yellow vellum paper in both Chinese and English. A heavy seal was appended at the bottom on silk ribbons. Colonel Chang had need of just such a well-connected, impressive young man as Johnnie, and during lunch he hired him to be his private secretary. His first task as a secretary was to arrange with the Allied Control Commission for the formal presentation of Colonel Chang's documents. Chang was also a man of the night, and they celebrated their meeting that same evening in some of Johnnie's favourite spots.

In due course, Johnnie arranged all the formalities, and at a brief meeting with Marshall Voroshilov and his aides, Colonel Chang was accredited as the Chinese Representative. Through the Allied Control Commission, they were allocated a grand old building in the suburb of Hitzing, near the Schönbrunn Palace, for the Chinese Mission. The house had to be repaired and redecorated; this, too, was facilitated by the Commission. Johnnie arranged for a shiny brass plate to be cut and mounted on the side of the entrance with the escutcheon of the Nationalist Chinese government etched thereon, advising all comers in Chinese, German, and English that this was the "Chinese Mission to the Allied Control Commission of Vienna. Business hours from 11 A.M. to 3 P.M." (Both Johnnie and Chang were late risers). During the alterations of the building, a nice apartment was built on the second floor for the colonel, and Johnnie, too, had a comfortable flat built for himself in the attic. Now the mission was open. The offices were well-equipped, and they employed a very attractive receptionist. Colonel Chang attended all the meetings of the Control Commission, and both the Colonel and Johnnie were invited to a variety of official functions. The Colonel was charming and well-educated, and so was his young secretary; they began to enjoy the social round of the diplomatic community. They filed all the official communications of the Commission and answered, when unavoidable, on the new and impressive letterhead of the Chinese Mission. They had also a good selection of official stamps, including Chinese visa stamps, cut for the use of the office, ready and waiting for business.

This business was not slow in coming. At this time, people from all over Eastern Europe, all kinds of refugees, right-wing, left-wing, the poor, the well-to-do, were arriving in Vienna, where they were given refugee status. But there they were stuck. None knew where their future would be. The quotas for Eastern European refugees to the United States were booked ahead for 20 years, and none of the other Allied countries were opening their gates. Through word of mouth, the news spread through the refugee community that for a rather hefty fee, the Chinese Mission would issue immigrant visas for whole families. (Don't forget that this was long before the advent of the glorious Chairman). But who, even then, would want to go and live in Japanese-ravaged Shanghai, or Peking or, Heaven help us, in Outer Mongolia? But everybody wanted to go to the United States, where the streets were paved with gold. So it did not take long for a smart fellow to figure out that if you had a permanent Chinese immigration visa, the road there could lead through the United States. And were the Chinese not accredited at the Control Commission and respectable allies of the United States? Through the whole war, had not Roosevelt coddled and supported the Generalissimo in every way? So it turned out that the American Mission was willing to grant transit visas to all in possession of a valid Chinese immigration permit. Of course you could not expect refugees to travel through the Soviet Union; goodness knows what gulags they would end up in!

And so people began to apply for Chinese immigration permits. First a few test cases, and then the trickle became a flood. Applicants were lining up hours before the mission opened its gates, disturbing the sleep of Colonel Chang and Johnnie with loud conversation while they waited. Of course, procedures had to be followed; first the fees had to be deposited, then the applications had to be vetted by "higher authorities." All in all, it took two or three weeks to get a visa. Johnnie was chief administrator. Business was good. Chang raised Johnnie's salary to levels unheard-of in those days, and the Mission acquired two cars: a Packard for the colonel and a snazzy BMW for his secretary. With the demands of social life, night life, hectic business hours, and meetings at the Control Commission, Johnnie could not be expected to keep up with his university classes, so he temporarily shelved his career. The Chinese Mission kept issuing visas, the Americans kept obligingly stamping in transit visas. Johnnie deposited the fees in the Mission's bank accounts, withdrawing operating costs. It could have lasted for ever.

By now, they had issued more than 200 landing permits. But unbeknownst to the Colonel, fate was preparing a heavy blow. In Philadelphia, U.S.A., the FBI discovered a Polish Jew and his wife who looked distinctly un-American, with expired visitor's visas in their passports, but valid landing permits for China. Fine, said the FBI, we'll send them on their way, but first let's check with the Chinese Embassy in Washington. Yes, but the embassy said we don't have a mission in Vienna. What! No mission! But you have a Colonel Chang accredited there. Chang!? We never heard of him... .

So one fine morning around 4 A.M., when Charlie Chang and Johnnie had barely had an hour's rest, the mission was surrounded by military jeeps with MP's from the four powers, and intimidating fellows they were, too. They dragged the Colonel and Johnnie half-asleep to the Auersberg Palace, where senior officers interrogated them separately. Johnnie was barely awake, but gathered his wits. In righteous indignation, he told the interrogators, "I am an innocent victim, the Colonel fooled me, just like he fooled the Allied Control Commission. Why, Marshall Voroshilov himself accredited him, so how can you expect me to be smarter than him." And so, after a while, they released Johnnie with apologies and a warning to be more careful in the future, and he promised to do so. This was the beginning of a long and fruitful relationship for Johnnie with the Auersberg authorities, particularly their American branch.

And Charlie Chang, you are asking what happened to him? Why, he was tried for serious felony and condemned to ten years' hard labour in a fortress prison by the American Military Tribunal. He actually spent quite a few years behind bars, but came out in the end, suave and sophisticated as ever. When last heard of, I think he was running the best Chinese restaurant in Vienna. He had, of course, married a wealthy Italian heiress. Or did I hear that a few years ago, he actually passed away, in spite of all finesses? As for the 200 or so holders of Chinese immigration visas, in transit in the United States, probably they are still on the wanted lists of the FBI today. Alas, none of them made it to China.

It took several days for Johnnie to bring me up-to-date on these adventures. We would get up quite late because of the exhausting evening programs that he laid on. For breakfast, we usually met in one of the two famous old coffeehouses, which (in keeping with both Viennese interest in music and Viennese fickleness) the proud "Vee-ahneris" named after Mozart and Beethoven respectively. However, neither of these composers was Viennese, although Mozart, a Salzburger, had been court musician at the Burg, while Beethoven, who towards the end of his life, lived in isolation due to deafness in Grinzing and did in fact compose there his "Ninth"—was German. For whatever reason, there was no "Café Strauss" in Vienna, although that would have been so appropriate.

Anyway, these cafés were very pleasant, warm, colourful places, where the headwaiter called everybody in the old tradition, not by name, but by his title: "Herr Baron", "Herr Graf", or "Herr Commerzial Rat", and if no title existed, then simply as "Herr Doktor". The coffee was good, and it was accompanied by delicious Viennese bakery products, "kippferls" and "semmerls", which were always fresh out of the oven, as you could tell from the marvellous aroma. The "Café Mozart" was just behind the Opera, next to the legendary Sacher Hotel, facing a little square in the back of the

Albertina gallery, which was attached to the Imperial Palace where all the famous Durer drawings used to be displayed. The Mozart had all the Viennese, German, and some Swiss newspapers hanging on racks, mounted on time-worn bamboo frames, and before sitting down we gathered up half a dozen to accompany breakfast. This café was frequented by most of the more successful local and expatriate black-marketeers; in fact, this was where they held office hours, negotiating while moving back and forth from table to table. Those were the days when for a price of a coffee or two and a few rolls, one could spend the day at marble tables and in comfortable armchairs, in relatively well-heated surroundings, and if you were on good terms with the cashier lady, a formidable Viennese matron, you could receive telephone calls and even place some calls yourself.

The Café Beethoven, on the other hand, located on Universitätstrasse, had mostly Viennese customers, mostly "Lateiners" (meaning having studied the Latin language), or academics as we would call them. In the mornings, it was not as crowded as the Mozart, but it had the same good coffee and other delicacies, as well as a famous hot chocolate, and in the back there were two billiard tables from the days of the empire; we spent many hours at this game. For lunch, we walked over to the Gabler Brau or Gosser Brau, both equally favoured. Here you could meet the growing refugee crowd and talk to the day's new arrivals.

These activities exhausted us, so in the afternoons we retired for a longish nap, to meet again before dinner in the lobby of the Kranz to plan the evening's entertainment. One evening, we had dinner with old friends from 1941 and 1942, Erwin Folinus and associates and Tibor Kant, who was a part of our motorcycle group and the only one of us who seriously worked right through those carefree years, determined to become the world's best magician. We met and walked over to one of Vienna's oldest restaurants, first opened in the twelfth century, the "Reichenberger Griechenbeisel" (Greek tavern of Reichenberg) just off Rotenturmgasse, behind the "Stefansdom," the Cathedral.

It was a good evening. Deep below the restaurant, the huge old wine cellar held some excellent pre-war wines from the Wachau, and we were in high spirits. All my companions had left Hungary permanently and were preparing to conquer the world beyond. Tibor Kant took me aside to try to persuade me not to go back to Hungary. I said that I had to go back to finish my education, and besides, I had no money. What would I do without it? After more drinking and talking, Tibi said: "You need no money, we'll stake you … to a new career." Tibi was known to be the brainiest of our lot, so I became curious. "What's on your mind?" I asked. "Look," he said, "the winter is over, and we'll all go to Bad Gastein together; you come with us, and we'll make a killing."

Bad Gastein was one of the most luxurious of the nineteenth-century spas high in the Alps, untouched by the war and already in full swing again. I remembered the often-told story of John Kolozs's aunt, the wife of Philip Weiss, the famous Hungarian banker. When she heard around the turn of the century that her nephew, Theodore Herzl, a young journalist, had become the founder of a movement called "Zionism", she asked in German: "Aber was will der Theo haben?" (what does Theo want?). She was told: "Er will, dass alle Juden nach Palestina gehen!" (he wants all Jews to move to Palestine). "Er ist verruckt," she replied, "Die Juden sollen nach Bad Gastein gehen" (He is crazy, the Jews should go to Bad Gastein). It seemed that everybody always went to Bad Gastein for luxurious holidays. Even the Emperor Francis Joseph had stayed regularly for decades at the Hotel Straubinger Hof.

Now after the second war, the Grand Hotel, a chateau-type structure perched on the hillside facing the magnificent Gastein waterfalls, was the "in" place. The top officials of the American Control Commission and the highest-ranking army officers, plus all the important American visiting firemen, the senators, congressmen, and captains of industry, always drove up there to take the waters and soothe their nerves after their trials and tribulations. Even Averell Harriman, an old customer before 1939, returned regularly. After the morning's healing bath and massage, after a good walk along the tree-lined promenade and a sumptuous dinner, there was nothing to do in these pre-television days before the advent of the gambling casino but to sit down in the hotel's card room to some pretty high-stakes serious poker. "So where do I fit in?" I asked. "Oh," said Tibi, "you come with us. We'll provide the playing money. You get into the game with me and some of the richer players, I'll make sure that the cards go your way, and you will win a fortune in a week's time." I could believe that; I had seen Tibi at his card tricks many times. "But why do you want me to be the winning hand?" I asked. "Because you look so honest and respectable," he replied. I said I'd think about it, but although I was tempted by the adventure, I declined the next day.

For a year after this, I heard little of Tibi and his gang. Then I read in the Viennese papers about a fantastic scam perpetrated on the U.S. forces in Europe. To protect U.S. dollars from speculation and to make sure that the millions of American soldiers in occupied Germany, Austria, and Northern Italy did not themselves enter the thriving black market with their greenbacks, the American Occupation Forces issued a special army currency, the so-called "scrip" money. This not very elaborate design was especially printed for the army, and all payments to the soldiers were made in this money, which could not be flooded back into America. All occupation personnel had to use this currency in the PX (Post Exchange) stores and among themselves. What scrip money they had left, when their tour of duty ended, the army cashier converted into drafts for real U.S. dollars to be changed into currency only back home.

Soon billions of this scrip were flowing out of the U.S. Army bank, including the U.S. Army bank in Milan. The PX stores sold anything that you could buy in American department stores or drugstores: clothing, nylons, Parker pens, cases and cases of scotch whisky at truly tax-free prices. All these goods could be sold again on the black markets of impoverished German and Austrian towns at fantastic profits. For example, a bottle of Scotch bought for $1.00 could be sold to a well-to-do German for $20.00. So of course a tremendous trade developed: scrip money paid for the goods, the goods sold to fetch real dollars. Scrip money was as good as gold. As a result, somebody had a million dollars' worth of scrip printed somewhere in Naples, Italy. The counterfeit was good, but there still was the risk of discovery by sharp-eyed PX cashiers. But the perpetrators were ingenious. They befriended the chief cashier of the Milan army bank, packed the million fake scrip dollars in wooden boxes identical to those regularly used by the bank, and the head cashier substituted them in the vaults of the bank for a million in real scrip money; then the group moved to Germany, and the scam was on.

It could have gone on forever, had the cashier, who always put the fake scrip box at the bottom of piles and piles of genuine million-dollar boxes, not gone on a well-deserved leave Stateside. Unfortunately, the army just then decided to hold an audit of the Milan bank for totally unrelated reasons, and of course the counterfeit money was found. The cashier was arrested by MP's in Baltimore, and he spilled the beans. Everybody was arrested except the brains of the operation, who got wind of the investigation and sailed on his new motor yacht just in time from the south of France in the direction of Casablanca. You think you know who he was? You guessed right. Tibi Kant, and for many decades, I never heard of him again after he sailed off into the sunset.

One day, not so long ago, I sat in a little Hungarian espresso shop in Toronto, Ontario. The husband of the owner, Pista Heczey, was another friend from motorcycling days. He sat down with a cup of coffee. "Guess who I saw just now when I visited Caracas, Venezuela?" he remarked, pulling out a snapshot. There on the deck of a very substantial "state of the art" cruising yacht, in white ducks, his feet stretched out and resting on the rails, a huge sombrero shading his face, with a twelve-inch Churchill sticking out of a handsome though somewhat ravaged face, I clearly recognised Tibi Kant. Perhaps if I had joined him on the trip to Bad Gastein, I would now be the first mate on his shiny vessel.

As the days went by, I began to understand the difference between life in Budapest and in Vienna. Hungary officially was no longer an occupied country, due to the peace treaty signed in 1947, but the Russians maintained a vast army there on the pretext that they had to maintain contact with their Austrian army of occupation. Austria and Germany, with Vienna and Berlin the seats of the occupying forces of the four powers, were occupied territories governed by the Allies.

But in Hungary, the Communist Party had slowly gathered absolute power. The secret police was all-powerful; all enterprises were nationalised, the right-wing parties annihilated. Most opposition politicians were either in jail or had fled the country. In other words, Budapest was on the way to becoming the capital of a Russian satellite, where in the name of their Soviet masters, the proletariat dictated. The situation was hopeless, and anybody who did not want to live in this totalitarian state, behind the Iron Curtain, had to plan to leave the country. And this was getting more difficult every day. Hardly any private individuals could now get hold of legal travel documents, but a mass illegal exodus to the West had begun to develop. At the time of my visit to Austria, it was not too difficult to leave, because the borders were not yet fortified.

Austria, on the other hand, remained an occupied country, a kind of buffer zone between western Germany, which was occupied by the Western allies, and the vast territory of the eastern European countries, which the Russians now slowly incorporated into their empire. They did not use a heavy hand in Austria, where they considered their presence temporary. The Iron Curtain was to be to the east of Austria.

Economically the country was far behind Hungary. Austria had hardly any exportable agricultural products and minimal industry, while in Hungary food and export goods were already plentiful. In Vienna, there was still strict rationing. In fact, the country had just arrived at the point where Hungary was in 1946. All kinds of adventurers had descended on Vienna, and the black markets were booming. In Vienna, coffee, food, and gasoline were available only on the black market. Even medicines were traded there, and penicillin, smuggled in from the West, was the hardest currency of all. It was not an accident that Carol Reed chose Vienna for his movie, "The Third Man" The film, with a generous mix of Viennese music and background, was and remains a very accurate picture of the seedy Viennese underworld of the era.

One of the climaxes of the movie was being photographed in the Prater during my visit, and Johnnie and I decided to go there to see what was going on. This we did on my last day in Vienna, in spite of the fact that the Prater was located in what had once been a beautiful park in the heart of the Russian zone. In the middle of the park, surrounded by its famous outdoor restaurants and beer gardens, now boarded up, sat the amusement area and its centrepiece, the giant Ferris wheel. For the climax, the protagonists were to take a ride in one of its cabs.

In the days of the monarchy, the central tree-lined avenue of the Prater was the scene of daily promenades of elegant coaches driven by uniformed coachmen. The occupants, ladies with parasols, charmingly greeted friends in other promenading carriages. The gentlemen, mostly on horseback, after their morning ride along Vienna's "Rotten Row," meandered through the park, joining the Corso, riding alongside and flirting. Some wore the uniforms of famous regiments, others morning coats and cravats. "Tout Vienna" was there; this was the Viennese equivalent of the Bois de Boulogne in Toulouse-Lautrec's era.

In 1948, all this was history. The working-class districts along the canal on the way to the park were drab and pockmarked by the war; the park was neglected. There were no coaches or riders, and the crowds of ordinary Viennese who used to visit the amusement area were nowhere to be seen. All was languishing under Russian occupation. I had heard that until just recently Colonel Podhajski, the commander of the Spanish Riding School, used to ride here regularly, exercising his beautiful Lipizzaner horses. But early one morning, as he was slowly riding back from his exercise, two Russian soldiers approached, grabbed the reins, one on each side, and ordered the Colonel to dismount. Podhajski was not easily frightened; standing up in the stirrups, he laid about left and right at the Russians with his riding crop until the surprised Russians let go. By the time they gathered their wits, the Colonel had galloped away and disappeared. After this, even he gave up riding in the park.

When it was their turn to police the centre, the Russians regularly seized people all over town, even in broad daylight in the Kartnerstrasse. These people disappeared in their hands, never to be heard from again. So the colonel was lucky. We had counterfeit Austrian identity papers and figured we were safe for a brief visit.

When built in the nineteenth century, the Ferris wheel was one of the engineering miracles of the era. Its designers used steel cables, instead of rigid spokes, to hold up the enormous wheel. It loomed high above us as soon as we reached the amusement park. We could not get very close because we found the whole area was cordoned off for the movie, but we watched from a distance as the wheel was started and stopped many times and one take after another was filmed.

We got back to the hotel safely, and the next day I got on the train at the Sudbahnhof for my trip back into Hungary. Soon we crossed the invisible line of the border, and the train came to a halt at the Hungarian border station of Hegyeshalom. This time the soldiers did not come out to the train, only the grim-faced customs officers. As they went through my luggage, presumably searching for seditious Western propaganda, I was acutely aware that I was in the hands of the State Security Forces. When they returned my passport properly stamped, I knew that the trap was sprung, that I would not be able to leave the country so easily next time.

Trench Coats and Shangri-La

The atmosphere during my absence from Budapest had become visibly strained. There was plenty of food, and unlike in Vienna, people still went to the restaurants, the theatre, and the opera, and walked in Vig utca for the noon-hour corso. But, as John Kolozs pointed out as we descended on the Stuhmer Espresso bar, the tension was almost tangible. A new phenomenon had emerged: more and more young people were walking around in brown corduroy jackets or grey/green long trench coats with belts. These were called "escape coats" by the cognoscenti. Those who planned to leave illegally first equipped themselves with sturdy clothing. Freedom was slowly but steadily diminishing.

Not long after I returned, the Communists with brutal threats forced the Social Democrats (the Socialists) to merge with them to form a new party, the "Hungarian Workers' Party." Because most of the opposition representatives were already in jail or had fled to the West, the "Workers' Party" now had a majority in Parliament. Naturally Matyas Rakosi, the Muscovite Stalinist despot, became the Party Secretary (the CEO). The Small Landholders' Party was still there, now in a minority, but Zoltan Tildy, its leader and the President of the Republic, was a frightened figurehead. Cardinal Mindszenty, the Catholic primate, was the only leader resisting the new order, and he had a vast following, but no representation in the legislature, as if that still had any role at all. The AVO, the State Security Police, was now all-powerful.

Now the curtain began to rise on the final act of Stalin's takeover. The semester came to its end, but I was not ready for the final exams because since March I had neglected my lectures, and so I had to postpone sitting for the exams until fall. John and I still walked in the old town, but we saw fewer and fewer brown corduroy jackets and trench coats. Perhaps the hot summer weather had something to do with this, but I suspected that their owners, like migrating flocks of birds, had flown away.

For the past year, I had had a part-time job with the respected architectural firm of Takacs, Detre, and Schall. I particularly enjoyed working with them because my role was to prepare renderings of the various current projects, work for which my earlier art studies had qualified me. The projects were mostly high-quality industrial buildings. Socialist realism had not yet spread to Hungary. I had just finished the perspective for a large factory, its design reminiscent of the works of the great German architect, Peter Behrens, particularly of his Fagus Works, which predated those of the Bauhaus School of Design, when suddenly the office was nationalised. I lost my job, and Takacs was drafted to become the head of one of the new Socialist architectural offices which the government now began to build up. All private architectural offices were dissolved and the well-known architects of Budapest forcibly drafted into four or five mega-offices. This was in line with Communist centralisation theory. Each office now had a particular specialty. One office did only agricultural buildings, another only industrial structures, the third, educational buildings, and yet another specialised in health-care services. Takacs, my former boss, became the director of the largest office, which looked after all buildings in Budapest, hence its acronym, Buvati. He immediately tried to recruit me as a designer, but I was able to deflect this invitation with the excuse that I had to study for my exams; in fact, I had other plans.

I began to withdraw from the night life of the declining city, although in the atmosphere of that summer, I was not able to concentrate on my studies. I tried to isolate myself from the constant flow of vile accusations and threats that poured from the Communist-controlled press and radio. This was possible to do if you stayed at home, but in all public places, through giant megaphones in workplaces, restaurants, and squares, one was constantly exposed to the "Voice of the People."

Just about that time, as I was driving one afternoon at a leisurely speed across Margaret Bridge in our "Darth Vader" camouflaged big Dodge motorcar, a small Citroen "Deux

Chevaux" overtook me. The driver, a woman, with short cropped blonde hair that waved in the wind above the rolled-back roof of her little convertible, glanced over at me as she was passed. Interested and encouraged, I accelerated and drove by her. Again I got a glance from the driver, so I slowed down and let her pass again. She had, I thought, an encouraging smile, and I started following her little car. By now, we were past the bridge and past the drive up to the Hill of the Roses, but I kept on behind her, getting regular backward glances as she drove along Margit Boulevard. It was an interesting pursuit. Suddenly she veered off Margit Boulevard to the left and entered a narrow street called "Ostrom utca" (Siege Street, so named in commemoration of the 1686 siege by the Christian armies of the Buda Royal Fortress, held by the Turks for 150 years). This street zigzagged uphill with a series of sharp turns towards the "Vienna Gate" of the Fortress. The little car made the turns nimbly, while the big Dodge had difficulty with the narrow street and the sudden bends. After each turn, there was a backward glance. I was right there behind. Just as the tall narrow stone gate loomed ahead, she suddenly stopped, and I had to pull sharply to the left to avoid her little car. Then I stopped, too, and got out.

By that time, she was advancing on me aggressively, an attractive short woman with an almost boyish haircut. After a few words, it turned out that she thought that the AVO was following her, and this worried but did not frighten her. I quickly explained that I was not the dreaded police, but a curious young man, introduced myself, and invited her for a coffee in the espresso bar in Fortuna utca, just beyond the gates. She was now relaxed and amused and suggested instead that I go on following her to her house in Uri utca for a drink— this was an ancient and elegant street, within sight of the Royal Fortress, lined on both sides with the medieval homes of the high aristocracy, dating back long before the Turkish occupation. Most of the owners had departed or lived only in a small part of their homes in those days of Communist rule. We drove by the Matyas Coronation Church (next to which now the Budapest Hilton Hotel stands, partially built into and around the ruins of an old monastery), and then after a sharp right turn, we stopped at a beautiful old baroque building with a garage (formerly a horse stable) attached. I parked curbside, she drove the Deux Chevaux into the garage, and in one minute we were sitting in a large elegant vaulted living room, its deep narrow windows overlooking the Fortress Promenade, a wide walk lined with horse chestnut trees. The far side is a crenellated breast-high stone wall with the Turkish cannon still pointing down, as they did when defending against the infidel. Beyond the wall, there is a sharp drop of several hundred feet of solid rock to the battlefield below.

It was a beautiful place, and my hostess Mrs. B.—Edna, as she suggested I call her—brought some glasses and wine, and we started a conversation which led to a strong friendship. Little did I know then that her garage would play a major role in my life.

After some glasses of wine, she told me her entire life story. Her father was a powerful well-known man in the political life of Hungary, but in his later years he was involved in a major scandal which affected the life of his whole family. Edna married young, had a son, but soon came to understand that men were not important to her life. Her friends were the Countess Elizabeth Szapary and the Countess Karolyi (Katinka Andrassy), who were part of a kind of Hungarian Bloomsbury set with Vita Sackville-West and Violet T relationships. Countess Karolyi was married to the famous "Red" Count, Gyula Karolyi, who at the collapse of the monarchy in 1918, took the reins of the new Republic for a brief time before the more extreme Communists under Bela Kun seized power. Because he felt very strongly that the 400 magnates had no right to hold on to their vast estates, which comprised 80% of the good arable land in the country and kept the peasants in virtual slavery, during his brief time in power he started the first Hungarian land reform initiative, dividing his own vast estates among his farmers and creating small but viable holdings, as an example to his peers.

The aristocracy did not forgive him for this treason, and after the collapse of the 1919 Communist regime, he and his wife were exiled. They spent the years from that time until 1946 mostly in France. The Communists did not forget him, either, and after the second war, invited him back to Hungary, where they returned to him a part of the Karolyi Palace, in the old town of Pest, while the rest of the building and its impressive main garden remained open to the public as a museum and relaxing green park in the centre of the city. As a further sign of gratitude to this much-maligned aristocrat, they appointed him Ambassador of the Republic of Hungary to France. Unfortunately, by this time, he was a fairly ineffectual older man, and his appointment was mainly a Communist public-relations exercise. His wife, Katinka, spent mostly of her time in her regained domain in Budapest, surrounded by her faithful servants—a further gesture on the part of the new Communist rulers—and in the company of her good friends, the Countess Szapary and Edna.

I now came to know this interesting triangle. I cannot say that I got to know the two Countesses well, but I ferried a jeep and a few other cars back and forth for them between the Karolyi Palace in Pest and one of the Andrassy Palaces at the foot of the Royal Fortress in Buda, and in the course of these favours, from time to time I was invited for a cup of tea.

Edna, however, became a good friend. We both found it convenient that we could enjoy each other's company without the fear of complications, and we began to go out for dinner or for drinks. It is through this friendship that I discovered Shangri-La.

In these terrible times, every second person one met and every second waiter and waitress in the restaurants, even one's own classmates at school, were spies for the AVO or suspected to be, warranting caution and curtailing any conversation beyond the weather. As a result, we went less and less to public places.

But one could not sit at home all the time. So one day, Edna and I went in search of an espresso bar she had heard of somewhere at the bottom of the Hill of the Roses, called the "Miniature." We found it on the lower slopes at the bottom of Ady Endre utca at the corner of Buday Laszlo utca. It was located in a corner building with a beautiful arched courtyard. The windows were cut high in a thick stone wall which probably dated back to before the Turkish occupation. The cobblestones around it shone in the light of a few street lamps. A simple sign read "Miniature Espresso."

Inside was a wonderful world, my Shangri-La during my last days in Hungary. The furnishings were elegant but faded, cast-offs perhaps as the former elite downsized its lifestyle. The upholstery, frayed in some places, was crushed velvet or brocade cloth, the tables, dark oak and mahogany; a small bar was located in the corner. There were quite a few people at the various tables, most with balloon glasses of brandy and small glasses of soda water before them. At a table in the back, a bridge game was in progress. All conversation stopped as we came through the door, and the rather well-dressed clientele sat uncomfortably still. A tall blonde with a very short page-boy cut came forward and seated us at a table. Surreptitious glances were cast in our direction, but Edna suddenly recognised a friend at a neighbouring table, and as they greeted each other, obviously as good old friends, our bona fides were established; people relaxed, and the conversation started up again. People had thought that we might be AVO spies. In fact, the place operated as a sort of informal club; all activities and conversation stopped when a stranger came in, and unless vouched for, spy or no spy, he or she would be frozen out of the place. We were only at the first stage of acceptance, but slowly, after many visits, we became part of the club. After a while, I brought John Kolozs along, and from this time on, as long as we remained In Hungary, this was our haven, our world in "Miniature," where we were safely separated from the world outside.

On this first visit, Edna and I sat watching everyone and everything around us and slowly polishing off many cognacs. There was a table next to the bar with some very military-looking gentlemen and their ladies. It was to this table that the tall blonde kept returning after serving customers. Later we found out that one of the men, Colonel Fedak, brother of the famous actress Sari Fedak, was the co-owner, and that the other owner was the tall blonde who was affectionately called Cilike, a diminutive of Cecelia.

The Miniature still exists, though of course all the habitués are long gone, as are the owners. It stands in the same spot, although not, I've heard and I don't doubt it, with the same atmosphere. I myself have never revisited it. Afraid of ghosts, I have never returned.

In the real world outside, the Cominform (the organisation through which Stalin administrated his vast holdings) denounced Tito, with dire future consequences to Laszlo Rájk, the police minister who was a great Titoist. Next, the Communist regime recalled the Hungarian ambassador in Cairo for consultation. His chosen name was Victor Chornoky. In reality, he was a member of the Bun banking family, a fact that he did not want to emphasise, all the more so since he had married the daughter of Zoltan Tildy, leader of the Small Landholders' Party and President of the new Republic of Hungary. Chornoky flew home dutifully; he stepped out unsuspectingly onto the tarmac, where two AVO officers waited to take him into custody. As he resisted, so the story went, the AVO was forced to shoot him on the spot. Everybody in Budapest heard this tale, and while we could not decipher the Byzantine intricacies of the plot, we figured rightly that now that the Social Democrats had been forced into a union with the Communists to form the "Hungarian Workers' Party", the next step must be the elimination of the Small Landholders' Party as an effective political organisation. Chornoky's execution was only the first shot.

And so it was. Only days later, in the middle of the summer holidays, Zoltan Tildy resigned as President and was put under house arrest in his villa, which was almost next door to our house. This event had many serious consequences for the country—it was evident that gradually the noose was tightening. For us, it had dire immediate consequences: Tildy's villa was surrounded by AVO detectives night and day, and at night the whole compound was illuminated by giant yard lights. Unfortunately, the light spilled over into our garden, putting us into a very unpleasant "limelight".

Father did not like this at all. He was also distressed by the never-ending audit of his old firm, now nationalised, which constantly turned up big and small problems. Among the small ones, the auditors found that Madame, our former housekeeper, who had become my father's trustee at the wine cellars and who kept a bunch of cats around to keep the cellar's rodent population under control, bought every week two litres of milk for the cats out of the petty cash. The auditors figured that this was a misuse of the Hungarian workers' rightful property and wanted to charge my father personally for three years' supply of milk (about 300 litres or 600 forints.) Father paid up, even finding some humour in the situation. More worrisome was the fact that the Ministry of Trade was trying to blackmail him into becoming head of the new Communist Wine Export Combine, called "Monimpex". Father avoided this by pleading ill health. Next, they threatened to charge him with sabotage if he did not lead the annual trade delegation to Switzerland, ironically to sell the wines that had been stolen by the government from him and from other members of the Export Association.

The next step undertaken by the Marxists was to move Szakasits, former head of the Social Democrats, into the largely ceremonial post of President, which had now become vacant due to the house arrest of Tildy.

Back in Shangri-La, Edna and I both laid siege to Cilike, the charming owner. She was impervious to Edna's advances, but I was delighted to find that she reacted to me in a friendly way. These were times when people were drinking quite a lot, and the Miniature offered every opportunity. We arrived there normally at around 8 o'clock in the evening and stayed until closing time, which was about 1 A.M. As the evening progressed, more and more cognac was consumed, and people moved around from one table to another until around midnight when they began to drift away. Countess Julia Apponyi and her husband, a Polish nobleman and ex-officer in the Austro-Hungarian army, usually left first. At that time, she owned the most fashionable *haute couture* house of Budapest and was a very hard-working woman. She made an interesting impression: tall, her head a striking reminder of her father, a famous diplomat, whose Roman nose and tall gaunt figure were known to every Hungarian schoolchild. He also had a lantern jaw, well hidden by a luxuriant pointed white beard. In Julia's case, the beard was missing. As the crowd began to thin, Cilike would pour four double glasses of brandy and bring along her cigarette case to join Edna, John, and me. When it was closing time, she ushered us out and remained in the bar alone. I soon found out that she had a lover, a famous Hungarian writer called Laszlo Passuth, who lived in an apartment above the Miniature, his windows facing into the arcaded courtyard, and after closing, that is where Cilike disappeared. Nevertheless, I felt that I was making some progress. I did not have the intellectual prowess of Passuth, but I was not stupid, and I had youth on my side.

I began to come down to the Miniature on off nights alone, without John and Edna. One night, outwaiting the last customer, I found that Cilike did not rush away. Instead, she suggested that I accompany her to a little pub a block away for a late meal. There was a gypsy band in the trellised garden, and by and by, as we finished eating, they moved closer, and I began to ask the *primas* to play some really beautiful love songs for Cilike. Soon we were both singing with the band and drinking more and more of the light white wine. Cilike knew many beautiful Hungarian songs and had the band play them for me. It was a classical romantic Hungarian courtship where each party talks to the other through the songs. To do this properly, you had to know literally hundreds of songs and, if the gypsies liked you and the mood was just right, this could go on all night. We both knew the songs well, and I certainly did tell Cilike how I felt. The pub closed at 4 A.M., and just before the end, she asked the gypsies for one more song—an old Transylvanian song. The lyrics of this song in Hungarian went like this:

"Erd, erdo, erdo, Maroszek i Kerek erdo;
Madar Benn az Elso Madr Benne a Kerito,
Monjatok Meg annak a Madarrak,
dalolja Ki nevet a babamnak,
Csardas Kis angyalom,
Ered faj a szivem nagyon"

which can be roughly translated as:

"Forest, forest, forest, deep forest of Marosszek,
A bird is the leader there, the beater,
Tell that bird to sing out the name of my love
Refrain: My little csardas angel,
My heart aches for you..."

Without the beautiful haunting melodies of the gypsies, the text sounds banal, but for me, with Cilike singing the words while the violins carried the tune, they were beautiful, thrilling. And when Cilike reached the part where the girl asks the bird to sing out the name of her love, she substituted mine. When the tune died off, she said, "To hell with Passuth! Come walk me home." It was closing time, and the gypsies were packing away the instruments as we left with uncertain steps. We were very drunk. Cilike lived only a short distance away in Zarda utca, but it took us quite a while to negotiate the cobblestones. She lived in a beautifully furnished whitewashed apartment, where any walls which were not covered by shelves and shelves of beautiful books were decorated with exquisite folk art and handicrafts. The bedroom even had a typical Hungarian "bubos kemence", a whitewashed corner oven with a rounded shape. Cilike's apartment had belonged to Sandor Maray, a very famous Hungarian writer, who had long ago escaped to Rome. How Cilike happened to inherit it, I never asked.

No sooner did we get inside than Cilike pulled me into the kitchen, where she proceeded to remove from the cupboard dozens of bottles of the finest cognac and other liquors and, pulling the corks, began to pour their contents into the sink, singing and calling out, "Goodbye, Passuth!" with each bottle. This apparently was Passuth's stash, and she exorcised his presence from the apartment by pouring them down the drain. Only when the last bottle went into the sink did she take me to the bedroom, where next to the "bubos kemence" and abutting on it was her large double bed.

That night, I discovered that the borders of the Miniature's Shangri-La extended as far as Zarda utca. In fact, Shangri-La was everywhere where Cilike was. And in all the time we had together, I never knew her to leave these boundaries but once. After this, through osmosis, everybody at the Miniature came to understand our changed relationship. Passuth was gone, I was in.

Cilike, who was about ten years older than me and much wiser, knew that our time was limited. She knew that, like everybody else of my generation, I would have to leave the country. When slightly intoxicated, she used to say, "Gyuri, you and Johnnie will be gone soon, into the wide world beyond, and Cilike will be working in the 'Red Star' hosiery factory." But Cilike had a very close friend somewhere in Latin America who kept writing to her faithfully. I like to think that she got out of Hungary and escaped the fate of life in the "Red Star" stocking factory—her metaphor for a totally Communist life style. Meanwhile, there was no reason to mourn, and I spent every evening in Shangri-La, and my nights there also.

Departures

By now, many of our friends had left, and more were going every day. Towards the end of the summer, a friend of John's, Andras Gyorgy, who worked in the government department for lumber export, was to go on an official mission to Austria, where he intended to abscond, never to return. He had accumulated 400 gold "Napoleon" coins, each worth about $12—at that time a major fortune. He could not take these with him on an official mission and had them sewn into two rough jute bags, each weighing about four pounds, which he left in John's care. As soon as he could, he would make arrangements with a diplomatic courier to take them to him in the diplomatic bag. Andras left, and as he intended, departed from the delegation in Vienna, where he proceeded to build a bridgehead for other friends who would follow. He lived in the Pension Jandaschek, and from there he kept up a lively correspondence with John, regularly inquiring about "those (meaning the coins) who were left behind." The coins were well and safely hidden in John's little apartment at the bottom of the Hill of the Roses.

The Communists, led by the Muscovite Matyas Rakosi, were systematically progressing, tightening the noose. Rájk, the friend of Tito, a nationalist Communist, was already a target of the Stalinist Communists and was replaced as Police Minister by Janos Kadar; Rájk became Foreign Minister. By now, the Social Democratic Party had been eliminated by the Communists, the Small Landholders' Party intimidated, its head, Tildy, under house arrest, the leaders and deputies of the opposition parties exiled. The Communists decided that the time had come to take back all the farms the government had carved out of the confiscated large estates in the 1946 land reform and given to the poor peasants as a political bribe. Late in August, Rakosi made a speech announcing government support for the formation of large agricultural cooperatives. Officially the farmers were free to join or to remain independent, but following the long-term Marxist agenda, within a couple of years all the farmers were forced most brutally into the cooperatives.

At the same time, a purge began within the Communist Party, the Hungarian Workers' Party, which resulted eventually in the expulsion of former Social Democrats and other unreliables. More than 100,000 were expelled. Suddenly the government announced that it had arrested the entire management of Standard Electric, the American ITT-owned communications company. Caught in the net were an Englishman, an American, and of course the Hungarian company president, Geiger. All were accused of spying against the people's democracy. Those of the alleged coven of spies who were Hungarians were tried and executed in short order; the Hungarian girlfriend of the Englishman was tortured to death, and the whole enterprise was confiscated. I was not immediately aware of how the consequences of their actions would influence my own life.

All opposition had been eliminated; the agricultural takeover was underway, and spies had been shown to be operating in our midst. Now, according to the prearranged schedule, the Communists turned against their last but most formidable enemy, the Catholic Church, whose tentacles reached into all elements of society. From now on, the gloves were off, and open warfare prevailed. The conservative Cardinal Mindszenty was a formidable opponent, surrounded and supported as he was by the clergy and by what remained of the old aristocracy, particularly represented in the person of Prince Eszterhazy, he whom I had observed taking his holidays in the postwar years in Balatonlelle with his faithful secretary and the actress, Melinda Ottrubay.

In the Miniature, although all this was known, discussion was avoided; after all, we were in Shangri-La.

My father was getting ready for the forced trip to Switzerland which was to happen in September, and I was getting ready for my exams, although my heart was not in my preparations; it was definitely in the Shangri-La with Cilike. I even began contemplating staying in Hungary, though not very seriously perhaps, for Cilike the realist, referring to herself in the third person, kept saying, "You, Gyuri, will be long gone to the West, while Cilike will be working at the knitting machine of the 'Red Star' hosiery factory."

But the Miniature remained what it always was, the ultimate refuge from the Marxist reality. Being there felt like being in the salon of the *Titanic*, where the music played on and the champagne kept flowing right to the very end when the ship slipped into the icy cold of the Atlantic. It was still possible to abandon ship, but time was running out.

Once in a while, I still went to Vig utca for an espresso at noon and to visit Kernyalszki the haberdasher, who was fitting me for some shirts. One Monday, as I was talking to him, he showed me a bolt of beautiful raw silk. I found it too expensive, but he told me that the Friday before he had delivered 24 shirts of the same material to Lexi Strommer. Knowing that by now Lexi's business was dead, I was surprised. What else did he buy, I asked? Kernyalszki said the same number of shorts, many neckties, and two new suits. Knowing that Lexi, who was a very big operator before the currency reform, had lately fallen on tough times, the next question was logical: "Did he pay for all these things?" "Mr. Strommer is one of my best customers and I am not worried about him," said the haberdasher. I did not reply, but I thought it probable that Lexi had left the country. Indeed, as I found out later, just about the time that I had my conversation with Kernyalszki, Lexi and his wife Hanna checked into the elegant hilltop Winkler Hotel in Salzburg, penniless, but complete with pigskin suitcases and 24 new silk shirts, all set to start a new life.

I figured that now Lexi was gone, the *Titanic* did not have too much time. I still could not leave because of the exams and the diploma, but my father did go on the official trip to Switzerland with the usual group of government people. There was only one difference from previous trips: this time his passport, validated for one trip only, was carried in the attaché case of one of two secret policemen who were accompanying him with orders not to let him out of their sight.

Eta and I saw him off at the railway station. When we drove home, we found a car with two secret policemen across the road, watching our house. From that moment until he returned three weeks later, we were under constant observation by relay teams. At night, their job was made easier because the entire area was lit up by the yard lights at the villa of Zoltan Tildy, who was still under house arrest. The "People's Republic" did not want to run the risk that we would follow my father out of the country while he was in Switzerland. He phoned regularly, and in a prearranged code, indicated that soon after his return, we would all leave.

During my father's absence, two unusual events occurred. As always, one rainy evening, I went to pick up John Kolozs for a trip to the Miniature. I drove up into Bem Jozsef utca in the direction of the Miniature and pulled up opposite John's apartment. To my surprise, I found him standing on the side of the road in his "escape coat," thoroughly wet. He got into the car with some difficulty. We drove off, and he told me that when he came home that afternoon, the faithful caretaker, Mrs. Szatmary, rushed into his apartment to report that a couple of detectives had come to her door inquiring about him. What they wanted to know was how he made a living. John had nothing to fear because he lived on the allowance his father gave him and was a student at the University, but this was not the time to get caught with 400 illegal gold coins under the bed. He quickly put the two heavy bags into the deep pockets of the trench coat and had been walking up and down in the rain waiting for my arrival.

Of course we went to Shangri-La, and with two cognacs to help clear our thinking, tried to figure out what to do about the gold, which was now sitting heavily in his coat pocket, hanging on a coat hanger within easy reach. I told John that because our house was under constant observation, I could not risk taking it home. After several more drinks, I got up to go to the washroom. This was outside, a square box about seven feet high with its own rooftop, built into the far corner of the high arcaded courtyard. I noticed that all kinds of furniture of Cilike's was piled up on top in the space under the arches. Near the edge, a rickety antique table had been placed, upside-down, its legs stretching upwards from a carved skirting. An idea occurred to me. I told John, who was 6'2" tall, that he could reach up and place the packages into the space between the table legs. I believed that nobody would be able to reach up like John and that the package would be safe and invisible. It seemed like a good temporary hiding place. From that day on, we came early to the Miniature, around 5 P.M. We never came in the daytime, although Cilike opened up around 1 P.M. John would go to the toilet, check the hiding place, and, assured that everything was all right, we would address ourselves to the evening.

Now the AVO had run wild, and the second unusual event which took place in my father's absence was in direct consequence. An old business associate and friend of my father's, Zoltan Reisman, phoned me in an agitated state. He told me that he had had to flee his villa just minutes before the AVO had come for him. He was calling from a public phone booth downtown, asking for my help. I told him to stay put, took our car out of the garage, and rushed to pick him up. The detectives standing across from our house cast inquisitive glances, but seeing I was alone and without luggage, they relaxed.

I found Zoltan waiting anxiously, and he jumped quickly into the car. Apparently as president of the Hungarian Wine Growers' Cooperative, he had been continuously fighting with the Communists, opposing their efforts to force small farmers into the huge Kolkhozes—the collective farms. The members of the cooperative were all quality-conscious wine growers, their memberships in the cooperative, a marketing association, dating to the 1930's, and they had no intention of putting their valuable farms into a government-controlled combine. Because he stood by his members, Zoltan was accused of sabotage, a very serious offence. Luckily he was tipped off just minutes before the police arrived, and he and his wife left their villa in a hurry. All he carried with him was his briefcase. I told him that our house was under observation and I could not take him there. Finally we drove to John Kolozs's flat, where we discussed how we could get him and his wife out of the country. She had already gone to the house of close friends where the police would not think to look for her.

We knew of a group of Czechoslovak smugglers who at this time were running an underground railway to Vienna via Czechoslovakia. This border in that direction was quite easy to cross. Czechoslovakia was another Iron Curtain country, and at that moment few Czechs were leaving. From there to Vienna was also a smooth trip. By evening, we had made contact with these people, who agreed to a pickup after sunset the following day for a fairly large fee. They would arrive with their car at John's place and drive our friends over the borders.

Now the problem was what to do with Zoltan for the next 24 hours. Our house was out of the question, and because of the recent visit of the AVO to John's apartment, he could not keep him overnight, either. Hotels were not possible because all guests had to fill in a form with all their data on checking in. This form went instantly to the local branch of the AVO for checking. Finally we came up with the only logical solution. We drove to an ancient all-night Turkish spa and steam bath, where in better times Hungarian gentlemen used to go after a night's revelry. Here, following a steam bath and massage, one could rent a small curtained cubicle with a narrow cot on which to sleep off the effects of unwise consumption. So far, in these places, one did not have to register and fill in forms. Soon Zoltan, John, and I, after a massage and cold shower, were all sitting in the very hot water of the spa's main pool. Steam was constantly rising towards the arched cupola, where it collected in great tufts. The light from the many-coloured glass skylights filtered through the steam, leaving us with a surreal glow. All sounds reverberated back, eerily multiplied. We watched the other bathers for suspicious moves, but nothing happened. The AVO had not yet infiltrated the Midas spa. Around midnight, John and I had a final shower, and after seeing Zoltan into his cubicle, we went home.

The next day, we all congregated in John's little flat waiting for dusk and the smugglers. I told Zoltan that by now my father and the delegation with his personal keepers were on their return trip and checked into the Hotel Kranz in Vienna.

I suggested that he and his wife go there after a safe arrival in Austria. Soon darkness fell, and a rainy night descended on the district. True to their promise, the smugglers arrived with a huge low-slung torpedo-shaped Tatra automobile with Czech license plates.

Zoltan and his wife stepped into the car, we shut the doors, and they took off towards Margit Bridge. In a few seconds, they melted into the foggy rainy darkness, and only the glow of the taillights could be seen for a short while longer. We were quite relieved to see them go. Mrs. Reisman had become quite loud in her excited state, and we were apprehensive, not that many people were abroad in this night of fog and rain.

Now it was time to go to Shangri-La and join the friendly crowd. In addition to the usual contingent tonight, there were a few new guests. Julia Apponyi brought along with her two of her best models. They were marvellous-looking girls, tall with beautiful bone structure, but not as emaciated as their French or American counterparts. Viki at the time was the top model in Hungary; in addition to her marvellous figure, she had unique deep dark eyes the size of saucers.

John went out to check on our hidden gold. All was in order. The night progressed in a predictable fashion. When Cilike finally closed down the bar, we all walked down the steep cobbled street towards Zarda utca, singing and feeling no pain at all. We even forgot the AVO that was lurking around out there in the darkness somewhere.

Next day, as I was at home having dinner with my stepmother, the phone rang. It was my father calling from the reception phone booth of the Hotel Kranz. He told us in a circumspect way that Zoltan and his wife were sitting at his table relaxing after the excitement of their escape, while Father's two guardians watched unsuspecting from a table in the corner of the dining room.

In another two days, my father was back in Budapest, and the armoured guards across the street suddenly evaporated. Father came back more or less decided that we must fold our tents and leave soon. In fact, he had made arrangements with

Mr. Kelemer, one of the great wine merchants of Austria and an old friend, to have fake Austrian identity cards ready for our arrival. He took passport photos of all three of us with him on his trip, and Mr. Kelemer promised to have the cards ready when we arrived. But I had not yet completed all my exams, and there was another "but"—our grapes were ripening, and it looked as if a marvellous crop was almost ready for harvest. So we kept postponing the decision to leave.

By now, Budapest was terrorised; the AVO captured important victims daily, and the battle with the Catholic Church became open warfare, with the AVO slowly gaining the upper hand.

My Uncle Julius, who was still the technical director of the Raba truck factory in Gyor, was accused by the Communist workers of favouring the absent Swiss capitalist owners, rather than the interests of the People's Republic. The AVO came and took him to 60 Andrassy utca. For about a week, he had been held incommunicado there.

His arrest occurred at the time the news of Marxist manoeuvres and AVO atrocities first began to filter out beyond the Iron Curtain via stories spread by Western papers and the BBC. The Rakosi regime wanted to counteract these rumours and invited all kinds of so-called "fellow travelers" from the West to visit, hoping that their faith in Communism would blind them to the obvious and encourage them to report favourably. The most important naive mouthpiece of the Left at that time was the "Red Dean of Canterbury," a tall gangly Anglican clergyman, who in addition was also a staunch enemy of the Church of Rome. So in due course he was invited to Budapest, where he was the guest of the government in an archducal palace. He was feted royally and taken to see agricultural cooperatives, factories, and the newly nationalised Catholic schools, while in the evenings he enjoyed the theatre, state dinners, and the opera. The Dean was duly impressed and held press conferences praising the system. One of the English journalists asked if in his whirl of activity he had been shown the dungeons of 60 Andrassy utca. Unfazed, the official host answered that they were next on the agenda.

The rest of the story I heard from Uncle Julius after he was unexpectedly released. The day before the Dean's visit, a tremendous cleanup operation was begun at Number 60. Prisoners being tortured, usually in order to squeeze out "confessions", were moved to the underground cells, where they were piled in like sardines and their treatment suspended. The upstairs cells were quickly repainted and cleaned out, the corridors were washed down, and even a few plants were placed in strategic corners. The brutal AVO personnel were removed, and jolly-looking moustachioed old-time policeman took over their duties. Those prisoners who had not yet been interrogated, who did not show signs of AVO brutality, and who had not yet acquired the pale complexion and vacant look of those under "treatment" were moved to the cleaned-up cells and told that an important foreign visitor was coming and that it was in their own best interest to cooperate. Uncle Julius was a prisoner in this category and, much to his surprise, along with others, he was brought up to the clean cells, given a shower, and issued new prison clothing. The prisoners found brand-new mattresses on the prison cots and were issued towels and handsome utensils.

The day came for the Red Dean's conducted tour. When the tall clergyman in his dark suit and dog collar, accompanied by Lt. General Gabor Peter of the AVO and other immaculately dressed high-ranking officers, entered the long first-floor prison corridor, the cell doors were opened, and all the intact prisoners lined up outside the doors in their spanking new outfits. Uncle Julius was there, and his six-foot figure stood out among the prisoners.

The Dean looked into a few cells and slowly walked past the line-up. It was really no surprise that his eyes lighted on Julius. He stopped and addressed him in English. Julius could not speak that language, but was fluent in French. Before anybody could jump in to interpret, he answered in French. As luck would have it, the Dean also had a good command of that language, and he asked Julius if he had been well-treated and if he had any complaints. Julius answered that he was well-treated (this was true up to that moment) and that his main complaint was that he was there and not at home with his wife. Julius was not a hero, and this in fact was the answer that the Red Dean wanted to hear. A few more questions, the Dean moved on, and the inspection was over. At the next press conference in the lobby of the Parliament, the Dean told of his visit to Andrassy utca and praised all that he had seen. He expressed surprise after all the unfair reports that he had read about this institution. The regime was delighted and sent the Dean home heavily laden with gifts. Julius, too, that lucky man, was released from jail and sent home, the charges dropped for the time being. When everything settled down, the AVO resumed torturing and brutalising as before, and "confessions" poured out of the unfortunate innocent victims.

I passed a few of my exams and drove down with my father and Eta to the vineyard for the harvest. The weather was gorgeous, the harvest plentiful. Sitting on the hilltop under the shady porch of our house, sipping and tasting the fresh most, we looked down at the ancient vineyard sloping towards the reedy shore of the shimmering lake and found it difficult to imagine that this would be our last harvest. Then back we went to Budapest, where rumours were spreading about the arrest of Mindszenty's secretary and severe measures against the Church.

At the Miniature, everything was as always, the pleasant evenings, the friends, but one could not deny that the vibrations of the listing *Titanic* penetrated even beyond Cilike's brocaded curtains. Every day, John and I faithfully checked the hiding place of the gold hoard. It was always there, undisturbed. John was back at lectures in his final year, and I regularly hung around at the school, listening to the oral exams of others.

One afternoon, my mind was only barely concentrating as friends delivered their knowledge of the complex structure of the "Hagia Sophia", the great Byzantine cathedral, currently the main mosque of Constantinople, as part of their study of the history of modern architecture. After the orals concluded, we walked over to a nearby pub to celebrate with a couple of spritzers. Suddenly an uneasy feeling seized me. Although I never visited the Miniature in the daytime, an inexplicable instinct told me that I should go there. I knew that Cilike was opening at 1 P.M., and I got into the car in a hurry. Arriving at the Miniature, I saw a handcart being wheeled out of the courtyard by a handyman. He was accompanied by the cleaning lady, a friendly middle-aged woman with a kerchief around her head. I got out of the car just as they reached the corner and said hello. I noticed that the old table that had hid the sacks of gold on top of the washroom was now sitting on the cart. Its bare legs were stretching upwards, and I did not have to be as tall as John Kolozs to see that the two bags of gold were no longer there. My breathing practically stopped and I stared wordlessly after the two of them as they trotted down the hill towards Margit Boulevard, the table legs swaying as the little handcart bounced over the cobblestones.

I rushed into the bar, where luckily I found Cilike polishing some glasses behind the bar. "Cilike," I said regaining my composure, "come bring two cognacs and sit down with me quickly." Cilike, who never saw me there in the daytime, let alone asking for drinks so early, coolly filled up two big balloon glasses and came around the bar. After a sip of cognac, I told her how we had hidden the gold in the table that was now being rolled down the hill. She said, "You should have told me earlier," and at first got angry; then, ever practical, she phoned for a taxi. "I am sending the table to have it repaired, and I have to rush to catch those two before they have time to look into those bags."

As we went outside, the taxi came up the hill, huffing with asthmatic grunts suitable to its age. Cilike jumped in and was gone. I went back to the bar, sat down, and started in again on the cognac as I waited. About five minutes later, I heard the sound of the taxi once again, and Cilike was back. She came in, carrying the two unopened bags. "I caught up with them on Margit Boulevard," she said, "and asked them if they seen the two packages of cutlery I forgot in the table. The handyman pulled them out from the deep pockets of his overalls and gave them back to me. He was quite embarrassed and said that he had been intending to bring them back after the table was delivered. So here they are."

Exactly at that moment, John, also driven by inexplicable instinct, came in through the door, and we told him the whole story, which luckily had a happy ending. Cilike, ever practical, said that the gold could not remain at the Miniature, but she agreed to hide it temporarily in her apartment. So after putting up the "Closed" sign on the door, she locked up, and the three of us went to her place. Only then, when we (and the gold) were safely inside, did she give us a stern lecture about our irresponsible action, which could have exposed her to real trouble.

When she finished, she said, "Now we will celebrate. The gold is saved, and its owner, whoever he is, should pay for the celebration." We could not help but agree, and bringing out her sewing kit, Cilike took out her scissors, expertly cut the thread, and ripped open the bag. The beautiful shiny gold coins spilled out. Cilike took one Napoleon coin and sold us two bottles of Dom Perignon from the "Miniature" stock that just happened to be in the refrigerator. We toasted the handyman, who did not look in the bags, we toasted Cilike, who recovered the loot, we toasted Sandor Maray, the writer, who had left his apartment to Cilike, and I believe we even toasted Passuth, the writer who made himself permanently absent. We toasted each other, and then we just drank all afternoon until no champagne was left. Then Cilike carefully hid the bags, in our presence, inside Maray's beautiful Hungarian peasant oven, and the three of us opened up the Miniature for the night's business.

From now on, we did not have to check daily on the gold as we had before, but for the next two weeks, every so often Cilike would suggest that we celebrate the miraculous recovery of the gold, we would dig out the bags from the oven, and Cilike would extract another coin to pay for more champagne. It was quite fortunate that finally Andras Gyorgy's messenger came from Vienna to pick up the bags (now about 12 coins lighter); otherwise we might all have expired of D.T.'s.

Now relieved of our grave responsibility, John and I resumed normal drinking—about four or five double cognacs a night. In these last hours on the listing, sinking *Titanic*, drinking to excess was the accepted way to obliterate thoughts of impending disaster. All our friends in and out of the Miniature were drinking uncontrollably, although perhaps the denizens of Shangri-La were in the lead.

The Underground Railway

My cousin John (not Johnnie with whom I played in the park as a child) who was a few years older than I, was an assistant to Professor Szegfu, a member of the history faculty of the classical university of Budapest and a serious Catholic scholar. Professor Szegfu had collaborated with Balint Homan (the pre-war minister of education) on the definitive multi-volume "History of Hungary", which appeared in the early forties. John had a considerable role in its creation and had done many years of research for this important and famous book.

Now in 1948, Professor Szegfu, who during the war had begun to drift leftward, was rewarded by Rakosi with the Hungarian ambassadorship to the Soviet Union; his partner, Professor Homan, who remained faithful to his right-wing ideology, currently was incarcerated for his politics in the prison at Vac. John, the careful scholar, was still at the history faculty, deep in his studies. Through Professor Szegfu, he was also closely connected with certain Catholic political parties, in particular with the opposition Democratic People's Party, which was known to be Christian centrist and which had won 16% of the vote in the 1947 elections. As I mentioned earlier, immediately after the election, the Communists set about obtaining an absolute majority, first by forcing a merger with the Social Democrats, then by neutralising their coalition partner, the Small Landholders' Party. At the same time, they eliminated the opposition parties such as the Democratic People's Party of Barankovics, simply by finding all kinds of irregularities in the way that representatives had been nominated and in the electoral lists. In these manoeuvres, the AVO played a key role, and by early 1948, all the leaders of opposition parties were either in the cellars of Andrassy utca 60 or in exile, and so were most of their parliamentary representatives. My cousin, John, being not too active a sympathiser, had managed to survive so far.

John lived on Margit Korut in a large apartment close to John Kolozs, but our lifestyles were so different that we met only rarely at family get-togethers. Much to my surprise, one evening he appeared at Shangri-La around 8 P.M., looking for me. I, of course, was present as usual and asked him to join our table, where I was sitting with Julia Apponyi and her husband, Viki the model, John Kolozs, and Cilike. He was introduced around, but he did not sit down and asked me mysteriously to sit with him separately so that we could have a few words in private. We moved to the far corner to a small table away from the group. After a small cognac and a very strong Turkish coffee, which Cilike brewed for him especially, he began to talk. His brother Feri had been the chief engineer of the Standard Electric Company, whose entire management, including the two foreign directors, the Englishman Sanders and the American Vogeler, had been arrested some months earlier and together with Geiger, the Hungarian President, were being prepared by the AVO for a show trial. The company itself had been seized by the Communists and Feri left in place temporarily by the government; because of his technical expertise, they could not afford to arrest him immediately. However, my cousin John told me, he was continuously interrogated, sometimes at his office and sometimes at AVO headquarters, and it became obvious to him that his arrest was inevitable. After careful preparation, he and his entire family managed to slip away under the very eyes of the AVO and successfully escaped to the West. Now John felt that because of his political connections and his brother's escape, his arrest by the AVO was also imminent. He had come to ask me if I wanted to escape with him in two days' time. He had a connection with a former Catholic opposition member of Parliament who had arranged an escape route. I told him that I was not finished with my exams and therefore was not ready to go. He explained that with the AVO after him, he had to go within two days if he wanted to get out at all. The cost of the escape would be $300, and needing a trustworthy partner to share the expenses, he had come to me.

After some more discussion, I said that I could not go, but suggested that he take John Kolozs with him as my point man; I would come later. I promised to discuss the matter with Kolozs, and we agreed to meet in the morning at a small espresso bar on Margit Boulevard, just across from where John lived. I suggested that he join us at our table, but he declined and left as quietly as he had come.

Later in the evening, I put my cousin's proposal to John Kolozs. He was eager to go. It would be another year and a half before he could finish university, and as luck would have it, his father, who worked for the same government lumber combine as had our friend Andras Gyorgy, the owner of the Napoleon coins, happened to be in Budapest from Szeged, and John hoped that he would help finance the venture.

So next morning around 11, we waited for John at the espresso bar. He arrived punctually with another man, whom he introduced as Dr. Bela Haray, a former member of Parliament, who came from a small village near Mosonmagyarovar, and who John said would arrange the escape. He suggested that Dr. Haray and I remain in contact so that when my time came, he would be there to help. Dr. Haray was a good-looking, 35-year-old physician whose specialty was sports medicine. I found out his full story only after the two Johns were long gone, but he looked trustworthy, and because John vouched for him, we exchanged phone numbers, and then he explained the scheme.

Later in the afternoon, the two escapees were to meet him near the railway station in yet another espresso bar, and after settling the finances, they would all get onto a train and after following a circuitous route, never travelling directly towards the border, would arrive late at night at a small town not too far from Austria. There they would be met by two farmers and be taken to a nearby farm. They would spend the night there, and next morning, hidden in a hay wagon, they would be transported to another farm only ten kilometres from the border. They would stay there until darkness fell, when they would be guided across to Austria by the same young farmers. It was early November, and it was not cold; no snow had yet fallen, so it should not be too difficult to cover the last ten kilometres unseen, walking through the fields. They were not to take any luggage, just small overnight bags. Agreement was reached, John left with Dr. Haray, and Kolozs and I rushed to his flat, where his father was waiting. My cousin had asked me to come to his place at 2 P.M. because he wanted my help with some unfinished business and there was no time to be wasted.

John Kolozs's father listened to the arrangements and gave John his blessing, but when it came to the money part, he said he had none. Instead, he retracted his pocket watch from his breast pocket, and together with its leather strap which was attached to his buttonhole, he gave it to John. He then left to look after some business, promising to be back in the afternoon. To resolve the crisis, I quickly drove with John to our villa and luckily found my father at home. He listened to the story, opened up his large old safe, and counted out $200 for John as a loan. He also gave John the address and phone number of his friend and old business associate, Mr. S. Kelemer in Vienna, in case the two Johns needed any assistance.

After this, we had to rush back down the hill. I dropped Kolozs at the corner of Benn Jozsef utca and hurried up to my cousin John's third-floor apartment. Two huge suitcases were standing in the hallway, their bulging sides held together with straps, for otherwise they would have burst. John's apartment was large, and he sublet parts of it to two young women from the university. "I'll introduce you in a minute," he said, "but first come into my study so that I can explain things."

I followed him into a sparsely furnished room. On the desk, he had a piece of paper with instructions written out for me. It turned out that John had made arrangements for his luggage to follow him. He asked me to ferry the two suitcases to an address on Bathory utca. I looked down at the paper. "John," I said, "this is the house of the well-known banker, Gustav Hoffman. His granddaughter Sylvia was a teenage friend of our group. I have been at the Hoffman Palace many times in our high-school days."

"Well, never mind that," John said, "now the American Embassy is using it. Take the bags there, look for Mr. Tibor, and leave them with him; he is a friend of a friend, and he will see that they follow me to Vienna." "O.K.," I said, or something similar, and we lugged the two enormous suitcases to the car, put them in the trunk, and with John in the passenger seat, I drove to John Kolosz's place further down the street. There he was standing, waiting with his little overnighter. He jumped in, I drove them to the taxi stand on Margit Boulevard, and after a handshake, the two were off in a taxi, with my promise to follow them to Austria as soon as I could.

I decided, so as not to be conspicuous, that I would deliver the trunks only at night. So that evening, I set out for the Miniature as usual, but first I drove to the Hoffman Palace on Bathory utca. I parked on the street; it was completely dark, and the building seemed unoccupied. I walked through the arched entry into the courtyard, and as I got there, a door opened in the back building which used to be the stables, but in the day was the garage with staff housing. A small stocky man appeared, with a flashlight which he shone in my face. "What do you what?" a reedy voice asked. "I am looking for Mr. Tibor, I am here with some suitcases," I said. "Well, don't stand around here," he replied. "Drive your car in and back up to the garage doors and don't use your headlights." I slowly backed up to the garage door, which the men opened with an electrical switch. "Don't just stand there," he yelled at me, "move them in quickly." I followed instructions and by the light of his torch, I dragged the two bags inside. Only when the bags were inside and the garage door shut again did the man turn on the light switch. The floor of the huge four-car garage was packed solid with suitcases, rows of them side by side as far as I could see in the darkness. "Put them over there," he barked, and I did as I was told. Then the strange man turned off the light and reopened the door. As he walked me into the courtyard, I turned to him and said, "You know, some years ago I came here often, to parties and dinners for Sylvia, the granddaughter of Gustav Hoffmann."

"Never mind," he said, "I would not know about that, just get your car out of here as fast as you can, and no lights until you are out on Bathory utca." Without another word, the little man disappeared behind his door. I did as he said, and soon was crossing over the Danube on the Margit Bridge, wondering about the strange event. Only much later did I find out that the Hoffman Palace was actually the Counterintelligence Corps of the U.S. Army for Budapest, under the protection of the U.S. Embassy.

At the Miniature, everything was just as always, the same atmosphere, the same people, though minus John, but that night nobody noticed.

Around dinnertime the next night, the phone rang, and it was my father's friend, Mr. Kelemer, calling from Vienna. He spoke to Father for a few minutes, and then my father handed me the receiver. "I have some friends of yours here," said Mr. Kelemer, "would you like to say hello?" John Kolozs came on the line; then cousin John. Their conversation was quite guarded, but there was no mistaking the happy tone. After a few minutes of chatting, we said our farewells, and only much later did I hear from John the story of how they got to Mr. Kelemer.

Dr. Haray's two young farmers had marched them to the border, which at that time was not yet barricaded, and pointed to a trail that led to the Austrian village of Halbturm. "Go to the village, and there, in the morning, you will find somebody to help you through the Russian Zone to Vienna. Good luck to you." With that, the farmer boys turned back towards Hungary and their farms.

The two Johns followed the trail and around midnight reached the village. All houses were in darkness, lighted only here and there by a dim streetlight. The village seemed eerily deserted. They walked on and reached the village square. But here dogs began to bark, and they looked for a way to get off the streets. Across the square, the Catholic church loomed in the darkness, only the clock in the spire illuminated; it was 12:30 A.M. Next to the church, on a slight hill, stood the Pfarrhaus, the residence of the priest. It, too, was in darkness. They climbed the incline to the front door, and my cousin John knocked hard on the door; there was no answer. "Let's try again," he said, "somebody must be in there." After several more tries, they could hear some movement inside, but the door still did not open. By now the dogs were barking fiercely all over, and both were getting very nervous. My cousin John, a good Catholic, realised that the Lord's help was required, and in a firm voice called out in Latin: "In nomine Domini!" (in the name of the Lord). Slowly the door began to open. They eased in, and the door was immediately shut behind them; then a light came on, and peering at them from behind granny glasses was a portly man, with sparse silky blonde hair, his ruby cheeks suggesting many years of judicious imbibing of the good Burgerland wines. He had dressed hastily in a woollen housecoat, his crumpled night shirt showing over his brown checked felt slippers. He was the village priest, and he was obviously annoyed. "Come inside," he said, and led them to the parish office. There John told their story and enumerated his good Catholic qualifications, and the priest relaxed. "You must understand that this close to the Hungarian border in the Russian Zone of Austria, at night doors do not open easily. Who knows who is out there?" The priest told them that the border area had more than its share

317

of suspicious characters: gangster smugglers, Russian patrols, and sometimes Hungarian border guards illegally chasing escapees into Austrian territory. "But you are good Catholics and I will help you; now let's have some food and wine, you must be hungry."

His housekeeper, an elderly grey-haired woman awakened by the noise, appeared, and she needed no further orders. A jug of wine and bread and cheese were put before them, and they explained that they needed help to get to Vienna. The priest told them that next day, after Sunday mass, he would help organise their trip. He apologised to John that they could not attend mass, but it would be too dangerous because there would be many watching eyes. After mass, he would meet them in the village pub. This was the place, he said, to plan the next move. With that, he blessed them and let the housekeeper take them to the guest room. They slept well, ate breakfast, and then walked over the pub to wait for the priest.

The pub was across the green, a typical country pub, with many trucks parked in its yard. They went in, sat down in the corner, and ordered some wine. The villagers were all at mass, and only truck drivers were gathered at the counter bar, chatting quietly.

The two Johns talked together in Hungarian, John Kolozs wondering whom they should contact in Vienna. Andras Gyorgy, whose gold hoard we had so faithfully guarded in the Miniature, was one choice. But John felt that Mr. Kelemer would be the better bet. No sooner did he mention the name than one driver, a moustachioed Viennese, walked over to them with his glass of wine and said, "I heard you mention Mr. Kelemer. I am his truck driver, and I have a wine transport outside which I am driving for him to Vienna. Which Mr. Kelemer do you know? Mr. Fen, who was here yesterday, or Mr. Sam?" John said, "Mr. Sam." "Well, I'll drive you to his cellars in the wine transport; don't worry about Russian patrols, I know them all."

By the time the priest arrived, all arrangements had been made, and the two Johns arrived in Vienna that afternoon. At the Russian checkpoint, the driver handed the guards two bottles of wine, and the truck passed without inspection.

After Mr. Kelemer's phone call, it was safe to announce at the Shangri-La that John had arrived in Vienna. Everybody was surprised except Cilike, who whispered to me, "I told you before, you and John will go into the wide world and Cilike will stay and work the knitting machine at the Red Star stocking factory; by the way, how come you are still here?" In those days, sometimes even the walls had ears, and so I answered carefully, "I am going to stay and work for the state architectural office led by my former boss, Mr. Takacs."

In fact, Takacs was now calling me every couple of weeks to ask when I would finish my exams and join the office. It was becoming quite difficult to fend him off, and this began to worry me. Equally worrying was the news that the Marxists had cajoled a few really prominent Catholic celebrities over to their side. A whole "cadre" of dissident Catholics now began to make statements in the press, disagreeing with the policies of Cardinal Mindszenty, the fighting head of the Catholic Church in Hungary. The most prominent among this group were Zoltan Kodaly, the world-famous composer, the head of the Conservatory of Music and creator of the Kodaly system of musical education, which even today is followed in many countries—most interestingly in Japan, with great success— the journalist Joseph Caucellier, a Communist puppet, and Professor Szegfu, the historian, Hungarian ambassador in Moscow, and fatherly mentor to my cousin John. Rumour had it—and it turned out to be true—that Rakosi had sent this trio to Esztergom in a final attempt to force Mindszenty to accede to the Marxist government's demands and subordinate the church to the will of the regime. Kodaly went reluctantly, not of his free will, Mindszenty later wrote; the journalist was to be the mouthpiece of the government's policy, but it was the heavyweight, Szegfu, the historian, who chiefly put the case.

Mindszenty listened to them, but his reaction was totally negative—he was preparing for martyrdom.

I now began to understand the reasons for my cousin's hasty departure. Everybody knew that the arrest of the Primate was imminent after his negative response to the delegation. In fact, I was quite sure that the government, knowing the inevitable outcome, had made this last approach only to show how conciliatory and patient it was.

Looking back to that time, I am sure that the regime position—on the face of it—was quite reasonable; the government wanted the separation of Church and State and the end to the influence of a foreign state (the Vatican) in the internal affairs of the country. This state of affairs had existed in America since the Declaration of Independence. The difference, as I see it now, is that in America there was religious freedom, while in Hungary the Marxists wanted to control the church, realising that it was not just the focus of faith, but a spearhead of stubborn resistance.

At the Shangri-La, as practically everywhere where well-meaning patriotic Hungarians met, Mindszenty became the symbol of resistance to the evil Russian-dominated government. What the outcome of the struggle would be was unfortunately clear to all of us.

I began to work harder at my studies and to prepare seriously for my departure. Dr. Haray had proved himself a reliable man who delivered what he promised, and I decided to keep in close contact with him. Many friends of mine wanted to leave now, and I figured that I could keep his underground railway busy until my time came.

One Man's Story

The elegant coffeehouse and confectionery called Lukacs had stood on the corner of Isabella and Andrassy Streets for as long as anybody could remember. The coffee and cakes they served were famous, and the atmosphere was long regarded as similar to that at the Viennese confectionery, Dehmel. At Lukacs, there were gleaming mahogany wall panels with ancient prints and cozy little separations for discreet flirtation, done up in grey-blue tones; at Dehmel's, there was gleaming mahogany and rich red upholstery. But while Dehmel's was a stone's throw away from the "Burg", the palace of the emperors, Lukacs's was actually in the building complex of Andrassy utca 60, the infamous headquarters of the AVO. For that reason, all of us had avoided it like the plague ever since the AVO started operations.

So it came to me as a shock that Dr. Haray, when I called and proposed that we meet, suggested that we do so at Lukacs. Nevertheless, I arrived at the appointed hour and found him sitting in one of the isolated booths, drinking Viennese coffee covered with whipped cream. I sat down with some apprehension and ordered a hot chocolate, which was always good for soothing the nerves. I asked him why we had to meet here, and he told me that he knew the AVO and that there was no safer place in Budapest to meet. None of them would pay any attention to us—they could not imagine anybody having the gall to plot in their bosom, so to speak. We had lots of time on our hands, and so I asked him about his connection with the AVO. He told me his story, and it was a fascinating one. He came from a village very close to the Austrian border, where his Catholic father was a peasant farmer. He showed outstanding intelligence at the elementary-school level, and the village teacher, in those days a talent scout for the Catholic church, recommended him for higher education. He was sponsored to enter studies at the Benedictine Gymnasium in Pannonhalma, and during his eight years there, he distinguished himself both with scholarship and with athletic ability. He made up his mind to become a physician—theology held no interest for him—and the church gave him well-deserved scholarships at the University Medical School, where he progressed with distinction.

Medical school demanded tremendous effort over a number of years; there was little or no time for relaxing or resting, particularly during the years of internship, and Haray, after reading about its powers, began to practice yoga seriously to exploit his hidden sources of energy. By the time he graduated, he was a yoga master, and he chose as his specialty sports medicine, joining the National Institute of Sports Medicine, which after the war began to get the attention of the government; all Socialist states offered the populace "bread and circuses", and sports fell into the "circus" category. Haray's career prospered, but he never forgot the debt he owed to the Catholic church, with whose help he had lifted himself out of the village environment, and he kept his contacts there. He first joined Catholic youth organisations as a teacher of yoga, but eventually he was drawn into the world of Catholic politics, the politics of anti-Communist resistance. When the Marxists, according to their scenario for winning the country through "democratic" means, allowed all kinds of new parties to enter the 1947 elections (the second postwar so-called "free" elections) with the aim of splitting the right-wing (anti-Marxist) vote, he became a founding member of Barankovics's new Catholic party. He ran for elections in the border district of his home county and was elected to represent it in Parliament under Barankovics, the party leader.

The party had 16% of the vote and expressed a strong courageous voice of opposition for the short period that it existed. By January 1948 (barely two months after the elections), the Communists, according to the play's script, had discovered irregularities in the nominating procedures. A parliamentary committee consisting of Communists and social democrats took away the parliamentary immunity of all the members of the party and expelled them from the legislature. By this time, the leader, Barankovics, had fled the country, but when Dr. Haray and his colleagues left the Parliament building, the AVO was waiting at the door.

We all knew that horrible things happened at Andrassy utca 60, but until now, my only first-hand report came from Uncle Julius, and he was lucky in his brief experience. Bela Haray now quite coolly related his story. When he arrived at AVO headquarters, he went through the usual reception. After the paperwork, he was taken for interrogation, and two

AVO officers, one of them a colonel, questioned him all night. They were trying to get him to implicate the other members of his party. Dr. Haray refused to be used in this way, and when the Colonel lost patience with him, he was ordered to remove his prison garb, and several very strong AVO men worked him over with rubber truncheons. He willed himself into another level of consciousness and became impervious to the pain that was inflicted. For one week, torture was alternated with short periods of sleep and interrogation. They wanted him to make him confess that his party, together with the high clergy led by Cardinal Mindszenty, had plotted the restoration of Hapsburg rule and planned a revolt to restore the huge estates to the magnates of Hungary, whose leader was Prince Paul Eszterhazy, the wealthiest of them all. These estates had been distributed to the peasants by the Marxists. He admitted nothing; more beatings were followed by more questioning, to no avail. After one week, during which he did not have more than a few hours' sleep, the AVO colonel ordered him taken downstairs and said, "We will give you time to change your mind; we'll teach you a lesson."

As it turned out, "downstairs" meant being taken through the basement and sub-basement to a long subterranean corridor, at the end of which a trap door was opened. He was lowered by a rope at least another three levels into a pitch-dark dank hole. When at last he got his footing in the darkness in ankle-high water, the rope was withdrawn, the trap door slammed into place, and way high above him, a 200-watt bare light bulb hanging on a long cable was lit. He now had the first look at his surroundings. He was in a 10 x 10 foot space formed by ancient stone foundations which were on a level below the main sewage canal from which sewage seeped continuously, covering the floor with about a foot of slimy water. The only furniture was a bunk of rough wooden planks supported from the stone wall by two rusty chains, which were arranged in such a way that the bunk sloped away from the wall at an angle, so that every time the prisoner fell asleep and let go of the chain, he would roll down and fall into the slime. The light bulb cast a strong light, and all kinds of red-eyed rodents appeared to be watching him.

Bela's great luck now was that he was a yoga master. He got onto the bunk and spent the next eight or ten hours in yoga practice, transported away from his surroundings. He had no idea at first of the time of the day, because the lighting never changed. After a while, he stretched out and tried to sleep, but every time he relaxed, he fell into the water. He began to master holding on to the chains even in his sleep.

This incarceration was planned as total sensory deprivation with the additional horror of the rats. But Bela's discipline took over, and he structured his time: approximately eight hours of yoga, four hours of miscellaneous exercises, and sleep. He did not succumb to fear.

After what seemed to him like many days, the trap door, way above him, was noisily opened, and a basket was lowered down to him. In the basket, he found an aluminum canister filled with tap water, a rough loaf of prison bread, and an aluminum bowl of gruel of indefinite content. He removed the stuff and stored it in a stone niche he had found previously. The basket silently ascended on its rope, and the trap door was dropped into place, the sound reverberating from the stone arches above. He decided to ration the food and ate only a little. He still had some left when, an infinite time later, the trap door opened again, and more food of the same type was lowered to him. This time, the basket waited. He understood, put the empty containers into it, and gave a tug. The basket ascended, and the trap door was banged shut. By now, Haray had a planned routine; he had even managed to figure out the passing of time. The basket kept returning, but as far as he could tell, it came irregularly, to confuse him further. He thought, "they don't want to kill me, just to break my resistance", and went back to his yoga and exercises. By now, he had trained himself to sleep without rolling off the sloping bunk.

Bela believed that he must have been in the dungeon about six months when one day the trap door opened, but instead of his usual basket, a large hammock-like seat came down to him, and a voice called from above, roughly: "Get in, don't waste time." He obeyed and was pulled up into the corridor from where he had descended (as he later found out) nine months earlier. Two AVO guards hoisted him up and made him scramble out on top. The trap door was dropped, and he was marched up through the narrow steps. Physically he was well because of his stamina, the yoga, and his exercises, but he decided not to reveal this. He had grown a long beard, and his finger and toe nails were long and broken off at different lengths. He finally arrived with his guards on the ground floor and was tossed into a cell. He sat down on the wooden bench, deliberately bent over like an old man, and wondered what would follow. He soon found out. The cell door swung open, and the AVO colonel strutted in, followed by his assistant. "My God, you stink", he said. "Now, I want to waste no more time with you, you scum bag. Either you agree to become our informer, or back down you go, where we might forget you forever."

Bela's brain was functioning better than ever, and he did not want to go back down, so he said slowly, "Yes, Colonel, I'll do whatever you want." But quietly he promised himself that he would never inform against his associates.

Half an hour later, after a lukewarm shower and the ministrations of a not-very-gentle prison barber, he was led back to the cell, where the Colonel was sitting at the desk, his assistant at a typewriter in the corner.

The Colonel was now quite friendly and told him that in the nine months' time he had spent underground, the Communist Party had made great progress, the Catholic resistance was breaking up, many important people were deserting the Church, and only a small group of recalcitrant clergyman and aristocrats now stood by the arch-enemy, Mindszenty; in the end, the People's Democracy would win and crush him. Many capitalists and people belonging to the upper classes were behaving like rats, trying to leave the sinking ship, taking with them what rightfully belonged to the people. Then he said that Haray's role in the future would be to merge back into his previous environment and watch and listen and report what he heard, particularly in regard to people planning to escape with their fortunes. Bela agreed, and a written protocol of his future duties and obligations was drawn up. A statement that he was not harmed during his period of incarceration and was decently treated at all times was included. Bela signed without hesitation, the Colonel and his assistant witnessing the documents. He was given a phone number where at all times he could call the Colonel if he had urgent reports. "Now get him out quickly," said the Colonel. "And mind, whatever you do, we will always keep an eye on you."

He was led to a counter where the clothing and belongings he had on him when arrested were returned, and he quickly put them on, pocketing his change and other belongings. He was arrested in January, and now it was late September, so he took his long winter coat on his arm, and the guards walked him to the entrance. The heavy oak door was banged shut behind him. It was a beautiful autumn afternoon, and the shadows of the old chestnut trees on Andrassy utca were slanting across the pavement in the light of the setting sun.

He shrugged and started walking towards the subway station on the corner of Isabella Street. When he got there, he began to feel a little better, even though his suit was hanging loosely on his diminished form, when he noticed the Lukacs café's lights coming on behind the heavy plate-glass windows. "What the hell", he said and pushed through the revolving door. He walked to the self-same booth where we were now sitting, hung up his winter coat on a peg, took the latest newspapers from the stand, and sat down.

He ordered a Viennese coffee with whipped cream and half a dozen delicious open-faced sandwiches and set about catching up with the news and overcoming the dietary deficiencies of Andrassy utca 60. Ever since then, two or three times a week, he had come here, at first with some anxiety, but finally believing that it was the only public place that the

AVO was not watching. Who but the faithful would dare to come here?

He found his old circle diminished by imprisonment or escape, but still existing, and he had no trouble fitting in. He kept the promise he made to himself and never reported on them. Now I understood my cousin John's connection with Dr. Haray. John was a part of this group; perhaps, as a historian, he wanted to observe history in the making, perhaps he was collecting material for a future book. John was always well-informed and had realised that his time was up.

Of course, Haray had to give the AVO something in return for his freedom. Coming from the Austrian border region, he could travel back and forth to his village, where he organised a few ex-army paratroopers, village cronies of his from childhood, to help some people across the "Iron Curtain." True to his contract, he faithfully reported on escapees, but he always waited until they were safely over the border. The AVO rushed to arrest them at home, but by the time they got there, the chickens had flown the coop.

Cousin John and Kolozs were not the first people that he had helped across, and he was ready to send more would-be escapees on their way. We agreed that I could send him my friends who wanted to leave, and he never failed me. Although he charged for each trip, his fee was modest, and he had expenses. Basically he was a true patriot whose spirit was never broken, and many people can thank him for their escape. I did my part without profit to keep the route open for myself, and perhaps for the romance. I felt that Bela Haray and I had inherited the mantle of the Scarlet Pimpernel.

Many years later, when I was safely in North America, I heard that Haray had been killed in a car accident. Thinking back, I began to wonder if at the same time my friend was "informing" for the AVO, he was also working for Western intelligence agencies.

My Dear Communist

It had been a few years since I last spoke to Marika Salusinszky. I knew that she had completed her university studies and had graduated with the highest honours in modern English literature. She remained a faithful party member, her idealism preventing her from seeing how monstrous the Marxist party machine had become. She had long ceased proselytising efforts in my direction, and I knew that she regarded me as nothing but a representative of the exploiting classes. But to my surprise, late in November, she phoned me and asked me to come and visit her; she told me that she was in bed with a severe case of pleurisy, a result of a flu infection.

Next day, I came to see her in Bathory utca. Her mother, Aunt Lili, let me in and escorted me through the once-magnificent apartment that used to house her husband's offices, and which for a few years after the war my father had rented for the Wine Exporters' Association. This organisation no longer existed because all the members, including Father, who was president, had been nationalised in March. Now the elegant conference room stood eerily empty as we walked past it towards the family quarters. Marika was in bed, propped up on pillows; she was pale and looked wan. I gave her two kisses on her cheeks and pulled up an armchair to sit near her. Aunt Lili brought some tea and small cakes, put them on a small table between us, and withdrew. I poured the tea, served Marika, and then sat down. I congratulated her on her academic success and asked about her plans. She was leaving before Christmas for England, where she was planning to carry on with her studies of English literature at Oxford. She talked about new English and American writers that I had never heard about, but I was convinced that they were on the official party list. But Marika was beautiful, and I still found the dusting of freckles on her pale face uniquely charming. With a wrenching feeling, I realised that this wonderful, earnest, idealistic young woman was hopelessly separated from me and I from her by the wall of her almost religious fervour and by my animosity towards all that she believed in.

I told her about my exams and tried to avoid all contentious matters. After a while, I gave her my best wishes for Oxford and kissed her again on my way out. Aunt Lili walked me to the door. As I went down the ornate marble stairway from the second floor, I thought of the happy days before her politics became a factor in our lives: the skating at the old skating club, the long walks, and that particularly memorable spring day we spent at the Budapest Zoo. The scene flashed in my mind: Marika laughing, feeding a giraffe, her blond hair, freckles, and blue eyes vivid in the sun. Soon after came that horrible summer and fall of 1944; Marika stood by me in the worst moments, and I recalled now with infinite sadness my happiness when I finally arrived home from the army and she was there, waiting and loving.

Perhaps she was hoping that the horrible wall would crumble as we sat together talking. Perhaps I could have made it happen, but I was not able to do it. I was sad, and I felt that this was the last time we would see each other. It was getting dark when I reached the street. I got into the car and drove around for a very long time in the misty November night. I never knew the route I took, but eventually I found myself in front of the Miniature, the warm friendly lights beckoning through the narrow slits between Cilike's heavy drapes. I went in and sat down, away from the group in the corner. Cilike came with a beautifully glistening balloon glass of her best VSOP. She did not ask any questions; she knew that something disturbing had happened. After the next drink, I joined our friends. It was a long night, and I never remembered how Cilike manoeuvred me to her apartment, but that's where I woke up in the morning, with a gigantic hangover.

The Last Months

A couple of days later, Father received an official order from the municipality of Bakacsony Tomaj, the district where our vineyard was located, ordering him to put up four young piglets for fattening and to deliver the four fattened pigs, butchered and prepared, the hams salted and submerged in pig's fat in large containers, sausages and head cheese made of the remnants, by the end of the winter.

Our vineyard was on top of a volcanic slope facing the lake. There was a house, a wine cellar behind it cut into the side of the hill, and a little further up, the house of the vintner, who lived there all year round with his family. Beside the vintner's, in his little yard, there was also a doghouse. All other land was tightly planted with rows upon rows of grapevines supported on stakes. There was no general farming, there were no pigsties, there was no food for fattening pigs high up on the hill. The order was nonsensical, perverse. But the last sentence of the order left no doubt that the local Communist Council meant what it said. In terse words, it stated that, should Father not obey, he would be arrested and charged with sabotaging the economy.

Badacsony Mountain, and beside it the smaller mountain of Badacsony Ors, had only tightly packed vineyards on their south-eastern slopes; growing conditions were very similar to the vineyards along Lac Leman, around Nihon, between Geneva and Montreux, where the best of Swiss wines had been cultivated since the days of the Roman Empire, when the grateful state donated the land to the ancient, retired veterans of the legions.

The vineyards on the Balaton were perhaps not that old, but certainly there were records: ancient documents dating to the Middle Ages, bills of lading in Latin, some of which were framed in our house, testifying to shipments from Badacsony to Saxony, to Cracow in Poland, and even as far as Muscovy. So, for at least 600 years, these blessed lands on the volcanic slopes had been densely cultivated with the best wine grapes, but in all these centuries nobody, but absolutely nobody, ever raised PIGS. The best and largest vineyard in Badacsony belonged to Prince Paul Eszterhazy. Other large holdings were owned by the great Transdanubian aristocracy, while many smaller vineyards belonged to the gentry, retired high-ranking officers, and senior civil servants, whose families had held them for many generations. Most of these families had general farming estates elsewhere, where in addition to wheat and corn, there was always room and fodder for pigs. The vineyards were unsuitable, and it would never have occurred to their owners to use their prize land to grow pigs. They grew liquid gold, the Badacsony wine, with the greatest love and care.

My father made a few phone calls to some neighbours, all of whom had received similar orders, and he called a friendly gathering at our place to discuss the matter. We drove down to the Balaton on the following day. The meeting was held immediately. To disguise its purpose, it was described as a wine tasting of the best of our wines from our cellar. My godfather, Feri Wiedman, was the first to arrive, followed by four or five others. A sandy cut led up from the lake highway to the first plateau, where there was an ancient fork with a beautiful baroque cross and a stone-carved crucifixion scene with the Virgin Mary at the foot of the cross, set into a fading, yellow-painted niche with stone cornices. Fresh flowers were always placed here by the farmers. The road to our house veered off to the right, but it was so difficult to negotiate the deep sandy cut that most of the guests left their vehicles there, or even down at the highway, and arrived on foot. Uncle Feri, my godfather, who weighed well over 200 pounds, could hardly make it. It soon turned out that all members of the group were upset and found the order incomprehensible. But most felt that some way would be found to work around it, although one realised that this was the end of bucolic peace in the vineyards. The Marxist government was now stretching out greedy claws.

A lot of good wines were tasted, interspersed with bits of good crusty bread, and after the meeting concluded, the vintner's wife served country-style snacks, more wine, and so on. But by late at night, no conclusions had been reached as to what should be done. Somehow everybody found their way down to their cars.

At six in the morning, Father, an early riser, shook me awake; he was getting ready quickly for our drive to Tomaj, where the District Council was located in the old municipal building, now decorated with a huge red flag with the hammer and sickle and the red star.

The meeting was brief. The chairman of the council, an avid Communist who had been sent from Budapest to Tomaj by the government, listened to my father's proposal that because he could not raise pigs in a vineyard, he would buy four fattened pigs when the time came and deliver them to the Council, butchered and prepared, in March. Instantly the comrade chairman became livid. "You are to obey the order of the People's Council to the letter, or else you will be arrested and charged with sabotage. The AVO knows how to deal with saboteurs."

Nobody ever spoke like this to my father, but he controlled his anger, and after a few seconds of silence, he answered, "I'll see what can be done, but you know that vineyards are not set up to grow pigs." The comrade yelled back, "I know nothing about your troubles; I only know how to enforce the orders of the People's Government. Now go—and don't forget your orders."

Father came out of the office without a word, but I could see the anger in his face. "Let's go to the village carpenter and see about building a pigsty." After some more silence, he said, "I can't believe that they want to destroy these vineyards that can grow only the finest of grapes, the finest of wines, and only with the devoted care and attention of the wine growers. They have developed these vineyards for many generations and cultivated exceptional wines on their individual small plots." But as we had found out, that's just what they planned to do.

The carpenter knew exactly how to build a fine pigsty: concrete floors, a small fenced-in run in front with a huge wooden trough for feeding, as well as a supply of running water, and he agreed to complete the work within a couple of weeks. We were the first to order this work, and he promised to prepare a contract for my father by the next day.

It was noon by the time an agreement was reached, and so we walked over to the village pub for some food. The publican was serving wine to his customers in tall glasses from a small barrel behind the counter, good local white wine, and there were siphon bottles of soda water, if desired, to make your own mix. But he was not his usual smiling self; he looked grim as he bustled around in his leather apron. The place was full, thick smoke furling under the smoke-darkened beams of the public room. There were a few farmers at some of the long oak tables, sitting on the wooden benches, drinking and smoking their pipes, but most tables were occupied by hatchet-faced urban-looking men, who looked us over arrogantly as we sat down in the corner. I could see that they were AVO men, sent from the city, and I had forebodings about their purpose. We had never seen them in this neck of the woods before. The radio kept blasting away with some folksy tune. By order of the Council, the radio had to be on all the time during business hours, so that the Party's propaganda and orders could not be avoided by the people even during their leisure time.

For lunch, the publican brought two deep soup platters of gulyas soup and delicious crusty peasant bread. The wine was served in a cheap decanter along with soda water. The conversation around us was hushed because the farmers were aware of the eyes and ears of the AVO. A very unpleasant atmosphere. I noticed one of the AVO men surreptitiously glancing at us, it seemed to me with hatred in his eyes, wondering what the two "pantaloon men"—a peasant expression for "gentlemen"—were doing here.

Suddenly the music stopped, and the harsh voice of a radio announcer cut into the silence: "We interrupt this program to bring you important news. This morning, the treacherous Cardinal Mindszenty was taken into custody with his retinue at the cardinal's palace in Esztergom and has been driven to Budapest, to the headquarters of the State

Security Police (the AVO) for preliminary interrogation. It is believed that in addition to plotting the overthrow of the People's Democratic Government and the restoration of the Hapsburg rule together with Prince Paul Eszterhazy, the Cardinal was actively planning the re-establishment of the large estates of the magnates, plotting the return of the lands distributed under the People's Government land reform. Along with the prince, he is also said to have been engaged in common currency crimes, stealing millions of forints from the people. Prince Eszterhazy, his secretary, and his mistress have also been detained by the security forces today and are under intense interrogation. It is expected that these vile criminals and agents of the American Government and of the Vatican will have to answer for their base crimes in the People's Court as soon as the preliminary interrogation is completed. Long live the People's Democracy and the power of the People!"

After a few seconds, the music resumed. I looked around and saw the stunned faces of the farmers, good Catholics all, and the triumphant expression of the AVO who no longer bothered with discretion. We finished our wine and food, and as soon as was possible without drawing attention to ourselves, we left the pub.

Driving back to the vineyard, Father said, "Now the end is near; it will not be possible to make any accommodation with this cursed government." As an afterthought, he added, "Now you have to finish your studies and get out of here immediately." This was the eighth day of December, and the miserable year of 1948 was about to end.

By now, Bela Haray and I were good friends; we met regularly at the Lukacs confectionery, and it turned out that he was a close friend of my old associate, Pista Kakonyi, professor of graphic arts at the Academy of Fine Arts. This was located directly across from Andrassy utca 60, and so Pista often came over for a chat and a good coffee when Bela Haray and I were meeting. At the end of the Siege of Budapest, it was with Pista that I, as his assistant, had manufactured out of a wooden block the stamp of the Russian High Command for "propuskas" (laissez-faire passes) to avoid capture by roving Russian patrols.

Pista was a country boy and closely connected with Catholic political groups. Alas, we both agreed that in the present situation, our simple stamp would not be adequate to outwit the sophisticated AVO, who were now hunting for bigger fish.

After a while, I discovered that the AVO had their own direct entrance to Lukacs's from the courtyard of Andrassy utca 60, and I began to recognise individual officers and agents. They came in to relax from the gruelling task of torturing people, and luckily they paid no attention to our more and more regular visits. I was very careful about the people whom I brought to Dr. Haray and was able to keep the underground railway operating regularly about once every three weeks or so.

The newspapers and the radio now intensified their attacks against Mindszenty and his "gang" as the government prepared for a show trial. This was to be pure theatre, stage-managed by the Communists. The language used was very similar to that used in Nazi attacks against the few patriotic Germans who in July 1944 had tried to assassinate Hitler: the Stauffenberg plot after which hundreds were executed in the most cruel way. We were afraid that similar fates were now to be meted out by the "People's Court."

I had managed to pass my remaining final exams, but my diploma would not be issued until the end of the second term at the university, in the early summer of 1949. Therefore, I could devote most of my time to organising escapes for friends, while spending the rest in Shangri-La, where the real world still did not encroach too much, although by now news reached us every day of the successful or unsuccessful escapes of friends, or alternatively of their arrest in the ever-widening circle of people implicated in the Mindszenty plot. Now the government was beginning to worry about the mass escapes, because the departures of wealthy citizens and intellectuals had seriously depleted the capital of the country, and they began increasing the number of checkpoints on highways and trains and also the vigilance and numbers of the border guards. There was talk about measures to close the borders completely, ostensibly to stop "foreign spies and saboteurs" from entering the People's Republic.

The pigpens were completed, and with their purchased fodder flowing into the trough, the hogs began to grow and fatten. Father still hoped that this would satisfy the Communist Council. Christmas came, and as always, our house was the centre of family gatherings. As usual, a large Christmas tree was erected, resplendent with the old decorations that I knew from my childhood. In addition to the decorations, hundreds of gold- and silver-wrapped "salon" candies were hung from all branches. These were basically soft candies made of sugar, some white and some chocolate-coloured. Children were the only ones who were willing to eat them; in our house, there were no children, yet by Christmas Eve, all the candies had disappeared from the lower branches. Our favourite dachshund, "Csombi", had figured out a way of sitting erect on her hindquarters, her long body stretching as far as it could, up towards the candies, and using her front paws, she managed to open up the paper wrappers and extract the precious candies without tugging on the branches. Our other two dachshunds were not as skilled, but they received their share, and Zsuzsu, the German shepherd dog patrolling in the garden, received extra-fine bones.

On Christmas Eve, the candles were lit, and the tree stood glowing in the semi-darkness of the living room. Eta's brother and sister-in-law came on Christmas Eve for dinner. This was the tradition in Catholic families, and after dinner they all, including Eta, went for midnight mass to the Basilica of Budapest, which this year must have been gloomy because most of the senior clergymen were in AVO hands. But masses of people attended by way of protest.

My mother's family, my darling aunts and uncles and their wives, came on Christmas Day. Presents were exchanged, but the spirit of Christmas was not there. Between Christmas and New Year's Eve, we drove to the vineyard and spent two nights. Everything was snowed under, only the stakes and the cut-back vines sticking out starkly in the snow. We climbed up into the drifts—I still remember the view of the crossroads cross, its base and roof snowed in, the Mater "Stabat Dolorosa" sprinkled with a dusting of snow. When we reached the house, a big fire was crackling in the oven in the living room, making everything warm and comfortable. The vintner and his family came for a visit and to wish us the best of the season, but the atmosphere was grim, in spite of the warm surroundings and the beautiful scenery outside. By now, the hate bombarding the country from the papers and the shrill radio programs could not be ignored.

Only the pigs were happy in their sty, slurping the plentiful fodder. They grunted with satisfaction as they rubbed against each other, their pink flesh glistening, bristling with wiry white hair. Eating, grunting, sleeping, they were happy in their secure home. But the butcher's knives were already being sharpened.

Back to town we went, the radio intruding on every mile of our trip, the attacks against the whole Catholic establishment flowing with venom.

New Year's Eve arrived, and of course a big New Year's party had been prepared by Cilike for the "Club". It was a cold clear night, all the stars twinkling above as I left our house, dressed in a dinner jacket and white silk shirt with little mother-of-pearl button studs, a tiny diamond in each centre twinkling just like the stars above. The studs were a gift from Eta to my father, who had lent them to me for the occasion. My black bowtie was hand-tied to just the perfect shape. The party had just started when I arrived. Cilike was in a beautiful heavy silk sheath made by Julia Apponyi's salon, her almost platinum blonde page-boy cut bobbing over the ice-cold blue of the dress.

The waters were certainly about to submerge the *Titanic*, and this was to be a party to end all parties. As the witching hour drew close, white-jacketed extra help—perhaps reliable

337

university students—began pouring drinks and serving all kinds of delicacies, compliments of the house. Just before midnight, the chef brought in a live squealing piglet, and for good luck, everybody tried to twist its curly tail. At exactly 12, the champagne began flowing, and we toasted each other and wished Happy New Year all around. Cilike went around kissing everybody, and she ended up by my side. She wished me the best of luck for the New Year, and I wished the same to her. It was a boisterous night, and after that, I can't remember all that happened; enough champagne was consumed to make us all forget the dire predictions for 1949, the year to come.

The first of January passed. It was a cold winter, and more friends disappeared to the West. John Kolozs's sister, Meta, and her husband, Jancsi Horvath, whom I knew from my Szeged sojourn in fur storage in the winter of 1945, had departed in the most daring way. They drove their car towards the Austrian border and just before Mosonmagyarovar, the headquarters of the infamous AVO major, which I first saw from the train on my visit to Vienna, they turned off to the left and took a narrow country road. This led to a small border crossing near the Austrian village of Monchhof. The border crossing had been closed by the Communists, but Jancsi knew that the road veered to the left near the former border station and for the next 10 km ran parallel to the border, with open fields on both sides.

He took the turn and when he saw no border patrols in the area, turned off the road and made a run through the frozen fields towards Austria. He drove over the fields which had been cleared except for the stubble for spring plowing, got back onto a road in Austria, and in ten minutes was in the small village of Monchhof at the head of the Neusiedler See. From there, the main road to Vienna awaited them, and in another hour, they arrived there. John Kolozs wrote to me with the whole story and urged me to follow the same route.

Since the episode of the pigs, my father had also begun to consider escape. It was an appealing thought to go over with the car *en famille*. Not only would we be through the curtain, but I would drive into Vienna at the wheel of my favourite car. I had suggested the idea to my father, and he was beginning to consider the risks.

I knew that he was serious when he told me one day that the time had come to dig up our gold hoard, which, carefully wrapped in burlap, I had hidden in the garden in the spring of 1944, deep in the earth among the roots of the seventh Lombardy poplar, counting from the first stone step to our entrance door. Equipped with a sharp trenching shovel, I sneaked out at 4 A.M., the quietest time of the night, counted out to the seventh poplar, and started digging. It was tough going in the frozen soil in the eerie illumination of the AVO security lights surrounding the Tildy villa. I worked hard, occasionally freezing up when the shovel hit a stone and made what seemed like the sound of a dynamite explosion. When neither the AVO nor our caretaker reacted to the noise, I continued digging. In about an hour, I had dug up the whole area around the poplar tree, but there was no sign of the gold. I gave up and replaced the earth, tramping it down and covering up the diggings with shovels of snow.

Father waited for me in the hall. I told him that the gold was gone. Somebody must have found it years ago and taken off with the loot—12 kilos of old gold, worth then about $12,000. Father was cool: "Tomorrow you must dig under the sixth poplar, and if it is not there, the next night you dig under the eighth. You must have forgotten the location." This would interfere with my visits to Shangri-La. Next night, I sneaked out again, determined to dig up both locations if necessary. Luckily the sixth poplar yielded up the treasure quite easily, and I lugged it upstairs after again replacing the soil. Fortunately it started snowing, and by daylight there were no tell-tale signs of my activity. We took the gold to Eta's brother for safekeeping. Once we were in Austria, we knew there were ways that we could arrange to have it smuggled out of the country.

The papers and the radio did not stop with their orchestrated reports of Mindszenty's interrogations and his "traitorous" activities, which the AVO, ever vigilant, had discovered just in time. His trial and that of his associates, including Prince Paul Eszterhazy, were to start as soon as he made a full confession, but no later then the beginning of February. No one had any doubts that with torture and drugs they would force him to confess whatever their scenario called for.

I escaped back to the Miniature. I needed the friendly atmosphere, the companionship of all the other passengers on the sinking ship. Most of all, I needed Cilike, who emanated calm and security, or so it seemed. I purchased a Sherlock Holmes-type Dunhill pipe from "Gallwitz's", the famous pipe emporium, which was located within a stone's throw of the former National Casino. Unlike the magnates' club, which had ceased to exist years ago, Gallwitz's was still there, surviving.

In fact, it survived the whole Communist era. In 1990, I went to the site of the original store and found that a milk bar stood in its place. But the faded sign saying "Gallwitz" was still visible on the facade. Encouraged, I went into the courtyard to look for the names of the owners of the apartments above. Sure enough, under the arcade, I found a hand-painted sign with an arrow pointing towards the staircase: "Gallwitz's, 2nd floor." I walked up, and there, in an old Biedermeyer living room, business was going on as usual. Even Mr. Gallwitz was there, aged but not broken. In some drawers, he still had a few precious Dunhill pipes, and I bought one from him. I am smoking it now, from time to time, as I write.

At the Miniature, my Sherlock Holmes pipe was admired. Mr. Gallwitz's Dunhill tobacco gave its own pungent aroma to the environment. John Kolozs and others were gone, but there were still customers; even Edna B. came in regularly.

One weekend, my father and I drove to the vineyard to see how the pigs were doing. There were ten of them, healthy and fat; the time for the butcher was approaching. We drove back to Budapest on the fourth of February, and once on the road, I turned on the radio. The Mindszenty trial was in progress at the People's Court. We heard the harsh attacks of the prosecutor, and then the questioning of the Cardinal started. In halting language, spoken by a broken trembling man, the confessions came. He admitted to having plotted, together with Prince Paul Eszterhazy, the overthrow of the People's Government and the restoration of the monarchy and the magnates' estates; he confessed that, with the Prince as his partner, he was guilty of the common "crime" of currency speculation. It was a pitiful performance, which my father thought nobody would believe. But the Communist press believed, or pretended to, and the whole world was inundated with this slime.

Pictures of the broken Cardinal sitting in court surrounded by his guards were flashed around the world. Stalin, the puppet master, and his acolytes were sensing victory and were delighted. They knew that this greatest enemy of the Marxists was about to go down in ignominy. By now, only the formality of the court's verdict and sentence, long prepared and rehearsed, remained to be heard.

Even at the Shangri-La, the Mindszenty trial could not be ignored. The boat was sinking. Everyone was now aware that the decks were all awash and that icy cold waters were seeping in over the threshold.

It was in these times that one day I took the bus up Bimbo utca to our house and at the Margit Boulevard stop met Ivan Balla, whom I knew from my motorcycling days. We discussed the Mindszenty trial, which was in its final throes; the verdict would be brought in any minute. Ivan told me that he had to get out of Hungary but did not know how. I told him about Bela Haray and arranged a meeting for the next day, February 8, 1949.

We met in the Lukacs café, and Haray arranged the usual route. Next day, they would travel by train to a certain farm, and from there, hidden in a hay wagon, Ivan would be transported close to the border and at night be guided over to Austria. I wished him good luck and departed.

This was the day that the Mindszenty verdict was delivered in the People's Court. All the accused were found guilty as charged. Mindszenty was sentenced to life imprisonment, his senior aides to from 5 to 15 years, depending on seniority. Prince Eszterhazy and his secretary got 15 years each, Eszterhazy for being the financial backer of the conspiracy, his secretary for carrying out the financial manoeuvres necessary. In vicious articles, the Communist press hailed this as a victory for the "People's Democracy"; the radio blared all day. We were at least relieved that there were no death sentences; it was evident that the government had not dared to go all the way.

That night, I succeeded in persuading my father that we all had to go, and he agreed that we should do so at once. The next morning, we put a few overnight bags into the car, as was usual when we left for the vineyard for a few nights and days. Eta instructed Juliska, the caretaker's wife, to look after the dogs, telling her to expect us back in a couple of days; then we all got into the car, and I drove off towards the Vienna highway. It was a cold grey winter day, and the highway was practically deserted as we sped westward through Gyor towards Mosonmagyarovar. After Gyor, we hit a lonely desolate stretch of road. The trees on both sides seemed to reach up bare arms towards the leaden sky, and the road was covered with an icy slush. Going at around 60 miles an hour, I saw suddenly two dark spots on the road ahead. I was approaching rapidly, and the two dark spots quickly took shape.

They turned into a Russian patrol walking steadily in the centre of the road, their machine guns at the ready. I gave a tremendous blast on my air horn and accelerated, steering straight at them. They stood their ground, and I had a split-second doubt about my strategy. More air horn. At the last moment, they jumped aside. As we flashed by, I could see their pale Russian faces under their fur hats, their eyes staring at the phenomenon of the hurtling black car, its passengers arrogantly ignoring them. For a second, I braced myself for a salvo from their machine guns. Nothing happened. As I looked in the mirror, they returned to patrol formation and receded from view.

In half an hour, just before the dangerous town of Mosonmagyarovar, we reached a small country road leading to the border on the left. I turned off, and at a leisurely speed began to drive on towards Austria. As John had described it, the road veered left just before the turnoff to the old border station, and we were now running parallel to the border line. On the other side, frozen fields marched off into the Austrian Burgenland. Here and there, nestling among the fields, I could see a few farmhouses in the distance. I was about 100 yards away from the border, traveling slowly, looking for a suitable spot to make my run. A few barren willow trees appeared to the right marking the banks of a small creek, frozen solid in the cold weather. A small curve ahead, and I slowed down more, mentally getting ready for what I believed would be a fateful turn to the right. I negotiated the bend carefully and ran directly into a hive of activity. A regiment of soldiers was stretched out along the border, and under the watchful eyes of a few sergeants and an officer, the men were busily drilling holes and erecting tall posts that stretched in a straight line as far as I could see. They were also erecting a guard tower. We did the only thing possible—we waved a greeting and slowly drove past—they paid scant attention. Half a mile farther, the fence posts, about eight feet high, were up in triple rows, and a detachment of men was stretching rows and rows of barbed wire on the posts. Farther down the road, concertina wire was being off-loaded from army trucks and laid between the triple fences. I had seen enough; the escape route was closed. Now I had to look for a discreet retreat. A narrow lane appeared, leading away from our road, back towards Hungary. I took it and was quite relieved when none of the border guards found this worthy of interest.

I kept driving on this byway, although I did not know exactly where I was heading. After about half an hour, a heavily laden hay wagon appeared on the road, headed towards the border. A sleepy farmer sat way up on top sucking on his pipe. It crossed my mind that Ivan Balla might be hidden in the hay, and I gave a blast of my air horn. The wagon moved on with its unusual midwinter cargo, and by the time I looked in the mirror, it had disappeared altogether in the gathering dusk. Many years later, Ivan Balla told me that, hidden under the hay on his way to the West, he had heard the hoot hoot hoot of my horn.

After some time, we found a major road heading towards the Balaton. We took it and in two hours arrived at the vineyard, an anticlimax under the circumstances. For a couple of days, we watched the pigs grow and then returned to Budapest.

We were some days late to cross the border and had discovered first-hand how serious the Communists were about closing down escape routes. I was depressed by the unsuccessful attempt, and so was my father. By the time we arrived back at our house on the Hill of the Roses, my father was limping heavily with a severe attack of gout.

In a few days, I met Bela Haray again. He already knew about the sealing of the border, but he was not too worried. He was getting ready to go to his village to investigate with his farmer friends the possibility of breaching this new obstacle. He assured me that he would get me across when the time came. Meantime, Father was quite ill and not in the mood to discuss further attempts.

March came, and spring would soon be with us. But in Budapest the mood was desperate. Everyone knew that the border was sealed, and now very few made escape attempts, most of them unsuccessful. The rumour spread that the wife and the daughter of the Hungarian managing director of SKF, the Swedish ball-bearing company, had tried to get across with the help of guides and that the daughter had stepped on a land mine which had blown off her leg. Nevertheless they had continued on, the guides carrying the injured girl. This was the first we had heard of the mine fields laid down by the border guards. All along the Austrian border, a 200-yard-wide strip in front of the triple wire fence had been denuded of trees, plowed up, and seeded with land mines interconnected by trip wires. A chain of watchtowers had been built along the fence, spaced so that the entire plowed, mined, 200-foot strip could be observed by the guards perched with their heavy machine guns atop the towers.

Theoretically now only birds could cross the borders. More horror stories began to circulate even at the Shangri-La, some of them no doubt started by the Communists to discourage further attempts.

For Easter, Bela Haray went to his border village to investigate the situation there further. When I phoned him the following Tuesday, he told me that it was urgent for us to meet immediately. I went to our usual booth at Lukacs and found him waiting impatiently. He had just come back from his village and found the construction of the fortified border completed, the observation towers manned by the border-guard soldiers, and other guards accompanied by German shepherd guard dogs patrolling constantly. The path of the patrols led between the Hungarian side of the triple fortified fence and the 200-yard-wide minefield. He also established that the patrols followed no regular pattern. The minefield was completed and interlaced by trip wires whose locations were being altered constantly during the daylight hours according to no set pattern.

This, Bela concluded, made it virtually impossible to cross the border. But he had some good news also: many of the border guards were local farm boys, and through them, his "smugglers" had found out that all the border-guard units had been ordered to Gyor, the major city straddling the Vienna-Budapest highway, for this year's May Day parade; the border would not be manned that night. This, Bela said, was a unique opportunity that I must not miss, because it would not come again. Immediately I decided that, with or without my father, I must go on May Day.

I went home, and after dinner, I told Father that I was going on May 1, without him if necessary if he could not make up his mind. It was not easy for me to tell my father this, but I did. Father was not used to ultimatums, and his immediate reaction was predictable: he said that he was staying and that I must go alone.

*Celebrations for May Day, 1949, promised to be the biggest
ever – and would provide the best opportunity to escape.*

In 1949, the May Day celebrations promised to be the biggest ever, being the first since the Communists had openly eliminated all opposition. Earlier in April, Matyas Rakosi had published a lengthy and forceful article explaining in no uncertain terms that People's Democracy meant now the dictatorship of the proletariat. What better way to celebrate this falsehood than with parades and accompanying hoopla organised on a gigantic scale!

For weeks already, all factories and other state-owned enterprises had been preparing elaborate floats and banners, all loud in their praise of Marx, Lenin, and Stalin as well as of the new Hungarian dictatorship of the proletariat, which had just taken away the last bit of freedom from the proletariat. Police, army units, border-guard units, and the AVO were all practicing for the great march past, learning to shout in unison the many prepared slogans. These parades would take place in major cities and in particular in Budapest. I had never participated in a May Day parade, but this year, it turned out that I would do so.

My determination to leave received a further boost next morning when I received a summons from the Party secretary of my former boss Takacs's Buvati office, ordering me to report for work without further delay on the day after the celebrations. This was serious business, because once I signed up for work, escape became as serious a crime as desertion from the army.

At breakfast, my father announced that although he was by no means decided, he and Eta would accompany me to the border and then consider the situation. This was a breakthrough and, I realised, as far as my father could go. May Day was only three days away, and I had a lot of preparations to make. There were pinball games ahead.

May Day! May Day!

I had one final meeting with Bela Haray to discuss details. With the border fortifications completed, there was no question of taking our car across, but we decided to drive on May Day towards Mosonmagyarovar. We had to have a good excuse to be traveling in that direction, and Father came up with the idea of visiting his former local agent in that town, Mr. Deutsch, a bearded Orthodox Jew who for decades had bought wines for my father in the Transdanubian area. Ostensibly the purpose of our trip would be to buy some wines for our wine cellar in Badacsony. Mr. Deutsch's firm was not yet nationalised, and Father made an appointment with him for the afternoon of May Day, telling him that we were planning to drive on to our vineyard. Mr. Deutsch did not ask any questions.

Bela Haray left immediately for his village to prepare the manoeuvre. I gave him Mr. Deutsch's address, and he said that as soon as we arrived there, I should go out to the car, open the hood, and tinker with the motor until somebody approached me, identifying himself and giving me final instructions.

Now I had to find a place to put the car until I could send some smuggler from Vienna to try to bring it over. It would not be possible to put it back into our garage on the Hill of the Roses because Haray was going to report us dutifully to the AVO as soon as we were safely in Austria, and the state security police would immediately descend on our house. So two things had to be resolved: how to get the car back to Budapest, and where to keep it hidden until we found somebody, as I believed we would be able to do, to smuggle it to us in Vienna.

The solution to the second problem came that evening in the Miniature bar. My friend Edna B. turned up, and I suddenly remembered that she had a large garage at her house on Uri utca, up in the Royal Fortress area, where no one would look for our car. Until then, I had not told anyone about our plans to escape except for Cilike, who had expected that my departure would come soon and was totally reliable. I quickly decided that Edna, too, could be trusted and told her of my problem. She immediately agreed to rent me the garage for a month for a fairly large sum of money.

Now, how to get the car back to Budapest? Bela Haray would have brought it back, but unfortunately he did not know how to drive. But finally this problem, too, was resolved. John Kolozs had an uncle in Budapest with whom we had spent many happy hours in better days in the nightclubs. Jozsi was a somewhat faded, aristocratic-looking playboy, the younger son of a once-prosperous Szeged family and always in need of extra income. I asked him to join us on the trip to the border and then drive the car back to Edna's garage, taking Bela back with him. He agreed to this job for a hefty fee.

Approaching the border with fireworks in the distance.

Now there was not much left to do. Father and I went to visit my uncles and aunts and said our good-byes. Eta visited her family members. Then I went from stationery store to stationery store, purchasing large quantities of red buntings, flags of the new People's Republic of Hungary and of the glorious Soviet Union, and in a Communist Party store I purchased large portraits of Lenin, Stalin, and the Hungarian leader Matyas Rakosi.

The day before May Day, I decorated our big black car with buntings and Communist slogans. Then in front of the hood, supported by the wide grille, I mounted Lenin's portrait in the centre and placed Stalin and Rakosi on either side. On top of them, I placed the two flags. By now the car looked like a large float in the parade, or at least the May Day car of a very important Party functionary. I stepped back to inspect the results of my labour, and I was very pleased.

For the last time, I proceeded to the Shangri-La to see Cilike, but this time I could not relax as usual, and I went home early. I had said my good-byes to Cilike before, and we parted casually. Our friends in the Miniature had no inkling of my plans.

After a restless night, I woke early, but not as early as my father. As always since his army days, he was up at 6 o'clock, and when I went to the garage, I found him there in the far corner, where a huge 19th-century safe was located. Its walls and door were heavy steel, ten inches thick. A complicated hinged key opened its lock, and a huge brass wheel in the face of the door had to be turned to retract the two one-inch thick bolts on each of the door's four sides from their slots in the door frame. Etched in the green enamel face of the door in gilt letters was the name of a famous Viennese firm that had manufactured it before the turn of the century. This was surrounded by replicas of gold medals which its manufacturer had won at the Paris, London, Bruxelles, and other famous world exhibitions. I had often admired the inscriptions on this massive fireproof box. To my surprise,

Father had the door open, and at first I thought he was removing some personal documents and papers that were stored there. As I came closer, I was in for an even greater surprise. Out of his old briefcase, he was filling up the steel shelves with neat, rubber-banded bundles of 1000-forint bank notes. "Have you changed your mind about leaving again?" I asked anxiously. "No, I have not changed my plan to come with you, but I am aware of the danger of falling into the AVO's hands near the border region, and should they interrogate us, what better proof that we were not trying to escape than having left a large sum of money in our safe. Nobody would do that if he planned to escape." I was aghast at the thought of leaving all this money there instead of taking it with us. At the same time, I realised that if we were caught with a briefcase full of cash, we could not talk our way out of the hands of the secret police. "How much are you leaving in there?" I asked. "100,000 forints," Father said. This was a large sum indeed, the equivalent of $5,000 at that time, enough money to live on in Hungary for five years. I tried to argue that we should take at least half the money with us. Father was firm; he calculated that it was the correct amount to prove our innocence should we have to do so. He locked the safe and, folding the key, deposited it into his briefcase with various other documents. We went upstairs again, and there Juliska, the wife of our caretaker, was waiting for us with the normal breakfast we would take before going to the country.

It was a bright sunny day, and we ate on the terrace surrounded by our three dachshunds waiting around for any offerings that mighty come from the table. Zsuzsu, the big German Shepherd bitch, came visiting from her patrol around the garden, with our ginger-haired cat riding on her back. It was a beautiful morning to remember, the overhanging branches of the big apricot tree laden with buds, ready to burst into flower.

We were in no hurry; the plan was to start on our way at 1 P.M. and arrive at the Deutsch house in Mosonmagyarovar at about 3:30 P.M.; we would then spend a couple of hours in the cellars, tasting and discussing the wines and waiting for instructions. I made a final call to Cilike, and then accompanied by the dogs, Zsuzsu on a leash, my father and I took a walk around the neighbourhood, which was quite deserted, everybody obviously having gone to the centre of town for the parade. At the corner of Pentelei Molnar utca lived a family whose beautiful young daughter Aniko and I had for some time carried out an innocent flirtation. Aniko was sitting on their second-floor balcony which jutted out into their well-kept garden; looking up, she smiled, and we waved and moved on.

By noon, we were back home, and shortly Jozsi, John Kolozs's uncle, arrived. To our amazement, he was dressed like a London City broker, wearing a bowler hat, morning coat, and striped pants, and carrying a furled bamboo-handled umbrella in one hand and a small dispatch case in the other. "Jozsi," I said, "why this outfit on May Day? We are not going to a fancy-dress party." "I did not think so," he replied, "but we are presumably driving a high party official, and I am dressed as an aide. And then, after the border, when I am driving the car back, should anything go wrong, should the car break down, I'll just get out and walk away, and who knows, perhaps it will be raining." He had a dry sense of humour, and perhaps he had a point, so I did not argue. I myself was dressed for the country, in flannels and tweed jacket; I figured I'd pass for the driver of an important personage should we be stopped by the police.

Exactly at 1 P.M., we took our small overnight bags and walked down to the garage, drove the car out, and Jozsi had quite a surprise at all my May Day decorations. "You see now how important it is to complete the image with a proper aide-de-camp next to the driver," he said. He got into the front passenger seat and sat ramrod-straight, umbrella in hand. Eta and Father got into the back, where they sank deep into the cushions. The dachshunds, and

Csombi particularly, Eta's favourite, tried to climb in too, and it took a bit of doing to close the doors. Juliska stood at the garden gate. I started driving up the slope, and as we passed her, Eta said to her, "Take care of everything, we'll be back in a couple of days."

We went through the driveway gate, and by the time I eased the car onto Torokveszi utca, Juliska had closed the gates and was standing there waving, the four dogs poking their heads through the fence, yapping. In a minute we were at the corner, and as I turned left into Pentelei Monlar utca, I looked up. Aniko was still on the terrace, standing at the balustrade. I waved at her, and she waved back, smiling. In the rear-view mirror, I looked back once more. By now, Aniko was reading her book. To avoid any celebrants in the streets of old Buda, I drove down Pusztaszeri utca, a back route on the Hill of the Roses and a short cut to the Vienna highway. Soon we had reached the highway and, gathering speed, were on our way. Everyone was quiet, wondering if we would ever see the villa on the Hill again.

There was hardly any traffic, and the suburbs whizzed by, the Dobogoko mountain blocking the view to the Danube on our right. Somewhere behind it, Nagymaros nestled in the great bend. On the left, as we passed under a footbridge and a huge industrial conveyor, I could see in the distance the castle of the Eszterhazy princes and its now-neglected ornamental lake.

After a while, the familiar sight of Almasfuzito loomed up, the Danube glittering to the right as the road straightened out and ran parallel to the freight yards. I slowed down as I reached the very spot where in 1944, after the huge air raid, Johnnie and I, escaping from the war, had hitched a ride from the SS officers as the oil tanker trains exploded and burned around us.

Tanker trains were there on the sidings still, and I was escaping once more, playing a new game on the pinball machine. The ball was rolling, rolling. Past the freight yards and back on the highway, I speeded up again; I knew that

Gyor was not very far away when we reached a narrow winding section of road with ancient linden trees marching by, regular as soldiers, their bottoms whitewashed to stand out in the night, to prevent accidents. After this stretch, the road turned again and broadened, running straight ahead. In a minute, I was on the outskirts of the city, where straight ahead was a police checkpoint with several policemen out in front. I bore down towards them and gave a long firm blast on my air horn, which was illegal on civilian cars and had its button hidden under the dashboard. (The regular horn, of course, was connected to a huge chromium wheel inside the even larger steering wheel). The police scrambled to stand to attention as this beautifully decorated car obviously carrying important persons slowed to a halt. Beyond the police barricade, I could see crowds milling about on the highway, ready for a night-long celebration now that the official parade was over.

As we came to a halt in front of the post, an old-time police sergeant stepped forward with a rigid salute. I rolled down the window, gave him the closed-fisted Communist salute, and in a firm voice said, "Comrade Sergeant, we are due in Mosonmagyarovar shortly, and I don't see how I can get through this crowd; I need help from you." "Yes, Comrade," came the answer, "I have two motorcycle police ready, and they will clear a path for you! Long live the People's Republic! Long live Comrade Rakosi!" He barked an order, and the two motorcycle cops kick started in unison at the side of the post building and drove ahead to the front of our car, signalling me to follow. I just had enough time to give one more salute to the sergeant before the two motorcycles, sirens blasting, roared ahead. I stepped on the accelerator and moved with them, the red buntings and flags on the hood fluttering in the breeze, the crowd backing away, letting us pass. They waved at us, yelling May Day slogans, and I could see their curious looks. But Father and Eta sat still, paying no attention. I sneaked a glance at

Jozsi—he was sitting ramrod-straight, but I thought that he looked somewhat pale.

In the city centre, the crowds became more numerous, but gave way obediently, cheerfully. In ten minutes, we reached the far end of the city, and the open road stretched towards the border. The motorcycle cops lifted their hands to indicate that they were stopping. I slowed down and came to a stop ten paces behind them.

They executed a textbook turn, one to the left, the other to the right, and saluting as they went by, accelerated back in the direction of the town.

All of us now had a delayed reaction to this dangerous crossing, and it took me quite a few minutes to regain my calm. By then, we were rolling on to our next stop at the Deutsch house in Mosonmagyarovar. We got there without further incident. It was a substantial country place facing a triangular greensward at the nexus of three village streets. I parked at the edge of this green space, and by that time Mr. Deutsch was already at the car, holding the door, helping Eta and my father out. Jozsi and I did not need any help; we were happy to stretch our legs.

Inside, Mrs. Deutsch, a charming roly-poly lady, greeted us with great hospitality; we all sat down, coffee and marvellous cakes were brought in, and a general conversation started about the difficult times. In a few minutes, I excused myself, saying that I had to check some malfunction in the engine of the car. I went out and opened the hood, and making the engine accessible by moving Lenin, Stalin, and Comrade Rakosi aside, got my tools out of the trunk, all the while surreptitiously looking about me. There was nobody in sight. I started working on the engine, taking out the spark plugs, brushing them, and pretending to be systematically looking for some defect.

After a while, a farm wagon came by; the driver, an old grey-moustachioed peasant, looked at me and the car curiously, but did not stop. When I had started cleaning the spark plugs for the third time and was getting quite anxious about my expected contact, I heard a young man approach on a bicycle, whistling. I looked up, but he went on with his bike, circling the little square and executing a few "figure eight" turns, drawing closer, than turning away, then coming back again. Obviously he was curious about my activities. I went on with the work, not sure if he were not an AVO spy. Finally he left his bike against a tree and, still whistling, approached the car. I went in deeper under the hood. Finally the whistling stopped abruptly, and I saw his cloth-capped head dodge in under the hood. For a while he studied the motor, then very slowly he said: "Bela sent me to give you the instructions." I looked at him, waiting. Finally he said, "Stay here until it is really dark. Then drive back to the Vienna highway and turn back towards Budapest. Two kilometres down the road, you will see a dirt road to the right. Turn off your headlights and drive down this road, slowly, until on your right you will see the huge upright of a draw well. Stop there, Bela and my brothers will be waiting there, but make sure it's absolutely dark before you start." "OK," I said and began to reassemble the motor, In a second, I heard the rattly sound of the bike as he started off again, whistling as he went.

I started the car to make sure that everything was all right and, shutting the hood, returned to the house. Mr. Deutsch was getting ready to take Father to the wine cellar to show him some wines. Mrs. Deutsch proposed an early dinner so that we should be able to leave before it got dark! Little did she know that we had the opposite aim. On the way to the cellar, I passed the latest information to Father. Mr. Deutsch's wines were excellent, and Father faithfully tasted them all, but I could see that his heart was not in it.

Mrs. Deutsch meanwhile chatted with Eta, but around 5 P.M., she summoned us from the cellar, and immediately the maid appeared with a sumptuous steaming stew, dumplings, and some wine. Obviously they were anxious to see us go, but we showed no sign of wanting to hurry. My father told one anecdote after the other, but they did not seem to strike the right chord. Finally Mr. Deutsch said, "I don't want to hurry you, but I have to tell you that Mosonmagyarovar has a very large AVO complement, and its Major is a fearsome sadist; they are always on the hunt for would-be escapees, and it's not good to be around here at night." I said that I knew about the infamous mayor. "We have nothing to fear," said my father. "We are heading from here to Badascony and are not worried." But the Deutsch family obviously was. Dessert and coffee appeared instantly. We drank our coffee as slowly as possible, but in the end we had to get up, thank them for the meal, and proceed to the car. Mr. Deutsch and his wife saw us off with great relief. By now, they must have guessed our real goal and were afraid of involvement. But by now it was really pitch dark, and luckily there was no moon.

As we reached the highway and turned back towards Budapest, I could hear the noises of revelry coming from the town centre. In a few minutes I saw the narrow dirt road, and switching off the headlights, I started carefully down it. After a little while, my eyes got used to the darkness, and I was able to differentiate between the pitch-black fields and the somewhat lighter ribbon of the road. Even so, I almost missed the draw well, its stork-like outline barely visible in the dark.

I stopped and got out. Bela and his farmer friends, two sturdy ex-paratroopers, were waiting patiently. Far away towards the west, I could see the lights of a few farmhouses; otherwise all was blackness.

We scrambled out of the car; my father and Eta had only now made their final decision, and opening the trunk, they removed half a dozen bags, including Eta's string shopping bag bulging with clothing, which they had smuggled into the car against my advice. Now it was too late to protest; anyhow, Eta assured me that she intended to carry most of them herself. In the confusion, my briefcase burst open, and my university documents spilled out. On my knees, I scrambled under the car, collecting the papers in the dark.

Luckily nothing was lost, and I was able to stuff them back into my bag.

Finally we were lined up at the side of the car; Bela Haray was anxious to get us off. The two smugglers, he told me, had sneaked away from a village May Day party and wanted to return before it ended to establish their alibis. He told me that earlier in the day they had driven a cow across the mine field all the way to the wire fence, and the cow had managed the 200-yard trip and come back unharmed. The plan was to follow in its footsteps to avoid the mines and trip wires. All the border guards were in Gyor, and the guard towers were unmanned. Now we said good-bye to each other, Haray and I embracing and wishing each other good luck in whispers. He got into the front passenger seat, and Jozsi shook hands all around and got into the driver's seat. Now all was in order and we waited for the car to drive off. Jozsi gently shut the door and grabbed the steering wheel, or so he thought. Unfortunately what he was holding was the chrome ring of the horn, and suddenly in the silence of the night we heard the blast of the gigantic dual horns. Jozsi did not know what was happening and did not let go. The sound continued. I ran around the car and pulled off his hands. The sound stopped. The silence was ear-shattering.

Suddenly from the distant village a flare went up, piercing the darkness, then another. We stood frozen, sure that an alarm had been given. But the flares rose gracefully and blossomed into beautiful fireworks, more and more rockets piercing the sky. They were May Day celebrations, not signals. I started breathing again. "Get started, Jozsi, and watch the horn, for God's sake," I said, wishing him and the car to disappear, But now he was extremely nervous, and as he tried to start the car, he pumped the accelerator and flooded the engine. It turned over, but would not fire. I grabbed him, dragged him out of the car, and jumped in: after waiting a few seconds, I floored the pedal and turned the ignition key. The engine began to turn, but the battery by now was weak. I hung in, willing the car to start. Finally, when I thought the battery could not turn the engine much longer, the spark plugs that I had so carefully cleaned a few hours earlier started firing; the engine caught on with a roar and came to life. I put it in gear and, carefully backing up, I turned the car around in the direction of Mosonmagyarovar and jumped out. Jozsi slid back into the driver's seat, and the big car lurched. I stood there watching as Jozsi went into the curve in the dark, the brake lights glowing in the night. I watched as long as I could see the brake lights turning on and off as he negotiated the winding road without headlights. Finally we were alone in the dark.

We were all anxious to go, and with the two smugglers taking the lead, we turned off the road into the freshly plowed, soft field. The smugglers said that we were eight kilometres from the border, a good two hours' march. It was tough going; my father and Eta were in heavy loden coats, each carrying three bags on straps on their shoulders, and Eta not used to walking. I walked close behind with my briefcase. After ten minutes' march, Eta asked me to carry one of her bags; a little later, she passed on another bag, and finally the last one. Father bravely carried on a little longer, but eventually he handed over his bags, too. After an hour or so of silent marching, I had all the bags hung from my shoulders. I must have looked like a laden Christmas tree if anybody had been able to see me in the darkness.

The sky was a shade lighter than the earth, which was inky black, the horizon just a vague line over the rolling fields. The switching of bags had taken some time, and suddenly I realised that we had lost our two guides. "Let's stop and wait until they find us," my father said. "How can they do that in the dark?" I asked. But there was no alternative; we had no way to figure out the direction in which we should be heading. So we sat down in the field, Father cool as always. "They are soldiers, they will know how to find us." Surrounded by all the bags, I sat there wondering what would happen next. It was nice to rest awhile. Suddenly, noiselessly, the guides emerged. Apparently when they realised that they had lost us, they began to circle around until they came upon us. Father whispered and suggested a new approach, based on some army experience. He took off his hat, hung it on the top of his walking stick, and gave it to one of the guides to hold aloft. Sure enough, the hat was just barely visible as the guide held it high enough to show above the horizon. We took off again, following the floating hat. We were managing to keep up with it fairly well when we suddenly realised that our guides had stopped ahead of us. When we reached them, we saw that ahead of us, just beyond some bushes, lay a railway track, a small branch line running left and right in a straight line. Whispering, I asked why we had stopped. One of the guides explained that it was the custom of the border guards to sit in the bushes at the edge of the line; from this vantage point, they could look down the track into the distance. The line of the track showed up light against the fields, and anybody crossing would be visible. So we sat down again, and one of the guides disappeared, silently circling around along the track, to see if the coast was clear. Ten minutes later he came back; all seemed to be well, the hat was raised, and we were on the move again. We scrambled over the railway signal wires that ran beside the tracks and crossed over without trouble. The guides said that the border was really close now. Suddenly the ground in front of us appeared lighter; it was no longer plowed earth. We had reached the mined strip of no man's land exactly at the spot where in the daytime the guides had driven the cow to the barbed-wire fence. Just barely visible, a couple of hundred yards away, I could see the machine-gun post on top of a guard tower.

While we stood in the field, one of the guides began to cross the minefield silently, following step by step in the indented tracks the cow had left earlier. Disappearing in the gloom, he went to scout out the lay of the land before taking us across. In the distance, I could see the lights of the Austrian village of Halbturm. As silently as he disappeared, our guide suddenly re-emerged and beckoned us to follow. Carefully and slowly following him in line, stepping only in his footsteps, we managed to cross the minefield.

We now arrived at the barbed-wire fence. The guides looked around, and not worrying any more about border guards, stopped whispering; in the strong flavourful accent of county Vas, the district they came from, one of them said, "No one is here; relax, and we'll cut the fence; then we'll help you across." The machine-gun guard tower was looming to our right, not more than twenty paces away. A well-trodden path along the fence, used by the foot patrols, led to it. One of the guides, seeing that I was looking at the tower curiously, told me, "You can walk up to it while you wait; there is no one there, and the path is safe." Then, without further ado, the two of them produced a huge wire cutter, a "souvenir" of their wartime service, and getting down on their stomachs, began to cut the strands of sharp barbed wire at the bottom of the first of the triple fences. Eta and Father sat down with the bags, and I cautiously walked over to the tower. It was a crude structure of wood piling with an open wooden platform about thirty feet up, surrounded by a low wooden balustrade. I could see the machine gun pointing down along the fence from under the sloping metal-lined roof which overhung the platform. Building up courage, I began to climb up the rough wooden ladder to get a guard's-eye view. I reached the top, but before I could climb onto the platform, the guide called urgently. I descended and hurried back to our little group. By now, our paratroopers had cut the bottom two barbed-wire lines of all three parallel fences and were cutting the concertina wires in between just enough to enable this dangerous sharp coil to be propped up so that when crawling across on one's belly, one could get through without injury.

May Day! May Day! The guards are away celebrating. Local farmers send a cow through a field up to the border to make sure there are no land mines at they cut a triple wire fence to to allow escape to the free world.

One of the guides crawled first, moving as a well-trained soldier would, to the Austrian side of the wire. From there he helped us as, one at a time, we, less trained and more worried, managed to snake across. Eta went first, both guides holding the wires up a bit, then my father. Meantime I began throwing the six bags, one at a time, high over the fence into Austrian territory. I went last, crawling carefully with the help of the second guide, who also crossed through. On the other side, when we were all finally across, the guides pointed at the dim glow of the Austrian village of Halbturm, showed us a trail between the fields, and said it would take ten minutes to get to the village. "When you reach the main street, at the third house you will see the lights on in the front clean-room windows behind the curtains. This is a signal from our cousin, the farmer, who is expecting you and will help you on. Approach the house carefully, because there are spies in the village. Now we must hurry to get back to the May Day party in the village before the local gendarmes begin to look for us." Wishing us Godspeed, they shook hands and disappeared under the fence, straightening back the wires as best as they could. Once on the Hungarian side, they disappeared without a sound.

Here we were in Austria, with the clothes we were wearing and our worldly possessions in six bags. I took the lead, with the bags hanging from my shoulders. Following the trail, we reached the edge of the village, where all houses were dark— it was around midnight, no May Day celebrations here—and the only illumination was a few dim street lights farther on. But, as the guides had told us, the third house down the street indeed had some lights filtering through its draped shuttered windows. To make sure that everything was all right, I went ahead, leaving Father and Eta in the shadow of some mulberry trees. In typical Hungarian fashion—this had been a Hungarian village before 1918—the gable end of the house faced the street. The entrance was through a small door which led directly to the porch and was part of a tall wooden fence which ran along the street in front of the farm to the side of the large horse barn, located with its barn doors also facing the street. I was about to knock gently on the door when it was silently opened by a tall farmer. "I was waiting for you, come in. Now you are safe." I waved to my father, and they came rushing. In a minute, we were sitting in a warm friendly kitchen being greeted by the farmer's wife, who immediately started brewing coffee.

My father said that we must immediately phone our friends in Vienna, who were planning to send a car for us. The farmer pointed at the phone on the wall, and my father dialled Mr. Kelemer's number. He was waiting up, having been alerted to our possible escape. My father and Mr. Kelemer spoke cautiously and circumspectly—after all, while we were in Austria, we were in the Russian Zone of Occupation, with Russian patrols all over the place, looking for escapees. Then my father handed the phone to the farmer, who explained that he would leave the barn doors open and that the driver should drive straight into the barn when he arrived. A Viennese car on the street would draw unnecessary attention from watchers who were everywhere.

After the call, Father explained that the car would arrive just before dawn and that the driver would immediately take us to Vienna to Mr. Kelemer's office. The driver would know his way around this rich wine-growing area of Burgenland because Mr. Kelemer bought wine here regularly and even had a few rented wine-storage cellars in the village.

Now there was nothing to do but wait. Food was offered, and the farmer chatted easily with my father in a dialect that I could just barely follow. Meanwhile, I looked around the kitchen, which was also the living room. It was obvious that this Austrian farmer enjoyed a much higher living standard than his Hungarian counterparts. In a Hungarian farmhouse, even a telephone would have been unheard-of. Periodically the farmer got up and went off into the stable just behind the horse barn. I thought that this was curious, and I saw that my father was wondering also. Around five in the morning, the farmer again went out and did not return for a long time. We were getting nervous when he came back again, his hands and arms glistening. He washed up, then asked us to follow him to the stable. There were a couple of horses in the front and quite a few cows in the back. A carbide lamp was burning in the last section. He walked us there, and we found a cow gently licking a beautiful tiny calf that stood shivering in the light of the lamp. "I just delivered the cow of this calf," the man said, "that's why I was coming and going all night."

As we stood there, we heard a car drive into the horse barn from the street. Rushing forward, we found Mr. Kelemer's big black Mercedes. The driver was just closing the barn doors. "Welcome to Austria," he said, "I have a few things for you from Mr. Kelemer." He opened the car door and brought out three Tyrolean hats, black with green piping and badger's-brush decoration, at that time just what an Austrian family would wear on an country outing. To complement the disguise, he pulled out of the glove compartment three Austrian identity cards, duly stamped and with our photographs, which Father had taken to Mr. Kelemer a year before, properly inserted.

"Now, if you're ready, we'll leave as soon as possible," said the driver, and our bags disappeared into the huge trunk of the Mercedes. We took one more look at the calf, and the farmer said, "A new life arrived here on this morning of the day you are beginning your new life."

Indeed, it seemed a good omen. There might be difficult days ahead, but I sensed that a long odyssey was finished. Canada, the Halifax docks, the Red Cross girls, the train ride to Montreal were in the future; they could not be foreseen, but I knew that those years that had called forth the greatest efforts of my life were over. The pinball games were ended. At the time of our escape, the term "Iron Curtain" was newly coined. To me, it still meant the great metal fire curtain in the Budapest theatres of my youth. Now the Iron Curtain had fallen behind us on the theatre of the macabre.

Eta and my father climbed into the back, while I took the front passenger seat. The driver started up the engine, and the farmer waited at the barn doors to close them the instant we cleared with the car. In seconds, we would be on the road to Vienna.

We put on Mr. Kelemer's disguises and drove into the future.

The New World

About the Author

George F. Eber was born in Budapest in 1923 and emigrated to Canada in 1950. A graduate of the Budapest Technical University, he opened his own architectural practice in Montreal and during Canada's Expo '67 was co-architect for the pavilions of 11 participating countries, including Germany, Holland, Iran, and the United States, working on this last project with Buckminster Fuller. Also for Expo '67, he designed and built Montreal's Alcan Aquarium. Following Expo, he consulted for clients all over the world, including Ansett Airlines in Australia and King Hussain of Jordan. For Ansett Airlines, he built the Hayman Island Resort on the Great Barrier Reef. He died in 1995, shortly after finishing *Pinball Games*.

Detail of the roof of the Dolphin Arena of the Montreal Aquarium, donated to the City of Montreal by ALCAN to celebrate Expo 67.

Firm of George F. Eber, Architect.

CPSIA information can be obtained at www.ICGtesting.com
Printed in the USA
LVOW012039051211

257941LV00003B/2/P